Churchless Christianity

Churchless Christianity

William Carey Library

PASADENA · CALIFORNIA

CHURCHLESS CHRISTIANITY
By
Herbert E. Hoefer

Published under agreement with APATS and Distributed by:

P.O. Box 40129
Pasadena, CA 91114 USA
Phone: 626.798.0819 • Email: publishing@wclbooks.com

Chapters 1 through 6 and the Appendicies,
First Published: 1991
by
Asian Programme for Advancement of
Training and Studies (APATS) India
&
The Department of Research & Publications
Gurukul Lutheran Theological College and Research Institute
Kilpauk, Madras, 600 010, India

Library of Congress Cataloging–in–Publication Data

Hoefer, Herbert E.
Churchless Christianity / Herbert Hoefer
p. cm.
Includes biographical references
ISBN 0-87808-444-4 (alk. paper)
1. Christianity — India. I. Title.

BR1155 .H64 2000
275.4'0825—dc21

00-046807

Cover Design: D.M. Battermann, R&D Design Services
Book Design & Layout : D.M. Battermann, R&D Design Services
OCR & Word-Processing: R.D. Battermann, R&D Design Services
Editing: Christine Shay, William Carey Library

Printed in the United States of America

CHURCHLESS CHRISTIANITY

Churchless Christianity:

a report of research among non-baptised believers in Christ in rural and urban Tamilnadu, India, with practical and theological reflections.

"I am the good shepherd; I know my own and my own know me......... And I have other sheep that are not of this fold; I must bring them also, and they will heed my voice. So there shall be one flock, one shepherd."

(Jn. 10:14, 16)

PUBLISHER'S PREFACE

William Carey Library commends this book to the mission community, not to champion every view contained herein, but to stimulate discussion, prayer and earnest study of the Scriptures, to the end that the world might be confronted with biblical worship and the true glory of God in Christ.

Contents

Preface

Dr. K. Rajaratnam, M.A., Ph.D. (London)
D.Th. (Budapest), D.D. (Serampore)
Executive Secretary, United Evangelical Lutheran Churches in India

I am happy to write this Preface for this book entitled "CHURCHLESS CHRISTIANITY" by Rev. Dr. Herbert Hoefer, former Director of Gurukul Lutheran Theological College and Research Institute, Madras. This research work has been undertaken about a decade ago and subsequently the data collected for this purpose was classified critically, analysed and vividly reflected upon by the author who brought out many insights about the newly emerging community known as "Non-Baptised Believers in Christ" (NBBC) especially in one of the southern states of India, viz., Tamilnadu.

During the period of research in 11 districts of Tamilnadu the author conducted personal interviews covering the full range of castes and creeds, women and men and young and old in the state. In the information he collected through interviews, questionnaires, etc., he arrived at some basic conclusions regarding the concerns of different categories of people. For example, I may mention, Hindus and Muslims who believe in Christ strongly but do not come forward openly for baptism have sincere and deep concerns regarding marriages of children, inter-family relationships, cultural identity and integrity, etc. These are genuine and real concerns which need to be studied and met in a suitable manner by the local Christian leaders. But there are some common characteristics for both NBBCs and Christians. Both categories are deeply interested in spiritual quest, experience of love and power of Jesus, in expression of gratitude, in possessing a sense of God's presence and power, etc. on one side and on the other financial and social insecurity, some mistaken or not well-informed ideas of Christianity, church structures, etc.

Interestingly, I noticed, some of the responses are very strong and positive in affirming Jesus as the "one and only incarnation of God" and "the only way to worship God is to worship Jesus." Of course there are some surprising facts expressed by respondents regarding the means and ways they came to know of Jesus etc. The author brought out the implications of this research for the ongoing evangelistic outreach and restructuring of church programmes.

These suggestions are appropriate and adoptable for the church. The parallel he drew between the early church's struggle with circumcision and the Indian church's struggle with baptism is well pointed out while the Church's proper attitude towards the people of other faiths and other castes is being discussed.

The last chapter vividly deals with, while the related literature produced by eminent Indian thinkers like Sadhu Sundar Singh, M. M. Thomas, Abhishiktananda and some western missiologists and thinkers, proposals for redoing Indian Christian structure of nurture and mission to accommodate the real needs, desires and concerns of NBBCs among the Hindu, Muslim and other communities. The fact which draws the attention of a critical reader is the suggestion of the author to "Christ-izing" the Hindu and Muslim culture rather than changing or rejecting it. The spiritual life and practice of Indian Christianity should be different from that of the west and this is to be realized in day to day Indian Christian life.

I am particularly happy that Dr. Hoefer's research on non-baptized believers in Christ in India follows a concern expressed in my report on 'The Structure of the Congregation in India' (1968) a study done for L.W.F. by an Indian team. This report referred to existence of non-baptised believers as a 'believing church' on the periphery of a 'proclaiming church' and called for ministry to this 'believing church'. Dr. Hoefer's research only strengthens strongly the need for such a specialised ministry. The findings also urge the theologians and missiologists to accept the challenge of the meaning of baptism in the religious and cultural context of India which may prove embarrassing to the traditional understanding of missiology and church growth.

I heartily congratulate the author for his outstanding work. I also appreciate the efforts made by the Asian Programme for Advancement of Training and Studies (APATS)–India and the Department of Research and Publications of Gurukul Lutheran Theological College and Research Institute, Madras, for bringing out these findings in the form of this publication.

I commend this book to every English knowing Christian, Indian or Western.

K. RAJARATNAM

Madras
Easter 1991.

A Word About This Book

The Rev. Dr. R. R. Sundara Rao, MA., B.D., Ph.D. (USA)
Dean, Research & Publications
Secretary, APATS —India.

Gurukul Lutheran Theological College
And Research Institute
Madras 600 010, India.

This book is an empirical study on the place of Jesus in faith and practice of Hindus and Muslims in the southern Indian State of Tamilnadu. This area has a long history of Christian mission, dating back to the 16th century; however the vast majority of converts have been from the outside major communities like Hindus and Muslims.

Yet, this study reveals that devotion to Jesus is pervasive in minds of people of other faiths. The author identifies and describes in detail, through 84 personal interviews and a statistical survey of Madras City, a particular group of Jesus-devotees he terms "non-baptised believers in Christ". This situation is prevalent throughout the villages and towns of the State, sharing the beliefs of Christians and practising their faith privately outside the Church. The statistical survey reveals that there are about 200,000 members of this "Churchless Christianity" in the city of Madras alone.

In the concluding chapters the author offers his proposals for the evangelistic mission of the church in India, based on the information gained in this study. In the past, Christian mission work has often been an attack on the culture and family structure of the nation. Baptism, in particular, has in many cases been used to alienate people from their "roots" and create barriers. The author suggests that the Church must repentantly yet gradually begin anew its outreach to the Hindu and Muslim population and the non-baptised believers in Christ can be our guides and emissaries. They are the ones who successfully integrate Christianity into the faith and practice of Indian culture.

This study also provides valuable insights about the Hindu and Muslim population and their response to the various forms of evangelistic and outreach methods. I wish that serious students of missiology and sociology will follow up this work with more detailed analysis and critical evaluation of the statistical material that is available at Gurukul Library.

As Dean of Research & Publications of Gurukul Lutheran Theological College and Research Institute, Madras and as Secretary of Asian Programme for Advancement of Training and Studies (APATS), a L.W.F. concern in India, which are jointly responsible for the publication of this excellent and insightful study, I extend my grateful thanks to all the persons connected with this publication. First of all, special thanks are due to Dr. K. Rajaratnam, Executive Secretary, United Evangelical Lutheran Churches in India for graciously providing funds through the above departments, to Rev. J. Adiss Arnold for correcting the proofs and to the IELC Concordia Press & Training Institute Vaniyambadi for the printing of this work.

I hope that this book will provide both insights and impetus to the leaders of the Church in India for their future strategy and work as they seek to serve the Church in Christ's name.

R.R. SUNDARA RAO

Madras
Easter, 1991.

Introduction

The purpose of this book is to describe a fact and to reflect upon it theologically. The fact is that there are thousands of people in the cities, towns and villages of India who believe solely in Jesus Christ as their Lord and Saviour but who have no plans to take baptism or join the church. The first two sections of this book describe the life circumstances and belief patterns of these people. In these sections I attempt to be as objective as possible so that other missiologists and theologians can struggle with the facts, perhaps more successfully than I.

In the third section I attempt to think through the facts theologically and practically. The facts for our reflection are a new, non-Biblical phenomenon — though there are some interesting Biblical parallels — so we must proceed carefully and tentatively. We are dealing with facts of modern salvation history, so we must be as faithful to the past and as creative for the future as we possibly can. In this section I offer some suggestions for rethinking our theology and church structures missiologically. However, my purpose is to stimulate new thinking among the readers, rather than to set forth a completely established theological position.

The material is arranged, therefore, so that the reader will go through much the same pattern of reflection as I experienced. The reader will meet the non-baptised believers in Christ from the rural areas of Tamil Nadu as I did (chapter one), and he/she will draw certain conclusions about them (chapter two). We will then proceed to Section Two giving the general research on faith in Christ among Hindus, Muslims and others in the four-million population of greater Madras city. Through a study of these facts we will continue to reflect on the nature of Christian faith and the pattern of Christian nurture which has been developing around us. Finally, in the last two chapters we will attempt to think through the practical and theological implications of what we have experienced.

Initially, I had thought to limit the book to the first four chapters. I felt that everyone should have simply the bare facts and come to his/her own conclusions. However, friends advised me that I would inevitably colour the facts with my own opinions and interpretations anyway. In addition, since I have presented and discussed this research with more than thirty groups over the past two years, the reflections I have gathered from those discussions also should be shared. At any rate, the point to be kept in mind by the reader is that the first four chapters are the most important. It would be best if the reader wrote his/her own Section Three before going on to read mine.

One part of this research is not presented in this book. Therefore, I will inform the reader briefly about it. In October 1980 we selected a random sample from the clergy lists of the three Lutheran Churches in Tamil Nadu and from the five Church of South India dioceses who responded. I wrote these pastors concerning my research among non-baptised believers in Christ and requested that they describe the non-baptised believers known to them in their own pastorate area (according to age, sex, caste, years as non-baptised believer, etc.) I also asked the pastors for their evaluation of the faith and practise of these people and of their relationship to the church.

The prime purpose of this initial questionnaire was to make contacts in a random manner with the non-baptised believers themselves — which I did during the first months of 1981. However we were also able to determine through the responses of the pastors that they generally have a quite appreciative attitude toward the non-baptised believers known to them and a quite open pastoral relationship. Of the 246 non-baptised believers identified by the pastors only concerning 6% did the pastors mark the question saying that they felt the person was denying Christ by not taking baptism. In most cases the pastors also reported that the non-baptised believer welcomes him and other church workers to his/her home. Their faith in Christ is public, and their relation to the church is as close as possible. My personal contacts with the pastors during the second phase of the research and my subsequent discussions with groups of pastors and church workers have confirmed this impression from the questionnaire.

My suggestions for more missiological church structures in Section III also reflect the openness and eagerness which I found already there among local pastors, Bible women and evangelists. Many are already bending and ignoring missiologically frustrating church practices in order that the call and nurture of the Gospel can readily go beyond the church walls. Their greatest frustration and anger is directed not against the non-baptised believers but against the rigid church rules and rigid congregational attitude which hinder the free flow of the Gospel into the community. They want to be servants of the Kingdom, rather than servants of the church. Hopefully the practical and theological discussion which may result from this research will provide some loosening of minds and structures so that these dedicated church workers can follow the lead of the Spirit to which their hearts are responding. Usually church structures and rules change only after church practices have already changed.

The two-pronged research effort has attempted to describe both the qualitative and quantitative dimensions of the sociological fact of non-baptised believers in Christ in India. As surveyed in the text, the acceptance of Christ without acceptance of baptism has been a long and pervasive fact of Indian mission history. I began my research by first attempting to answer the qualitative questions. Through my interviews with the individuals I wanted to determine how far their belief was genuine and orthodox. Once I was sufficiently impressed with the quality of faith to be found I wanted to determine how extensive this phenomenon was yet today.

A great blessing of our Lord on this research was the availability of three female graduate students from the Madras Christian College — Dept. of Statistics. They brought both Christian zeal and academic skill to this formidable task of surveying a random sample of the entire city of Madras. The Statistics Department had previously carried out such a research several times in making studies of City voting patterns. Now we were able to harness this skill for a missiological study.

At the time I didn't realize it, but it was particularly providential that the researchers were women. Since we were concerned to get a reading of the Indian society traditionally inaccessible to the church, the non-threatening character of both the research and the researchers was crucial. Traditionally conservative Hindus and Muslims, even women, were willing to answer questions asked by young women at their door on a hot summer day. Since most of the non-baptised believers are women and since women tend to carry out the religious responsibilities of social life, it was essential that the researchers have access to women respondents. Thank God that He plans so much better for His work than we do.

As I urge scholars to study this primary data, I want also to urge Hindu and Muslim scholars to add their insights. I personally learned a great deal for this study from orthodox Hindu friends in Ambur and Madras, from the inter-religious seminars we had at Gurukul (especially the dialogue with the RSS), and from 'high caste' Christians and non-baptised believers. They presented to me a portrait of Christ as captivated within the Indian church. I have made some analysis and suggestions from this perspective, but what we desperately need is that these mumblings of frustration become a rising chorus of objection which we can no longer ignore.

As people concerned that the Gospel of salvation reach all people, we must try to keep up with the leading of the Spirit of God. In this research it became evident that God was leading in ways which are not only personally surprising but also theologically and institutionally disturbing. I have tried to catch the upsetting nature of this data with my choice of title: **"Churchless Christianity"** Theologically and traditionally, those two words are mutually contradictory. However, the data presents us with just this contradiction. We are dealing with a fact of mission history in India. We have a "happy problem". We should be grateful that our Lord is able to carry us forward in His great mission and present us with such wonderful surprises.

As church leaders confront this data, their happy problem will be how to react practically. As I describe in the text, on the local level many pastors are already taking initiatives. However, they realize that many of their thoughts and actions are contrary to church rules. What should the church's reaction to this phenomenon be: ignore it? foster it? guide it? squelch it? In the dozens of discussions I have conducted with church leaders on this topic I have found all these reactions and many more.

My guess is that this movement of the Spirit will continue with or without us — just as it has up till now in the mission history of India. I would further anticipate with the gradual elimination of Western organizational influence in the Indian church that a uniquely Indian mission scene will develop — perhaps similar to that unfolding before us in nearby China. God will carry out His Kingdom work. The only question is if God's People will help Him or hinder Him.

In a research effort like this, the cooperation of so many people is required. This research was controversial, but, nonetheless, I received fullest cooperation at almost every turn. It is a testimony to the maturity, generosity and zeal of the Indian church that it is willing to consider and encourage even that with which it disagrees — in the hope that the strange effort might also result in the promotion of our Lord's mission in the overwhelming and complex challenges before us. I have already thanked so many people privately and personally, but I would like to record some general words of thanks here publicly if for no other reason than to illustrate the fine cooperation which church leaders at all levels provided in this effort:

I thank the President and Bishops of the India Evangelical Lutheran Church, the Arcot Lutheran Church, the Tamil Evangelical Lutheran Church, and the CSI dioceses of Madras, Coimbatore, Madurai, Tirunelveli and Kanyakumari.

I thank the fifty-four local pastors who responded to my initial questionnaire and the twenty who helped me with the local interviews. I thank their generous wives and congregation families who so willingly hosted me and provided accommodation.

I thank the Gurukul office staff especially Mr. Duraisamy, Mr. Joshua, Ms. Jayakumari who energetically and efficiently carried out the mailings and prepared the subsequent research documents.

I especially thank my co-Programme Secretary on the Gurukul Faculty, J. Adiss Arnold, who so ably and selflessly guided this research work. He helped me to formulate and interpret the questionnaires, and he carried out the taxing job of classifying all the castes in the Madras City survey.

I thank Dr. Gift Siromony, Head of the Statistics Department of Madras Christian College, for encouraging and guiding the survey of Madras City and for approvingly reading through chapters 3 and 4 of this book.

I thank Mr. David Ipe of the MCC Statistics Department especially, for he took up the implementation of the Madras City survey as a personal ministry, aiding me at all points in the work, from the several draft tests of the questionnaire, to the choosing and training of the researchers, to the final typing of the computer cards and seeing the material through the IIT computer.

I thank with great respect the three Statistics graduate students who carried out the survey in the heat of June all over the lanes and corners of this large city: Ms. Helen George, Ms. Shanta David, and Ms. Vanaja Pushparaj.

I thank the excellent typists who prepared all these materials for the press, Mrs. Shirley Malani of Kodaikanal School for chapter 1—4 and Mr. K.I.E. Victor of Gurukul for chapters 5—6. They, too, took up this task as a personal ministry, giving of their free time.

I thank the Gurukul Director, Rev. J. Gnanabaranam Johnson, and the Gurukul College Council for releasing me from regular programme activities so that I could pursue this special research on behalf of Gurukul and on behalf of the broader mission of the church.

Finally, I thank the mentor of the new Gurukul, Dr. K. Rajaratnam, who so energetically supported and guided our ministry even while away serving as Asia Secretary in the Lutheran World Federation. He commended this initiative and provided the funding for this publication.

Thanks above all to God who has entrusted to us His ministry of reconciliation and uplifted our lives into His great redemptive work among the nations.

March, 1983

Herbert E. Hoefer
Gurukul Lutheran Theological College & Research Institute,
Madras, India.

Because of changeover of staff at Gurukul and Concordia Press, it has taken seven years to bring this book to publication. In the meantime, several Gurukul faculty members had to step in as editors. The last one, Rev. J. Adiss Arnold, has indeed done yeoman service in overseeing all the final details — even while in the midst of completing his own doctoral dissertation. I thank him very much for his time, skill and dedication.

Dr. K. Rajaratnam has kindly agreed to write a Preface for the publication. Two successive Directors of Gurukul, Bishop Dorairaj Peter and Dr. M. Bage and Dr. D. W. Jesudoss, Principal of Gurukul's revived academic programme oversaw the administrative arrangements. Dr. R. R. Sundara Rao oversaw the original book jacket as Dean of Research and Publications for Gurukul. The staff of IELC Concordia Press and Training Institute, Vaniyambadi, faithfully brought the whole process to completion.

I made a visit to India in August 1990, to help with the final details. Because of the long delay, some of the statistical tables and some of the footnotes had been lost. We got everything together except some of the footnotes for the sixth chapter. I apologize to the reader for this gap in the publication.

At any rate, it was a great joy to be back with God's wonderful people of India, from whom I have always learned and received so much. I deeply hope and pray that this publication will be of some service to them in their great mission of God in that great land.

Herbert E. Hoefer
Pastor,
Luther Memorial Church,
River Falls, Wisconsin, U. S. A.

April 1991

SECTION ONE

Jesus' "Other Sheep" in Rural Tamil Nadu

CHAPTER ONE

"Who Are They ?"

(Interviews with eighty-four non-baptized believers in rural Tamil Nadu)

Various regions in Tamilnadu where the Author had interviewed NBBCs.

"Who Are They?"

Let us meet some of Jesus' "other sheep." These people consider themselves followers of Jesus, and they are considered such also in the general community. As per the survey I did among a random sample of CSI and Lutheran pastors in Tamil Nadu, the pastors also consider these people faithful disciples of Jesus. (The pastors evaluated only 6% of them as denying Christ by not taking baptism).

In the random sample of pastors I asked the pastors to list the non-baptized believers in Christ known to him in his parish area. I then visited those pastorates which had a significant number. In total, I interviewed 84 of the 247 NBBCs listed by the pastors. They were in typical cross-section socio-economically, spread out over nine districts of the state.

The interviews were generally carried out in the presence of the pastor or Bible woman/evangelist. The locus was according to the preference of the interviewee, often in the home unless the interviewee preferred to meet at the church or in the pastor's house. We would sit on the floor together. Since I speak Tamil, no interpretation was necessary. The duration was 45—60 minutes on an average.

I would open the interview with a prayer of thanksgiving to God for this opportunity to discuss as brothers and sisters in Christ, asking for His guidance as we shared with each other. Only in a couple of instances was I asked to teach on a particular topic. I would close with a prayer summarizing the joys and problems expressed. Generally the interview was a matter of their responses to my questions. Often toward the end of the interview period I would share with them some other experiences of NBBCs similar to them.

Several times I was asked for advice as to whether they should take baptism or not. My usual reply was that they should take baptism in a way which attracts and convinces their relatives. I advised them to visit each relative's home beforehand to explain their motivation for baptism. They might also offer to wait until their relatives give consent. Their goal should be to bring the whole family to Christ.

I usually began the interview with similar questions. However the course of the discussion would differ according to the particular problems and viewpoints expressed by the interviewee. Examples of the questions asked are as follows:

"How did you first come to learn about Jesus?"

"What attracted you about Jesus?"

"What benefit have you found in praying to Jesus?"

NB.: the Hindu term here for "praying" emphasises the idea of worship, the word "benefit" in Tamil literally means "good things"; thus, the literal translation of this important question would be: "What good things have you received in worshipping Jesus?"

"After receiving these benefits, what have you felt that Jesus expects of you?"

"If you have already received benefits from Jesus, do you see any need for baptism?"

"What practice of personal devotion and regular nurture do you follow?"

"Do you celebrate any Hindu festivals? If so, how do you celebrate them and why?"

"Do you celebrate Christmas at home? Do you go to Church at Christmas, Easter, Good Friday, or any other Christian festival?"

"Do you have cottage prayer meetings in your home with the Pastor and other Christians? If not, would you welcome such a thing?"

"How do you feel about a person of Christian faith wearing a *tilak*, putting a *kolam*, changing his name, etc.?"

"How do you try to witness to Jesus?"

"Do you expect problems ever arranging marriages for your children because of your Christian faith?"

"Do you have family devotions? Do you teach your children your Christian faith?"

"Do you plan eventually to take baptism?"

Bible Reading?

"Do you desire to take Holy Communion?"

In a few instances there was hesitation to discuss these points. I will note this when I describe the interviews in the next section. However, the vast majority were quite happy to discuss their situation and experiences. Most also showed surprising confidence concerning the correctness of their position on baptism and comfortableness concerning their more distant relationship to the organized church. As my initial survey of the pastors' opinions showed (ef. pp.) generally the church leaders show sympathetic understanding toward their situation. Their remaining without baptism leaves less problems for all concerned.

Now let us meet the individuals and groups with whom I spoke. I will describe briefly the setting in which the interview took place, but I will not reveal the exact village or the interviewee's name. I have those details in case anyone desires to make a responsible follow-up research. One might also contact the local pastor, for the NBBCs I was able to interview were ones well known in the community. There are many others, of course, unknown to anybody — except our Lord.

I will present the interviews beginning from the Southern tip of Tamiinadu and proceeding North. Thus we will begin in an area (Kanyakumari District) where Christians are one-half of the population and conclude where Christians are only 3%. I will add occasional notes on the relevant socio-cultural dynamics behind the situation described, since some of the readers may not be familiar with the dynamics of rural Tamilian society. I would request the reader to try to enter into the mind and heart of these "other sheep" of our Lord in order to determine empathetically their spiritual state. Only thereafter can we responsibly and creatively reflect on the theological and practical implications.

A Small Town near the border of Kerala, Kanyakumari District

The CSI pastor invited the two men to come at one time to his parsonage to discuss with me. The men preferred that I not come to their home. Both were of lower middle class, Nayar caste; one is a tailor and the other runs a small shop.

The tailor attends church regularly, but he goes to and from Church by a circuitous route in order to avoid the ridiculing comments of his Hindu neighbours. Twenty years ago a pastor's prayers had helped to heal his sister. He has a picture of Jesus in his private room at the back of his shop, but a Hindu picture in the shop itself. He celebrates Christmas in his home but not other Hindu festivals or rituals, for which he suffers ridicule from Hindu neighbours and relatives. He reads his Bible in the evening. His brothers and sisters also believe in Christ secretly, not being bold enough to go to church. His children also believe but they are not baptised. He says that he would have no objection to their baptism if that is what God wills for them and what they desire.

The small businessman does not go to Church, but he reads his Bible and prays before a picture of Jesus in his home. He had studied in a Christian school and thereby learned of Jesus. He has experienced Jesus' help in response to his prayers. He listens to Christian Radio programmes. He celebrates only Pongal. (N.B.: Pongal is a three-day festival in January, which is primarily a social event, involving the whole village community. Many village Christians also participate in the festivities, though avoiding the one or two traditional Hindu home rituals).

In the conversation, they jointly made the following statements:

They fear the reaction of their relations if they would take baptism.

They want to have a Christian burial.

They attend Christian public meetings, but their wives do not come along.

They expect Jesus to take them to heaven and to take care of their children.

They do not feel bad about not taking baptism, nor do they feel that God is displeased with them because of it.

God expects of them that they lead a decent life as a follower of Jesus.

They feel they should go to church.

If they take baptism, they feel they should leave going to the cinema, smoking and other bad habits. (NB.: Emphasis on cleansing one's life of bad habits is strong among many Protestant denominations, especially in Southern Tamilnadu where "low church" missions were predominant)

They do not try to persuade their wives to join their Christian faith, as it would only cause conflict in the home and among the relations. Now they are still accepted by their caste people and family members.

Their wives also fear that the family Hindu god would punish them if they ceased to worship.

The best way to reach their wives would be through Christian literature. If there were Bible women, they could possibly speak with them. Otherwise, only prayer for them is possible.

They expressed appreciation for the pastor and the congregation. (N.B.: The pastor spoke of the many conflicts and factions in the congregation, however. These men knew of the congregational life only through the regular worship).

They would not be interested to join in a cottage prayer meeting even if it was nearby.

They understood Jesus as teaching us to avoid a sinful life and to do good to others.

A Village near Martandam, Kanyakumari District:

The Lutheran pastor knew of this Nair family, though he had not had much intimate contact with them. (However, as a result of this interview he now visits them regularly). We walked through the rice fields to reach their home which is located on temple property just beside the wall of a large Hindu temple. They are quite poor.

This family is the physical and spiritual descendent of one Devasahayam Pillai, an officer of the Maharaja of Travancore who converted to Christianity in the early nineteenth century and suffered martyrdom. The Roman Catholic Church has constructed a small shrine in his honour on the roadside nearby. The old man of the house (now deceased) was aged eighty-nine years. He said that he was fifth generation non-baptised believer in Christ in his family. The widowed daughter has the same Christian faith, as do her four small children. One of the sons, who is a doctor in a nearby town, also is of Christian faith though not baptised. He has suffered blindness and the loss of both wife and son in his life. The other sons have no religious faith or practice, and they live elsewhere.

The family does not participate in any of the local Hindu functions though they rent from the temple itself. This has caused some friction with the local Hindu community, who at times threaten to vacate them from the house. Everyone knows of their Christian faith, but they do not practice it outwardly because it would irritate the surrounding Hindu authorities upon whom they are dependent. The elderly man is a retired Tamil Pandit, and the family survives only on his pension.

The family occasionally worships at the local Roman Catholic Church, but the priest does not come to visit them. At one point the priest had also advised them against taking baptism, as they would have to face many more difficulties in their life. They do not keep a picture of Jesus in their home, but they pray to Him. They have found no relief in their troubles through their prayers to Jesus for help. When he dies, the old man expressed that he wants to be buried in a sitting position and that he knows he "will be going to Jesus."

Another Village near Martandam, Kanyakumari District

The same Lutheran pastor took me to the home of a former teacher of his in his hometown. He is of the Pannikkar community, retired with his Hindu wife. They have only his pension to live on.

The man came to the Christian faith while studying in a Christian school as a boy. He believes that Jesus has saved him from his sins and will give him good in the future. He feels that he "lost his chance" to take baptism before he got married. After marriage he had to consider his wife and her family, and, most important, the marriage alliances of his children. (N.B.: Marriages are arranged only along caste lines, and relatives would not be willing to give their sons or daughters into a family where there might arise religious dissension and division). He expressed that this was the big problem also for "many others."

He says he goes to church occasionally and also to large public meetings. He observed that caste feelings also continue inside the church so he doesn't see any benefit in joining. He also attends temple worship and Hindu festivals, but he says that his prayers then also are Christian. He spoke quite dejectedly about his spiritual situation, for he felt compelled by circumstances to live "against his conscience."

In the same village we met a woman of upper middle class who is from the same Pannikkar community. Her father had appealed to the missionaries several decades previously, along with the above mentioned teacher, to construct a separate chapel for the five Panikkar families in the village on land which they would provide; however, the missionaries refused. After her marriage she had to join in her husband's religion, and her sons are leading devotees in the local temple. She complained that the local church no longer visits her house when they come on *bajanai* (N.B.: "Bajanai" is a form of carolling which is practiced on full-moon nights and festivals.) She no longer practices a Christian faith in any way.

Poovancode, Kanyakumari District

This next example I mention only to illustrate another aspect of the Hindu relationship to Christ. There are several high-caste families here who regularly call the pastor for any family function (e.g. opening a new business, moving to a new house, sending off to college, etc.) They also send their children to Sunday School and VBS, attend big Christian rallies, read Christian magazines, and listen to Christian radio programmes. However, when asked what they understood to be the teaching of the Christian religion, all they could reply was the Ten Commandments.

As we sat on the verandah of one of the houses and discussed, they spoke proudly of the harmonious way in which religions coexist in their town. They tried to take what is best in all religions. They have only Hindu worship in their homes because the festivals and customs are their "Family heritage." They do not pray to Jesus privately. They view Jesus as one of the *avatars,* but not sinless. When asked if he would object to one of his sons taking baptism, the father said he would not object if this is what the son sincerely wanted — though he also observed immediately that he does not see that Christians are any better than anybody else.

Such people - who are, of course, very numerous - I do not classify as non-baptized believers in Christ. They have neither the orthodox belief nor devoted practice which is expected of a follower of Christ. Jesus has no special place in their spiritual life, and they have made no break with their Hindu pattern of worship.

Nagercoil, Kanyakumari District

Around the beginning of the century, the "Zenana Mission" ("Zenana" is the term for Hindu women staying inside the house) of the LMS began work in Nagercoil. They opened several schools on caste Hindu streets for girls. The women missionary teachers would teach about Christianity in the schools, and they would visit the mothers of the girls in their homes to teach literacy and Christianity. They did not emphasize baptism in their ministry because the "Zenana" women had to live within Hindu households.

In the mid-60's the CSI diocese decided to give all their schools to the government, but these Zenana Mission schools were converted into meeting halls. Some of the teachers volunteered to leave the security and benefits of government teaching in order to continue the mission work as diocesan Bible Women. These Bible women now have a regular schedule of worship and Bible study for high-caste women in these meeting halls.

I visited three such meeting places and met groups of women ranging in number from ten to fifteen. Some were curious, some hostile, some inquirers, some non-baptised believers, and some baptised. They came from a variety of high castes. (N.B.: As long as the mission does not emphasise baptism or congregational membership, the women feel free to mix on this informal basis. Baptism is viewed and given as a free privilege of participation, rather than as a necessary requirement of participation.

At one place the Bible women pointed proudly to a small Hindu shrine just outside the small meeting hall. They said the local Hindu men had erected this shrine when they heard that the mission workers were going to use the building for Christian work. They tried to inaugurate the shrine by having the "devi" dance and receive possession of the spirit as a sign that the spirit had come to the idol. However, the "devi" never entered into her trance, though she tried several times, so the men apologised and left the shrine unused.

(N.B.: The incident demonstrates how popular Hinduism also discriminates between the idol and God. If a spirit is not known to have made its dwelling in the object, it is not worshipped. Jyoti Sahi tells an interesting story of some villagers in Karnataka in this regard in his article in "Christian Art in India").

Through events like this the women gained faith in the power of Jesus. They also had many personal experiences of the power of

the mission workers' prayers, so women from all backgrounds will come to them when in personal or family distress. These women are completely tied to the house and family affairs, and they find mental peace from their worries through the prayers of the Bible women. They came to the meetings out of curiosity and unexpectedly found new peace and happiness. Many witnessed in our discussions concerning the power of Jesus to heal their family members and to bring peace in their distress. A few spoke of the faith in Jesus which had been created in the hearts of their husbands as well through these experiences, but they will not come to church or kneel in prayer.

The major problem they all expressed in regard to baptism was the marriage of their daughters. When one woman spoke of having four daughters, all the other women assented a sympathetic "Aah." One woman said she would take baptism if God made this necessity clear in her own heart. (Later, one of the Bible women commented to me that she blames the church people primarily for these women's hesitation to take baptism; for if they would arrange inter-caste marriages, the major obstacle to baptism would be removed.)

However, all have a deep fear in their hearts over the anger and power of the family gods. They understand that they must worship only Jesus if they take baptism; whereas, now many keep a picture of Jesus among with the pictures of other gods in their *puja* room. If they take baptism and cease to carry out the family rituals, every family difficulty and calamity thereafter will be attributed to the women's failing to serve the family god. One woman expressed that baptism is not necessary, for one can pray to Jesus and receive His help also as an unbaptised person. The understanding in the families and community is that each person has the right and privilege to worship the god of his choice, the god which meets his/her needs. One woman specifically said that all gods are the same, but "my god is Jesus."

(N.B.: This understanding of religious reality and practice is called throughout India as "ishta devata". A god will serve those who serve it. It will punish those who are unfaithful to it. All gods are real forces and one must choose and experience the god whose help and protection one will solicit in life. Thus, there is a very personal, mutual relationship between the devotee and the god.)

Travelling one early morning on the government bus they put the usual Hindu morning devotional songs over the bus cassette tape recorder. One of the songs had the tune and theology of a Christian devotional lyric; but when I listened carefully, it was devoted to *Murugan,* not Christ. Another negative illustration of the same religious reality can be shown through the story, one convert, from the Nadar community, told me concerning his brother who also had been considering conversion. One early morning he had a vision in which *Murugan* told him that he would care for him if he continued to worship him. In order to prove his power and promise, *Murugan* told the young man, a cocoanut tree worker, that he should not tend his trees that evening. In such case, there would normally be no flow of sap into the bags the following morning. However, when he went to inspect the bags the next morning they were abnormally full. Thus, the brother gradually fell from the Christian faith. The village gods are a reality for these people to cope with. Jesus is understood as a god who must prove His faithfulness and power in competition with many other divine forces.)

The women also understand that many of the traditional customs of their Hindu community will come under question if they take baptism. Besides leaving the *pujas* which are an essential part of daily family life and of important community festivals, many feel they should leave the wearing of the *tilak* on the forehead, the putting of the *kolam* in front of the house, going to the cinema, etc. Others argued that the *tilak* and the *kolam* are simply cultural decorations. (N.B.: The "tilak" is the red spot placed on the forehead, traditionally representing the third eye of Shiva, emitting consuming fire. The "kolam" is the ricepowder decoration put by the women in front of the door each morning and evening traditionally to welcome the good spirits to the house. Most Protestants reject the *tilak* and some reject the *kolam* as external signs of identification with Hindu tradition. Roman Catholics practice these signs as cultural decorations and some innovatively avoid religious connotations by avoiding the red *tilak* — putting only a colour which matches their saree. A few spoke of how their children happily attended the mission Sunday School until they were told that going to the cinema and reading certain books were wrong.

In addition, certain common Christian customs would cause misunderstanding and offense among their Hindu family members. A Hindu woman removes her *tilak* and wears a white saree (worn by Pentecostal women on Sundays) only when she is widowed. In Christian prayer she is taught to cover her head with her saree, but in Hindu practice this gesture is only done to symbolize sorrow while on the way to a funeral. Similarly, Protestant social mores in the area are that a woman should not beautify herself with jewels or "manjal" (yellow sandal paste to make one's complexion fairer). Once again, avoidance of these things is a public sign of mourning in the general community. Family members and husbands oppose these practices because they become the subject of community ridicule when others see the woman in these inappropriate symbolic postures.

The women's practice of their Christian faith is confined to their private prayers in the home and to participation in the mission meetings as and when they feel the need for Bible study or special prayers. Many still go to the temple with family and friends, especially at festival time but they say that they only think of Jesus when they are there. One said that she was allowed to conduct a Christmas celebration in her home. All contribute to the mission financially, especially at festival time. They do not know about Holy Communion, for they have never seen it. Some had attended Roman Catholic worship but they did not like it because it was too much like Hindu worship.

Report of a Family in Kanyakumari District

Rev. S. Daniel, a faculty member at the Concordia Seminary, Nagercoil, told of a visit he had made to a Vellala headman's family in Kanyakumari district. Twenty years previously they had been ministered to by a Vellala pastor, who would hold worship in their home. However, subsequent pastors of different caste backgrounds had refused to treat them differently from others. When Rev. Daniel (a man of Vellala caste origins) visited them, he found that they were still exclusively Christian in their worship and belief and extremely happy to have a Vellala pastor minister to them. (N.B.: It is common experience that village families prefer the ministry of pastors/evangelists/Bible women from their own caste background. They are able to relate without any cultural barriers. However, it is also common experience that any church-worker of proven spiritual character or of effective prayer is welcome into any home.)

A Village near Tirunelveli

When I arrived at the CSI parsonage, three people were waiting for me. The pastor went about his other business, while I discussed with the non-baptized believers in Christ whom he had called together to meet me. I could not go into depth with any one of the group, for all were quite conscious of the presence of the others; and, being from quite different social backgrounds, they hesitated to speak freely before the others.

A woman of the Nayar caste spoke of how her husband and son have been believers in Christ for eight years. They both had studied in Christian schools and learned of Christ. The husband's father had a vision of Christ, and one brother also is a non-baptised believer. The husband does not join his wife in coming to Church, but he occasionally joins her for the big public meetings. They do not have family devotions, but worship Jesus along with the Hindu gods in their home. Their approach to the Hindu festivals is to carry them, out but to think of God, not Jesus specifically The woman felt there is nothing wrong with the *tilak* and *kolam.*

If all goes well, they hope one day to take baptism together. Now they are waiting for his mother to pass away so that her feelings in old age might not be hurt. Then they will decide in consultation with their relatives. I asked her what her relations say when she asks them to try Christianity. She said they tell her:

"Jesus is the Nadar God." However, even more disappointing and confusing for them has been the fact that none of their prayers to Jesus have been answered, "even at the meetings of Brother Dinakaran." They have many problems and no peace of mind.

A high school girl spoke, with much fervency and conviction about her Christian faith. She has learned about Christ at the Christian school, and she attends church regularly. She is of Nadar caste and so is the congregation. She does not think it is important to join the congregation but to worship Jesus.

The girl's big concern is her parents. She tries to avoid arguing with them about Christ, but they say that "The Hindu gods are better." Her parents will read the Bible and other Christian literature, but they will not come to the big public meeting with her. She is not worried about her marriage prospects because she is confident that "God will take care of it," She understands that God expects her to be "a good example so that her parents, will see and like Christ."

The third person was a young man of lower caste who earns his livelihood by playing the drum at Hindu festivals and functions. "All this is what I must do", he said, "but my faith is in Christ. Outside I am a Hindu, but inside I am a Christian." He also queried about the many denominations, expressing his confusion as to "which Jesus is the great one."

A Village near Pavoorchatrani, Tirunelveli District

The CSI pastor took me to the home of a couple, both school teachers, with three children. They are from Harijan background, while the local CSI church is Nadar and the Roman Catholic church is Harijan. Both studied at a CSI high school and teachers training Institute, and now attend church regularly. The husband told how he had prayed secretly as a youth that his parents would arrange a marriage for him with a woman who was a Christian.

Both expressed that they had found Christians most helpful to them in their life and thus came to appreciate the Christian faith. After three years of marriage they had no child; but after praying once in the church they had one. This experience deeply confirmed their faith. They expressed how they have always found strength in their difficulties, peace in their heart, and ability to attain good character through the Christian faith.

They do not celebrate any of the Hindu festivals, including Pongal, even though they consider it a secular festival. All the relatives on both sides are Hindu and they blame every difficulty which arises in their life on the fact that they fail to go to the temples. However, they feel financially secure and independent, so they do not care about their family's feelings.

They said that they plan to take baptism soon. No one had urged them to take baptism or explained to them its meaning, so they had not taken it very seriously. However, now they want their children baptised, but they feel that they should be baptised first. When I asked them how they feel about their children losing the opportunity to get government Harijan scholarships after baptism, they said that their children would not receive anyway since they both are earning a good salary. They also spoke of the witness value of baptism over against their Hindu relations, for then they will appreciate how much Christianity means to them.

Next the pastor took me to another nearby village where we entered the home of a retired teacher, who had taken baptism after many years of Christian faith (probably after completing the marriages of his children). However, the wife had not been baptised though she comes to church regularly, sitting in the back. They are of Mudaliar caste and live on Mudaliar Street. The wife never came onto the verandah where we were sitting, but listened from the kitchen. Therefore, I was unable to interview her.

The husband explained that he came to the Christian faith already as a boy through the visits of the Dhonavur Fellowship "zenana mission" workers to their home when teaching his mother to read. He also went to their hospital and attended public meetings there. He said that his son-in-law also had been healed through prayer to Jesus. Through his Christian faith, he had found peace in all his troubles of life. He feels the confidence of God's guidance in all the difficulties of life.

At first there was some opposition from his Mudaliar community. They said that Christianity is a "foreign religion." However, as they maintained all the social traditions of their community (zenana practices, marriage alliances, use of incense in the home, placing of kolam at the doorstep, participation in marriage festivals), the others came to respect their faith and keep social unity. However, they do not participate in the Hindu festivals. Now he feels that others recognise that one becomes a Christian today because his heart is changed, not for material benefit.

(Afterwards I discussed with the pastor what he was going to do when the woman died. He expressed his confusion and consternation, for everyone in the church and community knew that she practiced only the Christian faith; yet, the church rules would not allow him to bury her. No doubt, it would cause a great offence in the Hindu community if the church refused these final rites to one who had been so faithful. I advised the pastor to contact his bishop even now to get permission to bury her, in consultation with the congregational council.)

The pastor also told of two other people who were not available for interview. One is a 25-year old Chettiar forest ranger. Four years earlier he had gone to the nearby clinic of a private Christian doctor. The doctor advised him that he would get better in a month if he prayed to Jesus. The man was healed and converted to belief in Christ. Through him, his whole family came to the Christian faith and took baptism. However, he remains unbaptised because the security of his job would be jeopardised.

Because of their baptism, the family is suffering a good deal of persecution, even though they are big landlords in their village. The local Hindu workers refuse to work on their property, and other Hindu leaders refuse them water from the "Hindu well." The community leaders also insist that they give the usual annual tax for celebrating the Hindu festivals, but they refuse to give except as a voluntary contribution.

The Pastor also told of a local Nadar mill owner who finally took baptism at the age of sixty together with his wife. He has duly joined the local congregation as a member. There is a great deal of rivalry between the Christian Nadars and Hindu Nadars in the town, so now the Hindu employees in his mill, in his private management school and on his lands refuse to cooperate with him. His daughter also recently took baptism after working as a warden in a Christian hostel. Soon after his baptism the old man was in a bus accident, so his Hindu acquaintances quickly attributed this misfortune to his conversion. However, he pointed out that others in the accident had suffered greater injuries than he, so it was Jesus who had protected him.

A Village near Sampoothu, Tirunelveli District

We had to travel by bicycle to reach this remote village. We first met with the congregation leaders, and it was only with some difficulty that I persuaded them to take me to the non-baptised believers in the village. The congregation is a Harijan community, but the four NBBC families are of the lower sweeper community.

The congregation leaders stood with me as several of the men and women from the four families gradually gathered. We spoke together while standing outside the little collection of mud huts. The men confirmed that they do not join in Hindu festivals any more, but they come at Christmas to church and give their offerings. This statement evoked a comment from one of the congregation people about something these people had done in the worship service. A heated argument ensued between the two groups, which finally one of the congregation leaders brought to order, observing that these people simply did not know what was proper in church.

The men and women said that they would welcome it if the pastor and congregation people would come to their homes for cottage prayer meetings. Already now they bring their children when sick to the pastor or evangelist for blessing. They said they would have to discuss together about coming for baptism. They must arrange for marriage with their community in other village (Later I asked the congregation leaders if they would make marriage alliances with these people if they joined the congregation, and they quite adamantly said 'no'). They said that they do not ask financial help of the church, but they would like facilities like a place in boarding for their children.

On the way back through Tirunelveli, I stopped at another village. In speaking with the evangelist about my research, he pointed to a nearby house where a Mudaliar family lives. He said that they are secret believers who never come to church but go occasionally to big public meetings in other places. They became believers in Christ before coming to this village, but no one knows their history. They celebrate the Hindu festivals, but in a mild way. I did not feel it appropriate to draw attention to them in the community by going to visit them.

(N.B.: The subject of inter-caste marriages has come up several times in the discussions recorded so far. For people unfamiliar with the Indian culture, this may require some clarification. Most marriages are arranged by parents with a close family relative. The children have the security that this major matter is being handled for them in a responsible way. This pattern of marriage builds close family ties and mutual caring in times of crisis.

It is rare that parents will arrange a marriage with someone outside their caste. Such marriages usually occur among college students who get to know each other and force the parents to accept. Among less educated, village-level people marriage outside one's caste is unthinkable and highly problematic. A successful marriage is made up of many intimate attitudes, understandings and customs. These predispositions are formed deeply in one's childhood through the modelling of one's parents and relatives. Caste marriages allow for a broad foundation of mutual understanding on these intimate matters of life (e.g. how to discipline the children, how to handle money, how to relate to in-laws, the different roles of husband/wife or father/mother, types of cooking, practice of religion, use of leisure time, etc.). Therefore, marriages which follow family or caste lines provide a smooth transition for the new couple. In India people look to marriage for such family stability rather than for personal stimulation and enrichment (except, of course, among some urban, cosmopolitan couples). Parents arrange marriages for their children along caste lines because they want them to have as little difficulty as possible and to remain as close to the family as possible. When my father advised me as a young man "not to marry higher than you are", he was following the same principle).

Mukudal, near Tirunelveli

Once again, I had three people waiting for me as I entered the CSI Pastor's home. The CSI congregation is Nadar, and the Roman Catholic congregation is Harijan. A college student said that he has been in the Christian faith for some time, but he has decided not to take baptism until he secures a government job. He will lose the government reservation for his caste if he is baptised. A Nayar husband and wife revealed that they were waiting for his mother to die before taking baptism. A young man spoke rather casually of his recent baptism in response to the annual bishop's appeal to give teaching positions to new converts. However, he said that his wife hesitates to take baptism because of her parents' fears for the marriages of her brothers and sisters. They are Asari caste.

Sivakasi

Sivakasi is the location of the famous "secret Christians". In fact, they are neither "secret" nor "Christian." They are not Christian because they are not baptised. (According to my definition, if you are baptised, you are called a Christian whether you believe or not). Secondly, they are not really secret about their faith. Most practice it now quite openly, and all practice it quite tactfully. Perhaps we could most accurately call them "tactful believers in Christ".

Let us meet them. There are an estimated two hundred nonbaptised believers in Christ in Sivakasi, all Nadar women. There are about an equal number of baptised women, and about thirty baptised families, according to the local CSI pastor. They have a large chapel which was constructed through donations from the community, especially from the well-to-do husbands of the women believers. This unusual congregation is the result of the Zanana Mission workers once again. They began their work in the Sivakasi area in 1896, eventually opening thirteen schools for girls in the town and on the outskirts. These British women and their Bible women would visit the homes of the caste Hindu school girls to teach literacy and Bible to the mothers. They also developed a two-year series of booklets on the life of Jesus, on the lives of the saints, on the Ten Commandments, and on basic Christian teachings. Along with this went a five-year plan of memory verses. They would meet for classes in any home where the husband would allow, and there would be regular tests and prizes awarded.

This whole system has fallen into disuse since the British missionaries left twenty years ago. Now the work is carried on by four Bible women, but most of the nurture is carried out by the women themselves in home fellowship meetings around prayer and Bible study. I met only one woman who was a non-Nadar in these fellowship groups.

The missionaries also conducted an annual full moon convention at the end of June for three days, and this practice still continues, gathering thousands of people from the twenty surrounding villages. The popular belief is that a woman will be blessed with a child if she prays at this convention. There have also been thousands of adult immersion baptisms at this convention over the years.

The piety of the women is strongly prayer-oriented. I was called upon to address the evening service (at which the whole right side of the church was full of women, with only a handful of men sitting at the rear on the left side), and afterwards there was a long line of women with requests for special prayers through the laying on of hands. Through the prayers of the mission workers and fellowships they seek release from their physical ills and family problems. There are no poor people in this movement. They are "zenana" women who bring to their fellowships all the tensions and pressures of their restricted family life.

At the beginning of the work there was a great deal of opposition from the men. The Bible women would visit the women during the day when the men were out. The women would sneak off to church for the early morning or late evening service in the dark, saying that they were going to a friend's house. Often they would hide a second saree when they left the house, change into it at the friend's house, cover their head in the second saree to and from church, and return home after changing back into the first saree. The beating of wives for going to church was quite common in the early decades, and even two weeks before I visited a woman had been beaten by her son and her Bible torn into shreds. The older women speak quite proudly about their struggles in those days. It was a kind of women's liberation movement in a very male-dominated social system.

Even today the men keep themselves quite aloof from this Christian movement. They insist that the women carry out the traditional Hindu festivals, but the women said that they refuse to participate in the actual worship. Most of the men now allow their wives to carry on with their Christian faith and practices as long as they also carry on with their traditional cultural life, including the wearing of the *tilak,* putting of the *kolam,* preparing the home festivals, etc. The pastor said that some women come to him before or after they have been required to carry out a Hindu festival or to go to the temple in order to receive forgiveness. Even there, they say they pray only to Jesus when standing before the idol. Some women are not allowed to read the Bible in their home, so they do so in a neighbouring home or they keep it secretly in the kitchen and read in the daytime. Others say that they can pray only while lying in the bed morning and evening, not kneeling. Another controversy often comes when a believing woman dies, for some husbands insist on cremation ceremonies.

The proper relationship between faith and culture is a point of on-going controversy both within Hindu families and in the Christian fellowship. Besides the issues of *tilak* and *kolom,* many will question a woman if she puts too much white facial powder on, for it looks like Hindu "vibuthi" ashes on the forehead. One woman told of a vision she had showing two bullocks pulling a cart in opposite directions. That morning she took down all the pictures of Hindu gods in the house and kept only the Bible. Another woman commented, "I prefer to read the Bible rather than newspapers or magazines.

However, most of the women try to practice their faith in a way which also keeps peace and harmony in the house. These inter-faith domestic conflicts, as well as the usual family problems, are the main topics of their prayers. It hurts them that "the Hindu community thinks less of us if we are baptised, for they say that we have left our Indian traditions." The CSI traditions are more acceptable to the Hindu husbands than the sectarian and Pentecostal groups because their worship methods are so loud and their rejection of traditional culture so complete.

All of the women speak of their desire to be baptised. No children are baptised, except in Christian families. The boys attend Sunday School for a while, but soon the father takes them with him into work at the business. The girls are not baptised because it would affect the chances of their marriage arrangements, so each non-baptised believing girl must try to work it out with her husband later on. Most believing women try to arrange a marriage with the child of another believing woman so that at least the mother-in-law will support her daughter in the faith and not oppose baptism. In earlier days baptisms were sometimes carried out in the homes secretly at night, but now it is always done by immersion at the church, even if secretly.

Their women's major worry about taking baptism is that it will affect getting marriages arranged for their children. It seems that the community has now come to adjust itself to the reality of this Christian movement and to recognise that these women try to maintain some participation in traditional Hindu life. There seems to be more hesitation to take a daughter from a family where the husband is baptised, for they fear that she will not accept her Hindu husband and relations properly. The Hindu men of the Nadar community are generally involved in the big businesses of match-making, offset printing and fire works in Sivakasi. The Christian men are primarily teachers and office workers. Therefore, since marriages are arranged according to financial status, Christian wives of Hindu husbands must usually give their daughters to Hindu men in marriage.

The women commented that their husbands say "we will become poor if we become Christian." They will suffer loss of prestige in their society and loss of business prosperity. They would have to forego expensive marriage functions, luxurious living and enjoyable habits (like smoking, going to cinema, dressing well, etc.) In regard to Government discrimination against Christians in the allotment of scholarships and employment privileges unbaptised Nadar boys are eligible. Even if the mother is baptised, the children are still eligible as long as the father remains Hindu.

On the other hand, many Hindu husbands actively support the church. Before starting on a business venture or journey some husbands will send an offering and a request for prayer to the pastor. They will instruct their wives to pray for their health and prosperity in church.

The major interest of the Nadar men is their business. They find no time for serious consideration of religion. The Hindu religious functions are times for them to show their prestige and wealth in the community. They also do much business throughout the country, especially in the North, so they must be Hindu to be accepted. In addition, the requirements of successful business are practices such as black money, bribery, false accounting, deceit, etc., and these practices do not mix with Christianity. Unless one carries on such business practices, no one will do business with you. As one man put it, "If one becomes a Christian, he must work." He meant that a Christian cannot do business, but must work as an employee for someone else.

One NBBC man I met exemplified well this conflict of faith with culture and business realities. He had joined one of the discussions I had with a home fellowship of women. He sat nearby as we talked; but when we knelt to pray at the end, he walked off and stood at a distance. I sensed that he did not want to be on the floor with a group of women. (Later I learned that the gesture of kneeling is another gesture confined to mourning in the Hindu tradition). When I spoke with him privately about his Christian faith later, he indicated that he was planning to take baptism after another four or five years. Afterwards I inquired further of the pastor concerning this man. He told me that such a delay of baptism is quite common among believing men, for they feel it less mockery of Christ if they remain unbaptised while carrying on their business practices. In a few years, the man's sons will take over the business, and he will be free to take baptism.

(In the address which I gave at the worship service mentioned above I cautioned the women against "troubling" their husbands into the Christian faith. In their piety, they tend to emphasise the fear of hell and the imminent coming of the Lord in judgement. The acceptance of the Gospel should not be an act of fear. Secondly, the women must not use their Christian activities to socially embarrass their husbands. The question of wearing the tilak, for example, can be interpreted as a "victory" for the husband or the wife. Similarly, baptism should not be used to demonstrate a wife's dominance over her husband. Thirdly, the men seemed to react negatively to the attitudes of over-dependence in the women's prayers. The men are confident, proud businessmen who deal aggressively with the problems of life, whereas the Christian piety presented to them by the women is one of beseeching the Lord to solve every problem.

In general, entering into the Christian faith through baptism should not be interpreted as a cowardly act. Baptism should be a "manly" act of emboldening, empowering and uplifting by God for partnership with Him in the world. In a situation like Sivakasi, it may be necessary that a separate movement of men is encouraged, for the piety of the women is not attractive to the mentality of the men.)

Sattur

Sattur is only a few kilometers from Sivakasi, and its piety also is an extension of the zenana work. The CSI pastor took me first to the home of a middle-aged couple of some wealth. The wife is from Sivakasi and took baptism after marriage. For many years she had been pleading with him also to take baptism. He had been a non-baptised believer, especially frequenting the meetings of Brother Dinakaran all over the country. (NB.: Brother Dinakaran is a Nadar layman who is a high officer in the State Bank of India. He is a very popular preacher and healer in Tamil Nadu. He conducts training courses in Madras, and on the photos one sees everyone dressed like him in shirt and tie. He has a mass appeal, but his primary devotees are from the middle and upper classes).

Finally, the man went to a Bro. Dinakaran meeting in Delhi and took baptism in the Jammu River. However, he still does not attend the local congregation, though it is Nadar as he is. He asks, "Why should I take my Bible and go out on the street to church? Cannot God hear my prayers at home?" He said that he had attended a few early morning church services, at the urging of his wife, but he found no other managers or industrialists there. He said that other businessmen now think less of him because of his baptism, for he cannot show his wealth any longer at Hindu festival time. Yet, he said that he will not compromise his faith by doing these things. There are only two other Christian business men in the town. His relatives also failed to invite him to a recent funeral after his baptism.

He receives Bro. Dinakaran's magazine and plays his tapes at home. They said that they do not have family devotions, but each has his own private devotions. When I asked about the faith of their teenaged children, they said that it will be their own decision in due time. They encourage the children to go to church and to become Christian, and the children do enjoy the taped sermons and songs played in the home. However, when we knelt to pray at the close of our discussion, the children carried on with their own activities, even walking around.

I also had briefer interviews with a number of other NBBCs in Sattur. A young man of about twenty met me at the parsonage. He complained that he is unable to concentrate when he prays. He said that he cannot overcome his bad habits of smoking and telling lies, so he knows that he is not saved. Recently when he was sick, the pastor came and prayed for him; so he began to consider taking baptism. When I prayed with him, he only looked ahead, not down in concentration.

After the church service I met a middle-aged man whose wife is Christian. He said he prays to Jesus only when he is sick. The children are not taught about Christianity. He does not want to change religion because people will talk about him.

At the instance of his Christian wife after church, I went to visit a man in his mid-thirties, a teacher. He witnessed that his wife's prayers had healed him once when he was sick. She wants him to go to church and take baptism, but he said it "will take time." He pointed out that the people in the congregation are a "different caste."

I went out of town to the home of a newly married NBBC who had come to the parsonage to find me. He wanted me to speak with his wife. He said that he had been a fervent Hindu but came to the Christian faith at a mass meeting three years ago. Two years ago he said he received the gift of speaking in tongues (sound like Cornelius in Acts 10?) He wanted to take baptism and go to church regularly, but he is waiting for his wife to join him. For her sake he does not even discuss his faith in the home.

He said that he tries to witness to his Christian faith at work by standing for justice, but he does not speak directly about it. He attends Hindu festivals for the sake of family loyalty, but he only looks on. When he discusses Christianity with his friends, they comment that "one must lead a simple life if one becomes Christian," for one must give up betel-chewing, smoking, cinema etc. He said that he responds by saying that "the simple life is good."

A man in his mid-fifties came to see me at the parsonage. He said that he had been an unbaptised believer for eighteen years, regularly attending church. He had foregone baptism because of his wife and child; however, seven months ago they walked out on him. Therefore, he has now taken baptism, and he expects that the long-term illness he has been suffering must now improve because he "has been faithful". He expressed great resentment against his wife and son, saying that he does not pray for them and does not want them to come to his funeral.

I also met a middle-aged man who had studied in a Christian school but was a fervent Hindu until he had a vision ten years ago in which Christ told him "I am the Lord you are seeking." At school he had learned about proper moral living, but later a tract about removing bad character had a great effect upon him and turned him to Jesus to cleanse his life. He said he had freedom now from sinful character. He knows his Lord is with him and leading him, so he sees no need for baptism which is only something external.

The pastor also told of several other families in the town where the wives are believers in Christ. They are not allowed to come to church or to take baptism. He pointed out one huge residence in the middle of the town where all three wives of three wealthy brothers are known to be non-baptised believers in Christ, though no one knows how they practice their faith.

A Village outside Madurai

The CSI pastor took me to the home of a Christian man (about thirty years old) who married a Hindu woman. Only he was available. He said that he must write to the bishop to ask for forgiveness, and then his wife must take instruction and be baptised before their marriage can be reconsecrated and they be admitted to Holy Communion. His wife comes to church regularly, but he said no one has pressed her about baptism so she also has not thought much of it.

Next, the pastor took me to a family from Sri Lanka who had been attending church services fairly regularly, though not baptised. They were quite poor with five small children. They came to church seeking fellowship since they had newly come to the village. The Pastor also helped them to build a small shelter to live in. The man said that they had found no use in Hindu worship but they believe that Jesus will protect and help them if they act rightly. He said they would like to take baptism, but they lack the necessary money for the offering and for the special clothes.

A Village near R.S. Mangalam, Ramnad District

I bicycled with the local catechist to this interior village. We met with three men from a group of five high-caste families that had been coming to worship in a nearby chapel for a congregation of the same caste background for the past three years. We met in this chapel. They have small land holdings in this very dry, undeveloped part of Tamil Nadu.

They expressed that they had found new ability to overcome bad habits since practicing the Christian faith. They like the opportunity to train their children each Sunday in good habits through the Sunday School. They also appreciated the way the church helps the needy equally, unlike the government and they also expected some help from the church. They admired the way Christian teachers and pastors would help in approaching government authorities - who otherwise would simply ignore the petitions.

The men said that they still celebrate Hindu festivals for the sake of social unity, but they admitted that they do not feel good about doing so anymore. They do not like the way these festivals are celebrated and prefer the Christian way. They do not yet celebrate Christmas at home or have any private or family devotions. When asked what benefit they anticipate if they take baptism, one said that the demons would no longer be able to trouble them and another said that they would find help in their difficulties.

At another nearby village we happened to meet a thirty-year old man who spoke briefly about his faith in Christ. He said he had found that his family had stayed healthy and he found guidance in his difficulties since praying to Jesus. Now each night his family prays together for forgiveness and health. He said he would like a Bible and would like to attend a big public meeting. Back in the village where there is a large Harijan congregation, I discussed with the evangelist about the problems of high caste believers taking baptism. He responded that "they simply must come down and take." (The Tamil expression he used implies that they must leave their "high community" and join the church community.)

Paramakudi, Ramnad District

The local Lutheran pastor arranged for me to meet several young people at the mission compound. When I arrived, a boy outside the compound eyed me carefully, and later he was the one brought to me first. He is from a caste lower than the local Harijan congregation. The CSI congregation in town is Nadar and the Roman Catholic is Harijan.

The boy said he had studied for three years in a Christian school and learned of Christ. He said that he particularly liked the Christian opposition to idol worship and the Christian idea of forgiveness directly through prayer. He liked to read the Bible but now he does not have one. He prays twice a week or so at home, but he does not see that it is necessary to go to church. When he prays to Jesus, he finds that his problems are resolved and he gets mental peace. He had not considered what Jesus expects from him in response. He likes Christian radio programmes but cannot understand tracts and has not had time to take a Bible correspondence course. He said that he might attend if there is a public Christian meeting in the town, but it should not be on the mission compound.

The boy said that at first he had tried to persuade his parents and friends about the Christian faith. However, he found it only gained him anger, division and ridicule. His parents also have ceased trying to change his mind. His cousins are in a Roman Catholic hostel, so he hopes that they might become Christian; but the rest of his family is staunchly Hindu. He goes to Hindu pujas, like naming ceremonies as a member of the family, but he does not worship there. Similarly, he does his part in helping the family prepare for festivals at home, but he does not participate in the worship.

He said that he does not plan to take baptism, for "one is not a Christian because he is baptised." If he is baptised, he will have to change his name and all will know that he is Christian; and that is not necessary. It would also affect his government scholarship. Even after getting employment he does not plan to be baptised. "If I take baptism, I'll be a full Christian and all will know."

Later in the afternoon two high school students from a nearby village came to see me. Both had studied in a Christian school and traced their Christian faith to the influence of the first grade teacher.

Later, in seventh grade, an Every Home Crusade worker stayed in their village for four months and trained them up in the Christian faith and life. They said that their Christian friends in the village also encouraged them in the faith. They are Harijans, and they regularly participate in the local Harijan congregation activities.

One boy spoke of a skin disease which he had but which no doctor could cure. However, when he began praying regularly, it gradually disappeared. This cure convinced both him and his brothers and sisters about Jesus, but not his parents. He now prays at home alone or with his sister. His older two sisters are now married to Hindus, so they must celebrate the Hindu festivals and are not free to practice the Christian faith.

When they read the Bible, they found how to lead a good life and how their Hindu friends had been leading them on the wrong path. They give Christian tracts and magazines to their Hindu friends now. They felt that putting the tilak is not needed because it gives only external beauty, while it is internal beauty which is important.

One said that he planned to take baptism after completing his studies. The other said that he wanted to cleanse himself of the bad habits left over from his Hindu upbringing (anger, jealousy, bad words, etc.) and then take baptism. He was convinced that only if one prays to God with a clean heart will one stay clean. They understand that in baptism they will become God's child and be forgiven their past sins and given power to avoid future sinning. They desire to change their names at baptism because they are Hindu names. By taking baptism they will confirm that they are God's children throughout their life.

The pastor also told of their former servant lady who had been under possession of an evil spirit which would occasionally speak through her. However, he had prayed regularly with her and gradually she gained her freedom, for which she was very happy and grateful. While she was with them, she would attend church regularly; but now that she has gone to live in her son's home, she can only pray at home.

A Village near Uttamapalayam

While waiting for the CSI pastor to return (he had not received my letter before he left for a distant place), a layman from the local congregation took me to a wealthy cardamom plantation owner of Gounder caste in the next village. There was a small CSI chapel in the centre of the village and just opposite to it a large, modern prayer house. The land owner was just about to leave for his lands, but he stopped to discuss with me for some time in his comfortable living room, together with the layman.

He said that he was baptised last year after three years of attending Bro. Dinakaran meetings. Most of the men in his immediate family who have come to the Christian faith have also taken baptism now, but not all of the women, including his wife. He said that they left baptism as an option. One sister's husband, for example, is not baptised because he has not yet been able to get rid of his bad drinking habit. He said that they feel baptism should come at one stage of spiritual experience and progress. It should not be forced on anybody. When a person has reached that stage of commitment, he will come forward "to be fully true to Jesus."

The five converted families have joined together to build the separate prayer house, supporting their own pastor, seemingly a man from a low-caste background. They worship at 10.00 a.m. while the CSI congregation worships at 8.30 a.m. Thus, they could attend each other's services, and sometimes they have joint celebrations and evangelistic campaigns. He said they desire to stay away from congregational and denominational disputes through separate worship.

He said that he was able to construct the large building soon after his conversion because he had experienced so much more income from his plantations. His Hindu relations had countered by erecting large Hindu shrines at the roadside. When he constructed the prayer house, many people accused him of getting foreign money. (Indeed, even one pastor from that CSI diocese made the same accusation when I was sharing with a group about this man at Gurukul a couple of years later.) However, he says that he knew he would have such troubles after taking baptism, but "If one really believes in the Lord, He will lift him out of all troubles."

Later I was interested to discuss this prayer house with the local CSI pastor and lay leaders. To my great surprise, they felt no offence or resentment over the separate building and service. It was obvious that the low-caste Christians were happy that their landlord did not enter their congregation and dominate it. Similarly, the high-caste families, especially the women, could feel comfortable in their worship among their own people.

The landlord said the driving reason for the spiritual search which culminated in conversion to Christianity was the desire to overcome the bad habits in his life. He had gone to Sabarimala and fasted for forty days according to the Aiyappa cult requirements, but he still could not gain release from his sins. In Christ he found the forgiveness for his guilt over past sins and the strength for a new life.

His Hindu relatives have accused him of betraying "our forefathers and our status." But they also have seen the marked change in their life: freedom from bad habits, a real change of heart, peace in family life, greater economic prosperity. In reply to their complaint, he simply asserts that he has not changed religion at all: "Christ came to fulfill, so I worship the true Hindu God through Christ." He says that he has returned to the original Tamil religion of worshipping one God without the Aryan influences of pujas, idols, temples, priests, polytheism, etc. He said baptism is not a change of religion but an agreement with God.

He said that he did not see any reason to change his Hindu name when taking baptism, since conversion "is a matter of the heart". They left wearing of the tilak as an option, but they decided no longer to put the kolam in front of their house. For one or two years before their baptism they continued to observe the Hindu festivals, but now they decided that they must be true only to Jesus. He sees no reason why Christians cannot participate in Pongal.

He feels kneeling for prayer is a good thing, since it teaches humility before God. He said that he has married his daughters to Hindus of his own Gounder caste. Women do not have freedom of men, and they will have to cooperate with their husbands. They are not baptised.

He said the main obstacle to the spread of Christianity is the popular prejudice that it is a Harijan religion. People feel that the church takes advantage of poor people's weakness in order to make them Christian, "at least in name." By its own merits Christianity can spread in India. The problem is that the spirit of Christ is being obscured by the bad conduct of Christians, the differences between denominations, and the high exaltation of bishops. This is why he feels greater admiration for the Pentecostal denominations.

Uttamapalayam

The pastor took me to the home of a Muslim lawyer who is also a member of the "waqf" board. (N.B.: The "waqf" is the Muslim managing committee for their institutions.) The man did not want to answer questions, for he would speak what he had in mind rather than what I asked. He spoke at length about how Christians have not treated Muslims rightly and how Christians do not understand the Muslim mind. Christians have also written offensive and untrue things about Muhammad. They must appreciate all he did in history.

The lawyer pointed out that all Muslims already accept and respect Jesus as a great prophet. He admitted that Jesus had divine power and even that some of his followers, like Dinakaran, do also. Yet he maintained that Muslims can within their own religion use Jesus as a guide and actually "be strengthened in Islam through him". He said that almost every Friday sermon in the mosque refers to Jesus in this way.

In regard to his own spiritual life, he referred in passing comments to the following matters. He said that he is "greatly impressed by the Bible" and reads it daily. (He also commented that he has not studied the Koran.) The life of Jesus has deeply impressed him; and when he reads about the crucifixion, he "sheds tears." "I admit," he said, "that when I pray, I pray in Jesus' Name."

The man also lamented that Christians do not know how to approach Muslims with the Gospel. Although he had attended the mass meetings held by Dinakaran, he said that Muslims cannot be reached in this way. The approach must be personal and in a mild manner. He said he wanted to go to Madras to advise Bro. Dinakaran on this matter.

A Small Town near Uttamapalayam

The pastor took me to the home of the head of the local temple trust. He is a wealthy landlord of Devar caste whose family has built several schools and social service institutions in the town, he was sitting on the veranda of his large house when we walked up. He appeared nervous and uncertain about our sudden visit. We stood and talked with him only briefly, when he finally asked us not to continue because he did not want to be seen receiving Christian visitors (especially a foreign missionary!), for others would come and trouble him about this.

The pastor told me that this elderly man had been suffering for many years from a pain in his leg. When Bro. Dinakaran had a series of meetings here one month before this man had gone and put his hand over the pain as instructed by Dinakaran during the healing prayers at the end of the meeting. The pain immediately vanished. He then returned to his house and removed all the pictures of Hindu gods. He put a picture of Jesus into his puja room, and now worships only Jesus.

I asked him what he knew about Jesus, and he replied with feeling, "I don't know anything yet, but I want to learn." He said that he had secured a Bible a week ago, but a friend had asked to borrow it; so he had not yet had a chance to read. He said he was still in some confusion as to how to proceed in life. He planned to keep his position as head of the temple trust because otherwise his "family prestige would be gone."

We also visited a government officer in his office. He is a DK leader; so, since he knew we were coming, he had called five other DK members to join in the conversation. (N.B.: The "DK" is the "Dravida Kalagam," which means "the Dravidian organisation". It was founded by one E.V.R. Periyar half a century ago to organise the oppressed classes, especially the Harijans, against the dominant high castes, especially the Brahmins.) These men were not believers in Christ by any means, for they carried on the atheistic tradition of their founder. However, they reflect the social liberation thinking which undergird much of the mass movement toward Christianity among the oppressed classes in Tamil Nadu.

The men spoke of Jesus as a leader against the religious oppression of the poor. In this regard he remains as an important model and inspiration for the masses of India today as well. They particularly noted with appreciation Christianity's emphasis upon an upright life. They recalled how E.V.R. had preferred Christianity because a Harjan could become a priest and because there is no priestly or superior caste in the religion. However, the DK men roundly criticized the continuance of caste feelings in the church, as well as the corrupt practices of church leaders.

The pastor also told of another government officer in the area who had been inspired while in the Gandhian movement by Jesus' Sermon on the Mount. He had come to complete faith in Jesus when his prayer for the birth of a child was answered.

A Village near Coimbatore

A Harijan high school student came to the chapel where I was sitting, after the local CSI pastor had sent word to him. He said that he had Christian friends all through life and had joined in all the activities of the local congregation. He said that he had found answers to his prayers to Jesus and inner peace. His parents have no objection to his taking baptism, since he has already stopped participating in the Hindu festivals.

I asked him why he wants baptism when he already receives answers to his prayers to Jesus. He replied that he wants to give himself wholly to Jesus, to which the observing congregation people expressed grants of approval. He said he also wants to change his name at baptism so that others will know he is a full Christian. When I asked him about the consequences of baptism in losing his government scholarships and privileges as a Harijan, he seemed dumbfounded and confused. Apparently, he had not realised this consequence.

Several Villages near Chettipalayam outside Coimbatore

The Lutheran pastor took me to several villages where the Lutheran church has had mission work for many years. He pointed out that three chapels had been closed, for the members ceased to come when the missionaries left and no one gave them gifts any longer. Since they would have to forego a day's koolie if they came to church, the missionaries would pay them their wage of Rs. 5/- on Sunday. They often suffer unemployment if they are known to be practicing Christians because the local landlords won't give them work on the fields. If they are given work, they are expected to go first to the temple and then to the fields. Without economic security, these poor labourers feel unable to come to church and join Christianity, though they may like to.

Because of the long mission work in this area, especially through the schools, there are many non-baptised believers in Christ. The pastor expressed that he had at first resisted coming to this remote pastorate, but now he finds a real challenge in following up these people. However, he is quite confused as to how to minister to them. Some of them he is accepting to Holy Communion because he knows of their faith and their desire. He tells them that he is giving them this privilege on the understanding that they will eventually take baptism. The non-baptised believers are from Harijan and Backward Class backgrounds.

We met with five NBBCs from one village: two girl high school students, a housewife, and a middle-aged man. A man came into the church as we began our discussions, and I learned later that he was a Hindu leader in the community. The man's presence did not seem to disturb the people, for their Christian faith is well known in the community.

They traced their Christian faith to what they learned in the local elementary school. However, they said that they also continue to join in the Hindu festivals and temple worship because of family expectations, though thinking only of Jesus while there. Their families have no objection to their going to church, but they cannot celebrate Christmas at home. Earlier their relatives would come to church also, but now they ask why they should since they receive nothing from the missionary.

All five expressed satisfaction especially with the Christian teaching that there is only one God. They enjoy participating in the cottage prayer meetings, and three had been also to big public meetings held by Bro. Dinakaran. One said that she read the Bible regularly at home, but the other said only occasionally. The women said that they also go to Hindu homes to pray for them in their difficulties.

In another village, a 35 year old man told that he had learned about the Christian faith from a Doctor in a Christian hospital three years ago. He said that he had received both physical health and peace of mind there. He comes alone to church, but his wife and relations have no objections. Among his relations only one family is Christian.

One of the things he appreciates about Christianity is that one need not pay Rs. 100/- for prayer or priestly services as in the temple. He said that he no longer goes to the temple, and he expects to take baptism soon. However, he is concerned that the landlords will take him last for work the moment he converts.

In another village we met seven middle-aged persons from seven NBBC families. Each came to Christ in a different way. One came through an adult literacy programme run by the church.

Another had her baby healed by prayer to Jesus. Another had an ailment healed by Jesus. The fourth learned of Jesus in a Christian hospital. Another received Christian teaching in a Christian school. Another received the birth of a child through prayer to Jesus.

Because of their faith they have already suffered difficulties at the hands of the powerful high caste families. One rents from a landlord, and he has been threatened with eviction. All face problems in getting work on the fields, so they have considered to move to Coimbatore town to look for work. Some are restricted from using the local village well.

They said that for the last several years they have not been going to the temple. When I asked them what they would do if a Hindu god restored their child to health when ill, they said that they would not change their faith. They witnessed that for the past several years since they have refrained from temple worship, Jesus has taken care of the family, especially in that they no longer have bad quarrels and problems.

The pastor said that he knows of several high caste youth who have studied in the local Christian schools and come to faith in Christ. However, they keep their faith a secret from the families because it would mean being sent out of the house and thus the loss of all social and economic security in life. They ask who would then arrange a marriage for them.

Tiruvannamalai

This is a famous temple town in North Arcot District. It is another area of mass movements among the Harijans several decades back. I met the local Lutheran pastor, and he took me to the church where he left me and brought a Hanjan lawyer in his mid-thirties.

The lawyer frankly admitted at the outset that he has not taken baptism because it would ruin his chances of being promoted to the judiciary. He pointed out that a Christian clerk will remain in that category his whole life, while a Hindu clerk can expect to advance even to the level of Deputy Collector. He avoids going to church because he is afraid that someone will report this to the Collector. On Sundays he simply prays at home. He is happy to receive a visit from the pastor, however.

He traced his faith to his home. His mother had learned of Christ when she was in a Christian teachers training school, and both she and his father were non-baptised believers in Christ throughout their lives. All of the children were raised as non-baptised believers in Christ. As a boy he would attend church with his friends, and he has always preferred the dignity and order of Christian worship. His face contorted in disgust as he spoke of the way temple priests would withhold the sacred fire if one didn't put enough offering. He has been impressed with the way big Christian leaders will respect ordinary people. In the church educated and uneducated alike kneel to pray, while among Hindus they still observe the distinctions of caste heirarchy.

He told of a small incident when he was a college student which deepened his faith in Christ considerably. He had been visiting a Christian couple in Gudiyattam and had to leave by rented cycle in order to catch the train back. However, he could not get the lock undone no matter how much he or anyone else tried. Then the Christian couple simply prayed, and when he tried again the lock easily gave way.

The lawyer said that he does not receive any Christian literature or listen to Christian radio programmes or go to big meetings. He does not try to witness to his faith, but simply seeks to do good to people, keeping Jesus in his heart. If he joins the church at this point, he fears that people will criticize him for receiving so much government help as a Hindu Harijan and then forsaking his community.

The pastor then took me to the home of a college lecturer in his mid-thirties Above the entrance to the main rooms of his house hung a large picture of Jesus. There were no pictures of other gods in the house.

He told how he had studied in Protestant and Roman Catholic schools and even received first prize in Bible competitions. His father had done the same and was an NBBC like himself. His three sisters, however, are not of Christian faith "because the are not educated." His father expired recently and gave a last wish that his son should read the Bible in their village church service and hold a feast for the poor, so he plans to do that soon. He sends his children to a Christian school. His wife does not object in these matters because he says she knows not to think or act separately from him.

He said that he goes to church only on special festivals and occasionally he will attend a public meeting. They do not celebrate Christmas in their home. He also does not celebrate any Hindu festivals, except Pongal and other family festivals, remembering Jesus in his heart while not offending his relatives.

His friends and relations accuse him of atheism because he always ridicules Hindu customs and rituals. He says he welcomes church workers to his home for prayer and he has many friends among Harijan Christians. He strongly opposes Hindu attitudes toward Harijans.

The college lecturer stated that he is convinced he can be a better Christian witness by not taking baptism and thus staying within the Hindu community. He told how he often argues with relations, friends and colleagues about the merits of Christianity. Thus, he says one can be a follower of Christ without becoming a Christian officially. He says he is not concerned about possible difficulties in arranging marriages for his children because of his Christian faith, for he is confident that problem can be overcome.

He opposed the importance given to baptism by Christians. He emphasised that faith is what is important, while baptism is only a human custom. Baptism is supposed to be a break with caste-consciousness, but in fact Christians are as caste-conscious as anybody so baptism is meaningless. "Changing one's name, wearing a cross, and advertising one's faith are not necessary." Christians including himself - must be very different in their behaviour, but religion should not interfere with social customs. He argued that baptism may be necessary for uneducated people to enable them to break away from the external temptations of Hinduism. However with educated people there is enough inner strength so that this external break is not necessary.

He deplored the way Christians think that only they "can attain the Almighty." The fact is that most Hindus respect Christianity as a better path to salvation because it is attainable immediately. It is "the easiest way." Hindus find fault with Christians' behaviour and this is because so many Christians have converted only for financial gain. Christians should be positive in their proclamation of the faith, not ridiculing others' faith or disturbing their festivals. Bibles should be supplied to important people, not tracts which are simply discarded.

Back at the pastor's house I spoke with two elderly catechists about another NBBC who was out of station. He is a government social worker ("gramasevakar") who formerly was a follower of Mahatma Gandhi. While imprisoned once, he met some Christians; and after release from prison he went to the Christukula Ashram near Tirupattur to learn more about Christianity. There he decided to follow Christ, but Dr. Paton and Rev. Jesudoss advised him against baptism "unless Jesus speaks in your heart" because of all the difficulties he would have to face in his Mudaliar community.

The catechists said that the man now feels that he lost his chance then, for after his marriage he had to consider the marriage arrangements for his four daughters. They thought that he would take baptism after those marriage arrangements are completed, but they also told of his statement that he sees no necessity for baptism when "I have already repented and received forgiveness for my sins." He attends church regularly and speaks of himself as one of "the other sheep outside the fold."

The catechists told of his bold and continuous witnessing to Christ. They said that he takes tracts with him when he goes to the villages and distributes them there. As a prominent Hindu, he is allowed to speak at the great Tiruvannamalai temple. When he does, he always quotes the Vedas, the Gita and the Tirukkural pointing out how everything there is fulfilled in Christ. He points out that all other prophets are dead, but only Jesus is still alive as "the living God."

A Village near Mailpatti, North Arcot District

The Lutheran catechist took me to this village where there is a small Harijan congregation. In Mailpatti town the church runs the first school of that area, where high caste Hindus had sent their children for education until the government school was started. In the village we entered the home of a well-to-do Naidu landlord. Soon three more Naidu men came in. Two of them had come to Christ through attending the Mailpatti school. One testified that he had been healed by Christ at a Christian hospital.

The landlord said he had been to Madras recently to attend the Billy Graham crusade. He had also been to Thanjavur once to hear Bro. Dinakaran and "was really helped." He also joins in the public devotion at the Christian hospital when he is there. Three of them said that they celebrate Christmas at home, while the fourth said that he goes to church. On that day the two wealthy brothers will distribute food to the poor by hand, and they "receive blessing" in doing so. (The testimony of the one brother to his Christian faith turned out to be a surprise to the catechist.) They celebrate the Hindu festivals together with their wives for the sake of family unity, but they distribute food only on Christmas day.

In the home of the landlord one observes large pictures of Hindu gods in the main room as one enters. However, in the small, personal room of the man hangs only a picture of Jesus. The man spoke of how they think of Jesus when they go to sleep and when they arise each day. They spoke of peace in their heart as they follow Jesus. The teenaged son of the landlord told how he reads the Bible, especially the book of "Proverbs." He also joins in some of the congregational youth activities and cottage prayer meetings. The congregational worship was being held in a Harijan home, so I asked them if they would come to church if a chapel were built. They agreed that they would come no matter in what part of the village it was built. (Later the catechist told how sometimes these Naidu men would stand outside the home where Sunday worship was being conducted in order to hear the hymns and sermon. About a year later I was in that village for the dedication of a small chapel, but only the son attended that service. That boy also subsequently wrote me about joining in the seminary.)

I asked them if they had ever invited the congregation to hold a cottage prayer meeting in their home, but they said that others of their community would object. When asked if they would object if the pastor simply announced that they were coming, the landlord said he would have no objection. They also would like their children to go to Sunday School and to a Christian school. (Two of the men spoke of their poverty and struggles in life. Later I asked if the landlord helps such people, and the catechist said that he does not.)

One of these men eventually took baptism at the occasion of the church dedication. He had been attending church regularly in the town congregation of Mailpatti where he had studied. He said that he never goes to the temple or celebrates Hindu festivals. His

Hindu relatives say that this is the cause of his poverty. He said that he is ready for all this criticism and all the difficulties which will come if he is baptised. If he could only see some progress in his life, he would be ready for baptism. He said that he is not invited for congregational functions or cottage prayer meetings, though he would like to participate. He expressed a desire to join in Holy Communion.

Another well-known NBBC Naidu in the area, near Pernambut, often travels to the town of Ambur in order to attend worship. There he can attend anonymously, instead of with the local Harijans in his home village. The Ambur pastor told me that the man had once approached him for baptism, but he told him that church rules dictate that he must take it in his homeplace since there is a congregation there.

Madras City

The CSI pastor took me to the home of a 35 year old mother of three from Sivakasi. As we have seen already, she followed the practice of delaying baptism until she could work it out with her husband. He had earlier given permission for her and the children to attend church. She conducts family prayers in the home, but her husband only sits and observes.

The pastor was surprised to learn that the woman had recently been baptised by immersion at the chapel of an independent preacher. A Bible woman from that church had been visiting her regularly. The wife had been hoping that eventually her husband would take baptism with her, but finally she got his permission to do it on her own.

Recently the husband was ill, and she prayed for his recovery. When he returned to health, he also acknowledged that Jesus had healed him. For the past six months now, she said that he has not worshipped the Hindu gods. She has told him that this healing demonstrates "that Jesus loves you". She says that he fears to take baptism because of the reactions of his family members.

The pastor serves at a chapel which is in the midst of a Brahmin section of the city. He reported that there are always people from the community sitting in on the Sunday morning and evening services. At the New Year's Eve "Watchnight" service, he estimates that about two dozen Hindus come to Communion as well. He told of one Good Friday when a Brahmin lady suddenly came to him before the service to deliver a cover which contained Rs.250-. She said that her father had given instructions on his death bed that this cover should be given over to the local pastor. He had worshipped only Jesus as long as any one in the family could remember, and he had collected this offering from his salary month by month. When he died, the daughter said that his last words were "Now I am going to Jesus."

A Pastor in Madras City who was in my random sample gave me the address of a Brahmin high school boy whom he knew to be a non-baptised believer in Christ. I wrote the boy a letter informing him of my intentions in interviewing him and asking for a time and place where we might meet. The next day our Gurukul office received a phone call from a frantic woman when I was out. She was the mother of the boy and had opened the letter before it reached him. She pleaded that no one from the church come to see her son because she had several children to marry off.

CHAPTER TWO

"What Are They Like?"

Outline:

Traits of Harijan NBBCs

Personal Traits of High-Caste NBBCs
(ten traits described)

Worship Traits of High Caste NBBCs
(five traits described)

Common Traits among all NBBCs
(eleven traits described)

"What Are They Like?"

What is, then, the portrait which we may draw from this survey of non-baptised believers in Christ in rural Tamil Nadu? The people interviewed are from very diverse geographical, social, and religious backgrounds. Yet, are we able to discern any common characteristics or typical character within this diversity? If we are to derive any useful principles for our evangelistic and nurture ministries, we must strive to determine the natural avenues of approach.

Traits of Harijan NBBCs

One distinction which is immediately apparent is that between the situation of the Harijan NBBC and the so-called "high caste" NBBC. The situation of the Harijan non-baptised believer is much less complex though certainly critical. Except in the case of those Harijans who are of a "lower" caste than the local congregation (e.g. the Sampoothu sweepers and the Paramakudi youth), there is no social obstacle in joining the congregation. The Harijan NBBC youth have had long and strong friendships with Christian youth (e.g. the Tiruvannamalai lawyer, the Coimbatore youth, the two Paramakudi youth). There is no marriage problem, no class or caste problem.

The problem among the educated is the discriminatory laws which attempt to discourage further conversions among the Harijans by denying government scholarships, reserved seats for higher education and jobs, stipends in school and high school, free hostels for high school education, preferential promotions, reserved constituencies, etc. as soon as one becomes Christian. (In fact, I know of one case where an NBBC civil servant who was up for a preferential promotion had his house raided by the police in order to discover if he had a picture of Jesus on the wall. He got prior information of the raid, however, and removed the pictures before the police arrived. No doubt, someone who wanted the promotion in his place informed on him and someone who sympathised with his position warned him.) At any rate, the issue for most Harijan NBBCs is quite clear: come out in the open with your faith and lose your chances of material progress in life (e.g., the Tiruvannamalai lawyer and the Paramakudi boy).

The spiritual effect of this political and economic pressure can be most debilitating. Just as the high-caste person feels compelled to act against his conscience because of social reasons, the Harijan believer in Christ may feel compelled for economic and political reasons. A convert named A. Krishnan, for example, may take on a new Christian name at his baptism to symbolise his new religious commitment, but he may hide it by simply adding it as an initial in front of his old name in public use. Thus, if Krishnan's new baptismal name were "Joshua", he would call himself A. J. Krishnan thereafter. He knows he is compromising his Christian witness and his faith in God's promise over his life in baptism, but he fears to take the risk with the material welfare of his life and family.

Similarly, a few Christian parents (even pastors) will give their child a neutral name like Jeyakumar or avoid baptising as an infant in order to be able to register the child as a Hindu Harijan and receive the government privileges. When a Harijan NBBC sees converts and Christians succumbing to the temptations of compromise, he will naturally seek to find and justify ways by which he also can experience the abundant life both now and hereafter.

Among Harijan youth, therefore, a non-baptised believer in Christ will be one who is thoughtful and serious about religion but also desirous of material progress in life. The thoughtful person living in oppression will strive for liberation. Among high-caste persons their traditional religion contains a rich and compelling spiritual heritage to which they might quite naturally turn in a thoughtful and serious religious quest. However, as we have seen among the thoughtful and serious Harijans in the survey (e.g. the DK members, the Tiruvannamalai lawyer, the Chettipalayam people, the Paramakudi boy, the Coimbatore boy), traditional Hinduism often represents to them an oppressive structure which they want to reject and flee. Thus, if they reflect seriously on religion and seek spiritual and moral growth (e.g. the Paramakudi boys and the Chettipalayam people) Christianity becomes a live option for them.

We have seen a similar spiritual frustration among the uneducated people in Chettipalayam. Here the hindrance was not discriminatory government laws but discriminatory employers. These landless labourers could not stand up against the Hindu pressures like the landed Mukudal Nadar and Chettiar families could and even they have had to struggle considerably. The only relief for the Chettipalayam people would be to leave the place, as they were considering, and enter the big city slums.

Should they be uprooted from their home society in order to he baptised and thus cut off totally from all they know and love - and from those to whom they might naturally witness? (as the women were already doing in the Hindu homes)? Or should they remain as non-baptised believers in their home society, witnessing by sheer determination and fortitude? This is a dilemma facing all of the spiritually thoughtful poor in rural Tamil Nadu.

Thus, both among educated and uneducated Harijans we can expect to find non-baptised believers in Christ. What will typify them is their thoughtfulness about life and religion. The irony is that their very thoughtfulness will lead them to desire liberation and progress in life and it will lead them to seriously consider Christianity which then becomes a hindrance to this progress. They are caught in a tragic and unfair conflict of maturation. Later we will consider the practical implications of this situation for our evangelistic and nurture ministries.

Personal Traits of High-Caste NBBCs

Next we must consider the pattern among the so-called "high-caste" people. (N.B.: I use the term "high-caste" because it is the commonly used term for those whom traditional Hinduism has placed socially higher than others. However, my conviction is that all people are created of equal worth under God, and this aspect of the caste system must be opposed and eliminated.) The problem of NBBCs among these people is quite different. It is primarily social rather than economic or political. Many of these people are of solid economic status. However, where their economic position is insecure (e.g. the tailor and the shopowner, the Chettiar, the Sivakasi businessman), they too may hesitate to risk the disfavour of powerful people by making their Christian faith public or confirmed. In such cases, they have an added complexity, besides the social issue, to consider in regard to baptism.

The prime complicating factor for the high caste NBBC is his family. Firstly, he has the *problem of his personal marriage relationship*. Many of these people spoke of their desire to maintain harmony in their marriage (tailor and shopowner, Nagercoil and Sivakasi women, the Panikkar teacher, the elderly Nair man, the "gramasevakar", the 50 year old Sattur man, the Mailpatti men). There is a conflict between their divine responsibility to their wife/ husband and their divine responsibility to their Lord. Many try to balance these responsibilities by carrying out their faith in a manner which will not embarrass, upset, or alienate their spouse. The stability, peace, and harmony of the home is also their responsibility to maintain, and the difference of faith must be handled accordingly.

A second factor in the high-caste NBBCs family situation is the *attitudes of his relations*. Besides the personal emotional burden of hurting and alienating people near and dear to him, the NBBC must deal with the burden he inevitably places on them. The relatives fear for his family's welfare when he/she no longer visits the temple or worships the family or village deities (e.g., the Pavoorchatram teachers, the Mailpatti convert, Nagercoil and Sivakasi women). The tendency of the NBBCs is to accomodate these "weaker brethren" by both allowing them to carry on with their beliefs (e.g., the tailor and shopowner) and by going through the rituals expected by their loved ones - though at the same time praying to the Lord whom they believe can really accomplish what their relatives desire on their behalf (e.g., the Sivakasi and Nagercoil women, the Panikkar teacher, the college lecturer). No doubt, their relations know it is a charade, but they nonetheless appreciate that the NBBCs accommodate their feelings and maintain as much identity with the family as possible. The dying mother probably knows well enough what is planned after her death, but she appreciates their consideration for her feelings (e.g., Mukudal and Tirunelveli Nair families).

Of course, it may also be that the NBBC himself is the "weaker brother." He may have real fear - quite justifiably - over the *vindictive power of the family gods*. There will be a period — perhaps long, perhaps short-in which he himself seeks to continue to placate the traditional deities (e.g., the Nagercoil and Sivakasi women, the Tirunelveli Nair women), before committing himself totally into the care and power of Jesus. He may even be content to have his wife remain Hindu so that she might carry out this function (e.g., the tailor and the shopowner).

Thus, it is not surprising that a new believer will look for some confirmation of the power and care of Jesus before proceeding further. As Israel needed the Exodus experience and the disciples needed the Resurrection experience, so the Mailpatti converts wanted to see some solution to their problems. We will deal more with this topic when we come to discuss the common experiences of NBBCs a bit further on in this chapter.

Besides his extended family's religious feelings and fears, the NBBC must be *sensitive to his relations' social attitudes.* Especially in the village structure, the caste lines carry the weight of centuries of tradition. A high caste NBBC makes his kinsmen highly uncomfortable when he mixes freely with people of other castes, especially with Harijans. No doubt, by Christian conviction he must respect all people equally, and he must show it clearly in his attitudes and actions (e.g., the college lecturer, the Mailpatti boy, the "gramasevakar"). Yet, he will also respect the merits of the cultural pattern from the past in which so many people find meaning, security, social harmony, and mutual respect.

Thus, the NBBC does not flaunt his new-found freedom, as license to do what he wants no matter whose needs are ignored and whose feelings hurt. For the sake of the "weaker brethren" the Gounder builds a separate prayer house, the Panikkars request a separate chapel, the Zenana Mission encourages separate fellowship groups, the Vellalas request a home ministry, the Mailpatti Nairs request a chapel and the Pernambut Naidu attends the town services. If he alienates himself from his relations by an unacceptable style of social involvement, he forfeits all chances of influencing them. As the lecturer said, it may be that he can be a better witness "as a Hindu."

Fifthly, then, we cannot ignore the *close association in Indian tradition between religion and culture.* The NBBC is caught in a predicament where he wants to distinguish between these two in his life, whereas neither most of his Hindu kinsmen nor most of his Christian co-believers are able to. The common Protestant reaction to the close association of Indian culture with Hindu religion has been to develop a separate culture for the new religion: different devotions, different festivals, different names, different appearance, different lifestyle, different worship, gestures, etc. If you are to join this religion, you must get accustomed to its culture (cf. the problems expressed by the Sampoothu sweepers, the R. S. Mangalam people the Nagercoil and Sivakasi women, the Sattur "Cornelius"). This is the basis for all the accusations about a "foreign religion" and a forsaking of the family heritage (e.g., the

Gounder, the Poovancode people, the Mukudal Mudaliar, the Sivakasi women.)

The NBBC is *trying to change religion without changing culture,* even to the extent of asserting that he's not really changing religion at all (cf. the Gounder's beautiful argument). Unfortunately, he suffers from suspicion and rejection on the part of *both Hindu kinsmen and Christian co-believers.* Even if one is baptised, if one does-not participate in the mores of the Christian "culture", he will not be accepted. Sometimes the only way he can assert his cultural identity is by keeping aloof from the Christian community—which doesn't really know what to do with him anyway (e.g., the Gounder, the lecturer, the Martandam Nair, the Sampoothu Mudaliar). The consequence of this strategic aloofness is that the Christian community can then self-righteously judge the genuineness of his faith, and the NBBC ends up even more isolated and deprived spiritually.

The major blot on the Hindu caste system is untouchability. The traditional hierarchising of castes is bad enough (although those in this hierarchy do not seem to object to it). The great sin is the exclusion of fifteen percent of the population from any recognition in the social order (the "outcastes," or in Gandhi's new name for them: "Harijans," the children of God), and until recently, from any participation in the higher religious life. These attitudes toward the Harijans are a fact, even though their practical implementation is now illegal (cf. the comments of the college lecturer).

The vast majority of Christians are from the Harijan and backward castes. ("Backward caste" is the official government term for generally poor castes; the Nadars are so listed.) Christianity is thus viewed quiet naturally as a religion of the Harijans (cf. the Tirunelveli woman's report). To join the Christian faith is to leave one's traditional religious culture for the religious culture of the Harijan community. From the standpoint of the Christian gospel it may be a pride that we reach the poor and the oppressed. However, from the standpoint of the high-caste NBBC we see sixthly, that this identification *causes his whole family to be offended and alienated* (cf. the Gounder's observations). The popular Harijan attitude toward the caste Hindu believer is well reflected in the R.S. Mangalam evangelist's comment, vindictively implying that baptism does make a high-caste person a Harijan socially. The Harijan has centuries of feelings stored up against the caste Hindus, and the high-caste NBBC has to deal with this fact also. With attitudes like these on both sides to cope with, it is no wonder that NBBCs tend to stay aloof from the church by avoiding baptism. They can *keep their faith and still have a community* to live in. If they take baptism and join the church, they will be accepted nowhere.

It is no wonder then that many NBBCs "test the waters" before they jump in. Whether a person is from a caste Hindu background or a Muslim background, he comes from a tight, secure and deep social network. He *observes if he is included in the ministries and fellowship of the church* (e.g., the Mailpatti convert, the Martandam Nair woman, and even the Sampoothu sweepers who are in the same situation sociologically). The NBBC knows Jesus is not "the Nadar God but he suspects that the Christian church may be. If he takes baptism he is giving up a wonderful community; he wants to know - quite understandably - if there will be at least some community to replace it.

As a seventh characteristic, it is perhaps self-evident that the NBBC loves his family. Yet, we often neglect this important factor in his decisions about baptism. He wants to bring them to Christ so that they can share the joy and peace he has found. He is willing to forego the blessing of baptism and the strength of Christian fellowship if it might give him the time and opportunity he needs to fulfill this evangelistic task (e.g., the Tirunelveli girl, the Paramakudi boy, the Sivakasi women, the Madras Sivakasi woman, the Chettipalsyam people.

Because of the tightness of community in India, most major decisions are community decisions. *The NBBC will try to bring his community with him* in a matter as precious as his Christian faith. As he is united with his extended family in every other major decision, he should express and seek his unity with them in this matter also. (As mentioned in the previous chapter, this is how I advised them also.)

This love for his family may also result in the rejection of baptism for another reason. We saw three examples where faithfulness to the family tradition and to the example of the fathers meant remaining as a non-baptised believer: the Martandam Nair family, the Tiruvannamalai lawyer's family and the college lecturer's family. The family's love and respect for each other seals them in common commitment to Christ, but unbaptised. To take baptism would be to imply that everyone else was wrong. To remain unbaptised is to *affirm the peculiar mission of the family tradition.* This is a tradition which we may expect to spread among the high castes of the country if properly encouraged and cultivated.

In the extended family situation the NBBC *women are placed in the most delicate situation.* Not even their NBBC parents will encourage them to go against their husbands' feelings and wishes (e.g., the Gounder, the Sivakasi women, the Sivakasi woman in Madras, the Paramakudi boys, the Paramakudi servant lady). God's wish for a happy and stable marriage is once again recognised - and clearly given the priority. *The spiritual quest of the high-caste woman is not respected* if it might conflict with her familial responsibilities. In the stories of the Sivakasi women we have seen examples of the creative ways in which that conflict can be handled.

Tenthly and finally, we come to the most difficult problem faced by the high-caste NBBC: *the marriage arrangements for his children,* especially daughters. I have already given some notes on why relations hesitate to give their sons and daughters into families of different values and customs. It may be noted here that this hesitation extends even to a situation where only a brother or sister has come under Christian influence (e.g., the Madras boy, the Mukudal young man's wife). No doubt, disrespectful attitudes of some Christian leaders towards caste Hindus' religious and social feelings (cf. the college lecturer's and the Mukudal Mudaliar's comments) have provided grounds for this strong fear about Christian influence in the family. The fear is so strong that even the most sincere NBBCs had to respect it for the sake of their children thus forfeiting their privilege and desire to take baptism (e.g., the Martandam Panikkar, the "gramasevakar", the Nagercoil and Sivakasi women and so on).

In this respect we must also recall the observation of the Zenana Mission Bible woman that the major reason for this difficulty of the NBBCs is the refusal of Christians to give their sons and daughters across caste lines, even when there is a unity of faith. Our Gurukul Director Rev. Gnanabaranam Johnson tells the story of one time when he asked a Nadar Christian student of his whether he would prefer a non-Christian Nadar wife or a non-Nadar Christian wife. He reports that the boy replied immediately. "A Nadar wife, of course."

Worship Traits of High-caste NBBCs

The outcome of all these sociological and family problems is disassociation from the corporate life of the church. Many will attend services, but they won't get involved more than that. Especially conducive to this more aloof style of relating to the church, is the Roman Catholic style of worship. A person can walk in and walk out of a large cathedral, both during a service and any other time. One can participate in the prayers and processions anonymously, or one can light a candle privately. Where protestant churches are open all day long, I have seen the same pattern occurring.

The Hindu worshippers feel comfortable *using the church like they do their temple.* This is the first distinctive characteristic we note in high-caste Hindu worship practices. It is their style of worship. A few will keep up our Christian discipline of regular Sunday worship (e.g., the tailor, the "gramasevakar", the Chettiar).

Most will *utilize the church worship as they do the temple worship,* according to their need and desire from time to time and at festival time (e.g., the Martandam Panikkar and Nair, the Pernambut and Mailpatti Naidus, the Nagercoil and Sivakasi women, the Poovancode people and so on).

A second feature of the NBBCs' more "Hindu" style of Christian worship is *their emphasis upon and approach to private devotion.* There certainly is some use of the Bible (e.g., the temple trust head, the Mailpatti boy and convert, the college lecturer, the Muslim lawyer, the Chettiar); however, it is not a devotional use as much as an instructional use, which certainly is also appropriate. The major role in the NBBC's devotional life is given to the picture of Jesus in the home, especially among those who have not come under strong Protestant influence as in Sivakasi (e.g., the temple trust head, the Mailpatti Naidu brothers, the Vellala family, the shop owner, the Nagercoil women, the Tirunelveli Nair couple). Once again, of course, this is the traditional Hindu style of worship. It is not so much prayer and petition as honouring and praising. It is an identification of one's whole being with the divine being. At its best, it is a self-emptying so that one can be filled with the divine presence. It is meditation with thc goal of being possessed by the Spirit of Christ - a Christian "devi" experience.

A third feature of the traditional Hindu style of worship is the pilgrimage. The devotee may make a pilgrimage in order to find solace or solution in a particular need, or he may do it in honour of a special occasion. It may be to a holy place or to a holy person. He goes expecting to be transformed and uplifted. We have found most rural Tamil Nadu non-baptised believers in Christ *using the big public meetings* conducted by respected evangelists in a similar way (e.g., the Tirunelveli Nair, the Sampoothu Mudaliar, the Sattur businessman and "Cornelius", the Pavoorchatram people, the R.S. Mangalam 30-year old man, the Paramakudi boy, the Muslim lawyer, the temple trust head, the Gounder, the Chettiyar, the Mailpatti Naidu landlord). The large meeting allows the anonymity and aloofness from the church which they desire. At the same time it provides the instruction and inspiration which they need.

If he is a follower of a particular evangelist, he may go because a major campaign is being conducted somewhere. If he has a particular need, he may avail himself of any campaign which may be passing by. The non-baptised believer goes in the hope of being transformed and uplifted, and then he returns once again to his private devotion at home.

The next feature of their "Hindu" style of worship is somewhat more problematic and controversial: *the following of the "ishta devata" principle.* We have already noted how some non-baptised believers worship Jesus alongside their other gods. We have also seen that several have removed all other pictures from their house and kept only a picture of Jesus (e.g., the temple trust head, the Gounder, the lecturer, the Mailpatti Naidu, some of the Sivakasi and Nagercoil women, the Vellala family); however, even among these, the college lecturer would argue somewhat in favour of the "ishta devata" principle.

To some extent, as we have seen, the NBBCs follow this principle only as a matter of accommodation to familial or social feelings, not as a matter of personal belief. Several testified that they worship only Jesus anyway when they stand before the various gods. In general, when the NBBC feels secure enough socially and economically (as in the examples cited above), he carries through on his theological conviction and spiritual experience by keeping only a picture of Jesus.

On the other hand, we have here recognition that the response to God's power and love is not confined to the Christian religion. The NBBCs have here a corrective to some of our popular, unbiblical exclusivistic mission theologies. This is a point to which we must return in our theological reflections.

Finally, we all recognise in orthodox Hindu piety *a fervency and sincerity* which puts most of us to shame. There is a unique combination of searching and finding, reflecting and experiencing, experimenting and committing. Of course, these characteristics are found primarily among the elite few, but they provide an insight into the basic values of the culture and a goal accepted by all in the society. We find these same characteristics in the high-caste NBBCs.

The conversion stories and on-going piety of the "gramasevakar" the temple trust head, the Gounder, the Martandam Nair, and the Sivakasi women inspire us all - and also the surrounding Hindu community

As one further illustration of these characteristics I might mention a Roman Catholic Christian, another wealthy cardamom plantation owner in the Uttamapalayam area, who came to a new spiritual commitment through the ministry of Bro. Dinakaran in that area. In keeping with traditional Hindu piety he has now decided to leave his business to his sons and enter into the "sannyasi' stage of life by devoting himself for the rest of his years to preaching to the poor in the villages and spending one-tenth of his income for their uplift. When the social and economic security of the Indian devotee is provided and when he is inspired by the spirit of Christ he brings a fervency and sincerity to the Gospel which makes our ordinary church life pale into insignificance.

In summary, then, what is the portrait we can draw of the high-caste non-baptised believer in Christ? He is most often a sincere believer in our Lord and desires fellowship with the church but feels compelled to remain aloof in order to avoid alienating his kith and kin. Endangering the marriage possibilities of his children is his major worry. The woman NBBC suffers the greatest isolation. Because of his prime identity with the traditions of his own community, he expresses his faith primarily within the worship style of Hinduism: with fervency but privately. His major spiritual struggle is in relating his Christian faith to the realities of the family deities around him. His major desire is that his family and community might come to share the experience in Christ with him.

Common Traits Among All NBBCs

So far we have been analysing the peculiar characteristics of the non-baptised believers in Christ among the Harijan and caste Hindu communities. We have found in each case that they are believers in our Lord who have formidable problems to cope with in the exercise of their faith. We can only have the greatest sympathy and admiration for many of them. As we attempt to discern any common characteristics and traits within this diverse phenomenon, we must certainly begin by recognising that these people are marked by a *reflectiveness and spirituality which* are a considerable level above the ordinary, whether in the church or in general society. Although they are worlds apart in other respects, in this respect we find much in common between the Chettipalayam people and the Uttamapalayam people we have met in the above pages.

A second laudable characteristic we can find among the NBBCs of all varieties is a sense of *gratitude and faithfulness*. These people came to our Lord like many others with a need, and they are of the one in ten who have returned to fall at His feet to say thanks. In spite of all it costs them emotionally and financially, they boldly and publicly carry His Name because they have become convinced that 'He is Lord. From the Sampoothu sweepers and the old Madras Brahmin giving offerings to the Paramakudi Harijan boys and the Martandam Nair family giving their whole livelihood, we are inspired at the example of gratitude and faithfulness which these people provide us in the midst of their life struggles. The wealthy temple trust head could easily have paid several thousand rupees as a thank-offering in the local church, and all would have felt satisfied. However, his profound sense of gratitude and faithfulness had to be expressed in more than rupees.

As we have seen, in the midst of these struggles they come to our Lord in faith and hope. They choose Him among the plethora of gods and goddesses because they think He may have the compassion and power to heal them now as He helped the sick and the lame of His day. Thus, a third characteristic which we find in common among the NBBCs of rich and poor is their *turning to the Lord in a crisis of life* and experiencing His help.

The most common experience by far is the experience of healing. Fully ten times we heard this witness: the tailor, the Pavoorchatram Mudaliar, the Paramakudi boys, the servant lady, the Sivakasi and Nagercoil women, the Sattur teacher, the temple trust head, the Chettiar, and the Madras husband. Four times we heard the witness of the birth of a child: the Uttamapalayam government officer, the Pavoorchatram teachers, the Sivakasi annual convention, and the Chettipalyam mother. People often experienced this effective love of Christ through the prayers of his ministers: the Nagercoil and Sivakasi Bible women, the tailor, the temple trust head, the Sattur boy. Certainly they could have received the blessing, left their thank-offering and proceeded on their way until the next crisis struck. However, these NBBCs remained with their Lord in gratitude and faithfulness, as we have seen.

These people *experienced the love and power* of Christ in their personal lives. Among all of these people we find this personal experience as a fourth common characteristic. As we saw above, they face the real threat of "principalities and powers in high places" in their lives, so they need to know that Jesus is able and willing to care for them. A god may have the power, but he may not have love. Another god may have love but not power. A third god may have both but not care about me. All three are needed: God's love, God's power, and for me.

In the event of healing and help in distress, many NBBCs from all backgrounds experienced that Jesus loves and cares for them personally. Many had this experience in physical need, as we saw above. Others had this experience with a stuck cycle lock or an uninaugurated shrine or a bus accident; others in a personal revelatory vision (e.g., the Tirunelveli Nair father, the Sivakasi lady, the 40 year old Sattur man. They had their own "Red Sea" experience of deliverance and revelation, so they were ready to stand humbly and trustingly beneath Mt. Sinai to make their covenant of obedience with their Lord.

In spite of these convincing personal experiences, we find that the new believers in Christ are able to stand firm in this conviction with varying degrees of strength and steadfastness. One of the determining factors, which we have already noted in passing, is the financial security the NBBC has in his life. We saw this problem as a central temptation in the lives of the Harijan youths.

We find the same *spiritual frustration because of financial insecurity* in the life of the drummer, the Martandam Nair, the tailor, the Chettiar, the Sivakasi businessman, the Tiruvannamalai lawyer (and perhaps the Uttamapalayam lawyer?), and the

Chettipalayam people. Others of sound financial condition are able to stand strong and act confidently. They have only social persecutions to face (e.g., the Pavoorchatram Nadar and teachers, the Gounder, the temple trust head). The others must make a real leap of faith, taking their family and children with them (e.g., the Mailpatti convert). They need our prayers and our support.

Sixthly another common cause for some NBBCs' inability to stand firm in the Lord we can trace to *weakness of character and immaturity of faith.* We see the new believer in Christ setting out on his own to witness boldly to Christ, but in the face of concerted opposition he becomes confused and frightened. He retreats into his own private devotional life, adopting an "ishta devata" principle and giving theological rationalizations for his decision (e.g. the Paramakudi boy, the tailor and shop owner, the Poovancode people, the Sattur "Cornelius" and businessman). Another common reaction which we have seen is that baptism is unnecessary since one can receive Christ's blessing also without it (e.g., the "gramasevakar" the Nagercoil woman, the 40 year old Sattur man, and many others less explicitly).

They all know in their heart that such talk is just a rationalization, that they are "living against conscience , as the Martandam Panikkar put it. Yet, they do not feel inwardly strong enough to become what God has made them in Christ. The question we must deal with later is "Whose fault is it that these NBBCs lack the necessary inner strength?"

It is clear that these co-believers in Christ, then, have *many wrong ideas and incomplete knowledge.* For the most part, all they hear over the radio and in the mass meetings is "the milk of the Gospel." They are ready for "solid food", but they are not seated where it is served. They read the Bible, but like the Ethiopian Eunuch and the disciples on the way to Emmaus they require someone to make it all coherent. In short, they need the wisdom of the church. Many non-baptised believers we have found to be confused or uninformed about the meaning of baptism (e.g., the Madurai wife, the Pavoorchatram teachers, as well as those cited already above) and of Holy Communion (e.g., the Nagercoil women). They are advised in contradictory ways by church leaders (e.g., the Martaridam priest and the Christukula Ashram pastors). They look in vain for some direct, inner guidance (e.g., the tailor, the Nagercoil and Sivakasi women, the "gramasevakar"). Once again, we must begin to ask the question "Whose fault and responsibility is this?"

Eighthly, in spite of all their theological problems and misunderstandings, we discern a wonderful clarity on the essentials of the Christian faith. They seek help in their despair, but they look more for an assurance of *God's guidance and strength in their struggles*. When I asked them the question about what they had received from Christ, this experience of peace was the most consistent theme throughout their witness of faith and experience: the Pavoorchatram teachers, the Nagercoil and Sivakasi women, the Mukudal Mudaliar and girl, the Paramakudi boy, the U.S. Mangalam 30 year old man, the Gounder, the Coimbatore boy, the Chettipalsyam people.

These spiritual seekers are on the Indian quest for "shanti", and they have found it in Christ. They are still Indians, they haven't yet become Protestants. Only the tailor and shopowner and two dying men (the Martandam Nair and the Madras Brahmin) talked about the quest for heaven. The release from distress is not to be found alone in the hereafter. The peace of eternal life is already now, through life in Christ. It is good biblical theology.

These non-baptised believers also have another insight into the fundamentals of the proper Christian experience. So much of the evangelistic message they heard would have emphasized not only the quest for heaven but also the quest for forgiveness of sin. As the quest for heaven apparently was "filtered out" of the message these NBBCs heard, so also was the quest for forgiveness. They received the Gospel message in terms of their own Indian spiritual quest.

The assurance of 'God's forgiveness certainly is mentioned in the discussions (e.g., the Martandam Panikkar, the Sivakasi women, the "gramasevakar", and the Gounder), but in the conversations I had I felt that only in the Gounder's case was this assurance a particularly meaningful experience. With the others the mention of forgiveness seemed more mechanical, more a learned response than a heartfelt experience. The responses to my questions about the benefits from worshipping Jesus mentioned the experience of *victory over the power of sin*, never the assurance of forgiveness (e.g., the R. S. Mangalam people, the Paramakudi boys, the 40 year old Sattur man, the Gounder.) This a ninth common characteristic.

Furthermore, the moral value of Christianity is given prime importance also in regard to baptism. It is made the condition of baptism (e.g., the Sattur boy, the Paramakudi boys, the Gounder brother, the tailor and the shopowner). It is made the goal of baptism (e.g., the Paramakudi boys, the Gounder, the lecturer). The ethical life is seen as the one clear witness to the reality of the Gospel (e.g., the Tirunelveli girl, the lecturer, the DK members, the Tiruvannamalai lawyer, the Gounder). Perhaps we must sit and hear from these "other sheep" what the Gospel is for India.

When we come to the matter of how these non-baptised believers came to faith in Christ, we find a tenth common testimony. *Experience in a Christian school* is mentioned most frequently. In the rural areas of Tamil Nadu the mission organisations began many schools. The objective was both to uplift the masses with good education and to share the gospel of Jesus Christ. In the testimonies before our Lord of many who have gone before — it was the example and teaching of these village school teachers which made them take Christ seriously (e.g., the shopowner, the Martandam Panikkar, the Tirunelveli Nair, the teachers, the three Paramakudi boys, the Chettipalayam people, the Mailpatti Naidus). In the mission schools the boys and girls of all castes have sat together on the floor to hear and knelt together to confess the call of the Gospel. A couple mentioned the experience of a Christian hospital (one from the Chettipalayam village and one from the Mailpatti village), and several spoke of the ministry of other churchworkers. However, our survey shows clearly the strongest impact has been through the village Christian school.

Finally we must return once again to the less pleasant realities of our sociological problem. It is clear in our survey that the NBBC's *attitude toward the church is directly determined by sociological realities.* If the local congregation is of the same community as he is the new believer easily moves into it and appreciates it. If the social background of the congregation is not one he can feel comfortable with, he withdraws and often criticises. If the caste group is the same, he joins: the R.S. Mangalam people, the Pavoorchatram teachers, the Paramakudi boys, the Coimbatore boy, the Chettipalayam people. (The "gramasevakar", who attends the local mixed caste town church, may be considered an exception. As a person he seems to be exceptional anyway.) Those of different caste from the local congregation — whether "lower" or "higher"remain aloof, as we have already seen.

In this chapter we have tried to analyse both the distinctive traits as well as the common traits of the non-baptised believers in Christ whom we met in the first chapter. We have begun to appreciate the distinctive social, political, and economic problems in the midst of which they seek to remain faithful to their Lord. We have seen their strengths and their weaknesses. We have begun to see where we might help and where we might be helped. We have seen where our different methods of sharing the Gospel have been helpful and where not so helpful. Our next section will continue to clarify and confirm our thinking on these crucial issues. Only thereafter will we begin to consider what all this may mean to our traditional church thought and life.

The general portrait of the non-baptised believer in Christ in rural Tamil Nadu, no matter from what background he may come, is an encouraging one. He is a thoughtful and sincere person who takes his spiritual life seriously. He responds with gratitude and faithfulness when he has reached conviction about the love and power of Christ. Most often this conviction comes in some experience of healing, but it also often derives from the experience in a Christian school. The strength of his relationship to the church depends on whether the local congregation is of his own caste background or not. He clearly needs this relationship because of the financial, social and spiritual problems he faces. In spite of all these problems, however, he/she presents us with a clear Indian experience of Christ as the fulfillment of the traditional spiritual quest for peace of mind and a clean heart. The non-baptised believer of rural Tamil Nadu is an admirable person. Thanks be to God.

SECTION TWO

The Non-Baptised Believer In Madras City

CHAPTER THREE

"Madras, a Christian City?"

Outline:

The Questionnaire on Faith in Christ
(the bio-data and sections explained)

General Data on Hindus, Muslims and Others
(ten statistical tables analysed)

Cross-Table Data on Hindus, Muslims and Others
(statistics analysed according to bio-data)

"Churchless Christianity" in the City
(a summary analysis of the statistics)

"Madras, a Christian City?"

The Questionnaire on Faith in Christ

In the first section we have met Jesus' "Other Sheep" personally and intimately. We have come to some appreciation of their struggles of life and faith. We have begun to think about the implications for our theological understanding and practical ministry.

However, even though the survey reported in Section One was conducted in a random sample manner, much was left to the chance discretion of the Pastor (e.g., whether he responded or not, whether he knew about the NBBCs in his area or not). My own follow-up work also depended on my choice of places to visit and the availability of the NBBCs at the time. Therefore a more systematic objective study was required in order to get a more accurate picture of the general characteristics and numbers of the non-baptised believers in Christ.

We decided to carry out this scientific study in the city of Madras. We felt that this population is concentrated enough and diverse enough that we could get an accurate picture of the whole. We also wanted to get an idea of the urban NBBCs as compared to the rural NBBCs already surveyed.

We also decided to broaden the Madras City study in order to give us an idea of the place of Jesus Christ in the faith and practice of the whole population, not only the NBBCs. For our theological understanding and practical planning it is important to know the general background of which the non-baptised believer is a particular phenomenon. The questionnaire was designed in order to give us a clear idea of how Hindus and Muslims are already related to Christ and how we might best reach them.

I would refer the reader to the full copy of the questionnaire in Appendix I. For our purposes of understanding the results of the survey, I will now describe the highlights of the questionnaire used. Thereafter we will begin a study of the actual information gathered in Madras City.

The Bio-data

The first eight questions are the usual bio-data information used later to analyse how parts of the general population differ from each other.

Age: We began from age fifteen years, as we wanted to get a more mature opinion on the various questions. The first three divisions of age are every five years, while after thirty the divisions are every ten years. This division corresponds roughly to the greater percentage of younger people in the City population, as also our survey statistics indicate. From age forty the number of people in the population begins decreasing sharply. Thus, even though the age span is less, the number of people represented by the figure in each age group is approximately the same up to age fifty.

Sex: Our survey achieved a balance of 410 males and 400 females because Dr. Siromony found three female researchers for this work. The Muslim and high-caste women would have hesitated even to open the door to a male researcher.

Occupation: On this question we found out in the final tabulation that we made a serious omission. Many of the NBBCs turned out to be educated youth. We should have asked at this point if a respondent is a student, but unfortunately we omitted that category.

Caste: At this point we were interested to learn the differences between high-caste and low-caste respondents. However, we could not ask that question directly, so we had to ask the caste name and later classify according to the government register.

This question also raised some objection, according to the report of the researchers, for several respondents objected at this point, asking "You Christians don't follow caste, so why do you ask about it?"

Religion: We included the division of Christians into Orthodox, Roman Catholic and Protestant, thinking that others may want to use this information in order to study the attitudes and practices of these different denominations. For the information on the NBBCs, Hindus, Muslims, and others, these categories were eliminated, of course.

Education: Other social research has shown that pre-high school education does not provide really functional literacy. Therefore, when we consider the use of Christian literature, we must take into consideration primarily those of more than eight years schooling.

Income Group: This was another matter which was difficult to determine. We decided simply to ask our experienced and well-trained researchers to make a judgement on seeing the house of the respondent.

Native Place: In this question we were interested to determine to what extent a respondent's geographical connections and background significantly influenced his Christian experience, rather than the immediate Madras City environment. In specific, we asked if they had native connections to Kerala and southern Tamil Nadu, where there is strong Christian influence.

Section One: Opportunities to Learn About Jesus

We now come into the body of the questionnaire itself. The first section is the largest one. We asked twenty-one different ways in which a person might have learned about Jesus in his life. In regard to each possible opportunity we offered the respondent five answers, of which he was to choose one. For example, in regard to the first question on whether he had learned about Jesus in a Sunday School, he could have answered:

1. "*Yes,* I went to Sunday School, and I learned *much* about Jesus there"; or
2. "Yes, I learned *a little* bit"; or
3. 'Yes, but I did *not like* what I experienced there"; or
4. 'Yes, but I learned *nothing* there"; or
5. "*No,* I never had the opportunity to go to a Sunday School".

In this manner we hoped to determine which evangelistic approaches have had the best results and also which have produced negative results.

In this section of the questionnaire we also ran into a problem. The researchers interpreted the "learned a little bit" response differently among themselves. Two of them used the Tamil word "*konjum*" for "a little bit". This word can mean (depending on the accent given to it) a very small, infinitesimal amount. One of the researchers interpreted this question to the respondents in a comparative sense, asking whether one way is more or less than others. Thus, "a little bit" may reveal only a slight Christian influence in one set of answers and a considerable influence in another set of answers. It was a gap in our preparations beforehand; however, we still have an impression as to whether a respondent has had any influence at all through the particular evangelistic avenue.

The first division of opportunities to learn about Jesus is that having to do with exposure to Christian institutions in Madras City. Of course, there are many hospitals, schools and social service institutions in a city like Madras, so this influence will not be as great as in a rural area. However, it does help us to clear away any false impressions or stereotypes we might have had about the effect of our institutional work in an urban context. Question No. 16 refers to Velankanni. Velankanni is a much-frequented Roman Catholic healing centre associated with Jesus' mother Mary. It is located near Nagapatinam in southern Tamil Nadu.

The second division of opportunities contains the various mass media. In my initial preparation of the questionnaire, I never even thought of television and movies as opportunities for learning about Jesus. Prof. David Ipe suggested the inclusion of TV because of the pre-Christmas and pre-Easter shows he had seen explaining these Christian festivals. None of us thought of the cinema, however. Only when the girls went out on the pre-test trial run of the questionnaire, did they come back and tell us that this response was coming frequently and must be included. You will probably be surprised like I was when you see the results on this item. The item "Christian literature", as distinguished from Bible and tracts, refers to Christian magazines and devotional literature.

The third division of opportunities is opportunities of learning about Jesus through personal contacts. The term "Christian evangelists" was interpreted in the survey to refer to professional church workers, as distinct from any individual Christian. The items "marriage to a Christian" and "children studying in a Christian school" will naturally be rather infrequent, but for the sake of completeness we included them.

Section Two: Distribution of Bibles & Pictures

The second section was only two questions. We were interested in determining people's attitudes toward the Bible and Bible distribution, so we intentionally asked not only if they personally would like a Bible in their home but if they thought it is good for all homes to have one. Thus, our interest was to find out how favourable the respondents are to this whole evangelistic technique.

The second question in this section asks the same concerning the distribution of pictures of Jesus. This possibility arose from the experience I had with rural NBBCs. The picture implies a divine role and respect for Jesus in the home, and it is ever before the household's awareness. The Bible may be more informationally used, while the picture of Jesus is a more public and devotional commitment.

Section Three: Beliefs about Jesus

The third section gathered information on people's knowledge and understanding about Jesus. We need to know at what level the general population or parts of it are already so that we can take them further. Educationally speaking, it is a kind of "pre-test" in our public teaching programme.

In question no. 35 we placed one of the key items we used in determining the non-baptised believers in Christ in the general population. Response "e" stating "Jesus is the one and only true incarnation of God" was one of the indicators of orthodox belief in Jesus. The other indicator came toward the end of the questionnaire, as we shall see. Please note that the respondents were to choose only one response to this question, so they had to indicate in what regard Jesus means the most to them.

From question no. 36 to 44 we inquired various possible religious influences which a person might have had from contact with Jesus. Once again, my experience among the rural NBBCs influenced the choice of responses here: prayer, moral growth, and peace of mind contrasted with forgiveness of sin and attainment of heaven. We also tested once again the reciprocal responsibility in our Christian understanding of worship (no. 41 on "what God wants of me"), which the rural NBBCs generally failed to understand and we found the same results.

The third division of this section tested the actual facts known about Jesus. The emphasis of these questions is on those facts which relate to the possibility of seeing Jesus as a divine power to help me in my need, which was the crucial insight we found in the spiritual pilgrimage of the rural NBBCs.

Section Four: Experiences in Worship of Jesus

The fourth section of the questionnaire asked details concerning spiritual and devotional experiences the respondent might have had with Jesus, since this was a major role Jesus played in the life of the rural NBBCs studied earlier. The first division asks specifically about experiences in times of need, while the third division asks about general devotional practices. in the second division of this section, prayer for healing is brought in. Question no. 59 brings in the term "blessing" which is a very general term, but it conveys in popular usage a general feeling of satisfaction in devotion to Jesus. Question no. 63 brings in the specifically Christian emphasis on intercessory prayer in order to test if this Christian relationship to Christ exists also among Hindus, Muslims, and NBBCs. Question no. 68 is a Criterion for determining an NBBC.

Section Five: Preferred Ways to Learn about Jesus

Section five takes seven different evangelistic methods and asks the respondent to say if he would be open to an approach in this manner or not. The seven methods mentioned at this point are all professional methods. Thus, they are intended to help the church in planning its organised evangelistic activities. Unplanned contacts with families, for example, are not mentioned here but organised discussion groups are. It proves instructive to contrast this section with the responses to section one, for we are able to determine what methods are welcome but under-utilised.

Section Six: Family Situation of NBBCs

The final section of the questionnaire asks four questions directly related to non-baptised believers in Christ. No. 77 is the second key response in identifying an NBBC, for it adds the person's conviction as to the practice of the faith. No. 35 gave us the orthodox theological response, while no. 77 gives us the orthodox practical response. No. 76 helps us to evaluate how receptive Christians and others are to the religious approach of the NBBCs. No. 78 is intended to determine how much direct access Christians have to NBBCs, and no. 79 is intended to determine how much direct access NBBCs have to other Hindus and Muslims.

In most cases the researchers also took down the name and address of the respondents. This information is intended for purposes of professional verification. We did not feel it is proper to use this information to follow up the non-baptised believers discovered in the survey though it certainly was tempting.

General Data on Hindus, Muslims and Others

Before getting into the details about the non-baptised believers in Christ, we do well to look at the responses of the general Hindu and Muslim population. We will better understand the experience and position of the NBBCs if we determine the general spiritual environment in which they live among other Hindus and Muslims. We will also be able to discern where the non-baptised believers are on the total spectrum of responses to Christ. Of course, the information also has great importance for the church's general planning of evangelistic outreach, for we will find that the necessity before us is as much nurture as proclamation. There is a kind of Christianity already there waiting for us to encourage it to full bloom.

The tables of survey statistics referred to in the coming pages have been printed in Appendix II. Of course, there are many more tables, especially cross-tables, which have not been included because the information was not utilised in this analysis. The full set of tables is available at Gurukul for those who would like to study the material in more detail and depth.

Table One: Bio-Data

First we will look at the Bio-Data on Hindus, Muslims and Others (Table One in Appendix II). India is a country of youth. More than one-third of the population in Madras City is between fifteen and twenty-five years of age. (In rural areas it is around 50% because the death rate is higher.) Our work among young people, then, is most important, also because youth is the age of questioning and searching. After marriage; as we saw among the rural NBBCs, free spiritual decisions are difficult to make and implement. A similar survey in Japan revealed that almost all conversions take place before the age of thirty, and our experience in India is the same.

In regard to "Occupation" it is interesting to notice that only 2% of the people of other religions are teachers, while the statistics on Christians show 9.6% are teachers. (Note: This table on Christian bio-data is not provided in the appendix. The teaching profession, we saw in the previous chapters, is an excellent opportunity for Christian's influence, so we must be happy that a large percentage of Christians enter this profession.)

A comparison with Christian statistics also in regard to "Caste" is revealing. Almost half the population are high-caste Hindus, whereas among Christians the figure is only 10.8%. Indeed many of our high-caste converts have relocated to the cities, for they do not usually have a rural community to live in as the Harijan congregations from the mass movements provide. At any rate, the statistics further illustrated the loneliness and frustration which the high-caste NBBC will feel. We also recognise that we have very little access among the high castes through the Christian community.

Table Two: Opportunities to Learn about Jesus

Now let us move on to the first important section on how people of other religions have learned about Jesus. In order to be sure that the necessary manner of interpreting the tables is clear, I will read the first row of statistics on the Sunday School. The reader may please follow by referring to Appendix II.

Twenty-one Hindus and Muslims said that they learned much about Jesus from attending a Sunday School. Twenty-one Hindus and Muslims are 2.89% of the total 726 who responded to the question. Similarly, thirteen responded that they learned a little about Jesus by attending a Sunday School, which is 1.79% of the total. No one said that they attended but did not like what they learned, and only one responded that he attended but learned nothing at all about Jesus there. The vast majority never attended at all.

This last statistic, by the way, should make us consider making some special efforts to recruit neighbourhood children for this instruction. Our own Christian children would be the best recruiters. There is considerable impact on those who did attend, for childhood is the age of deep learning.

Let us take an overall perspective first on the results of the statistics in this section of the questionnaire. If we combine both "much" and "little" learned about Jesus, what is the ranking we find among the twenty-one evangelistic avenues?:

1.	Movies	65%
2.	Tracts	50%
3.	Individual Christian	48%
4.	Street preaching	45%
5.	Christian family	45%
6.	Radio programmes	43%
7.	TV programmes	38%
8.	Church worship	38%
9.	Christian weddings	30%
10.	Christian literature	27%
11.	Christian school	27%
12.	Bible reading	24%

Any surprises? I was personally surprised to find that the item I had not even considered for the initial questionnaire turned out to lead this list by a significant margin. These are the commercial movies shown for the general public in the cinema houses around the city. We have had a couple of commercial movies on the life of Jesus both in Telugu and in Tamil, and there have always been the English language epics like "The Bible", "The Ten Commandments", etc. Clearly the good news about Jesus is going out to people far beyond what the church is doing. Similarly, we find the Christian influence of secular TV standing high on our list.

In general, it is the mass media which brings the most pervasive impact on the city population. The Christian mass media of tracts, street preaching, and radio together with the secular movies and TV account for five of the seven top places in the list. Obviously, the mass media is a field where we should be developing personnel, techniques and materials which respond to this open door of opportunity.

However, before we get too enthusiastic about the mass media we should take a look at those opportunities to learn about Jesus which had a strong impact on the interviewees. We may recall at this point that the reliability of the "little bit" response is somewhat questionable because of the varied way it was administered. However, with the "much" response we know that we have a significant Christian impact:

1.	Individual Christian	29%
2.	Christian family	26%
3.	Movies	19%
4.	Radio programmes	18%
5.	Church worship	16%
6.	Christian School	15%
7.	Christian weddings	12%
8.	TV programmes	10%
9.	Tracts	9%
10.	Street preaching	8%

Clearly it is the personal, intimate, real-life contacts which have the deepest impact on people's minds and hearts. The witness of Christian living, whether by individuals or by families, is still the most convincing proclamation of the Gospel. (Remember what the little Mukudal girl said?) We have seen in our previous interviews that people are looking for an experienced Gospel, a power which gives peace of mind and strength of character. When they see that power at work, they learn more about Jesus than what they hear proclaimed at the mass meetings in the street preaching.

Nonetheless, it is still impressive that mass media like movies and radio remain in the third and fourth positions also in our second list of "much" impact. The mass media's major contribution is a superficial introduction which might whet one's appetite to look for more. However, a good movie can be a highly uplifting experience, and regular listening to the radio can gradually transform one's thinking. The power of the mass media is a fact on all levels.

Next, I would like to comment on several of the items specifically and briefly. I would invite the reader to make his own study item by item and to draw his own conclusions.

The Christian schools are not as pervasive a medium of Christian influence in the urban setting as in the rural, for there are many other good schools. Yet, the impact is considerable on those who attend. We must use this opportunity to have Bible classes for all, and not only morning devotions.

Similarly, Christian hospitals are few among many government and private hospitals in the city. However we must also recognise that those who enter these Christian institutions apparently leave with little new knowledge of Christ. We must consider ways in which the opportunity to learn about Christ can be provided in the hospital setting.

What has been said about our hospitals holds true about our social work also, according to the survey results. These statistics certainly argue against those who accuse us of using social work activities in order to convert!

A considerable number of Hindus and Muslims, fully one fourth have gone to Velankanni. However, only a few have learned much about Jesus there. It is a point for our Roman Catholic friends to consider.

Reading of Christian tracts, literature, and even the Bible seem to have little significant impact on Hindus and Muslims. As we saw already among the rural NBBCs, the Bible requires an interpreter. Even clearly explained information only reaches to head level. Personal experience is what reaches the heart. Thus our Christian literature must be considered with the mass media as more superficial medthod of outreach.

The large public meetings clearly have little impact on the Hindu and Muslim population of the city. Eighty-five percent have never attended, and only 3.5% felt any significant impact. These meetings have a greater attraction to the Christians (three-fourths have attended and half have learned "much") and to the NBBCs, as we have seen and as we shall see. Obviously, these meetings should be re-oriented more towards nurture of those already in the faith, since it is primarily believers who are attending.

Street preaching is shown to be a superficial mass medium, but as a mass medium it also clearly has its place. It does not bring deep commitment, but it does get some information out. The largest amount of negative feedback has come on this item: 1.2%. However, I was personally surprised that the negative reaction from the general public is so little, for the criticism of this medium by the elite of the church and of the society is considerable. Obviously, street preaching is not as bad as we may think.

The low figure on "Discussion with an Evangelist" is a definite embarrassment. At least in Madras City it is apparent that our churchworkers are not getting out into the general public. When we come to the fifth section on ways in which people would like to be reached, we will be even more embarrassed.

Although the number of people who have learned about Christ from their school-going children is small, it is significant that the impact is as great as it is. Only six people out of the 120 who have children going to a Christian school said that they have learned nothing about Jesus through them. We must consider ways in which we can plan for more parental involvement in the spiritual programme of our schools.

Finally, we see in the statistics, perhaps with some pleasant surprise, that many Hindus and Muslims actually come to church. It may well be that most attend the Roman Catholic services which, as we noted in the previous chapter, provide a style of worship which outsiders can more comfortably attend. However, whether at regular worship services or at funerals and weddings, the statistics clearly show that the church service is a significant evangelistic medium. No doubt, we must plan our liturgies and our sermons more intentionally with these people in mind, for they are there and they are listening. Through observing a people's worship one can gain a deep insight into their spiritual experience. This is the challenge before each pastor as he plans especially those services like festivals and weddings when he knows many Hindus and Muslims will be present.

Table Three: Distribution of Bibles, Pictures & Nature of Jesus

In Table Three of Appendix II we find the statistics revealing the attitudes among Hindus, Muslims and others about our distribution of Bibles and pictures of Jesus. Clearly there is much positive public opinion about this method of spreading the Gospel. Only 20% disagree that every home should have a Bible, and only 2% strongly. The negative opinion rises considerably when it comes to having a picture of Jesus in every home, as we would expect; however, more than two-thirds of the population agrees with the idea.

We have accepted and implemented this idea in regard to Bible distribution, however, from what we have seen now both among the rural and urban populations we should consider much more seriously the distribution of pictures of Jesus for every home. Knowing what we do about the meaning and function of a picture in the home, the offering of this method of relating to our Lord may be one of our most important and most neglected resources.

The other set of statistics in Table Three gives what people of other faiths think about the nature of Jesus. What is the popular Christology in the "churchless Christianity" around us? The vast majority of Hindus (the 9.6% response probably belongs to the Muslim population) obviously look upon Jesus as another god like *Murugan* and *Ganesh*, the "ishta devata" principle. Although we may find such a description unsatisfactory as it stands, it also reveals a broad acceptance of Jesus' divinity among the city populace. We will see later that people also widely accept His humanity, so we are not too far from consolidating into an orthodox Christology. It is encouraging to know where people are already at as we think of approaching them so that we can plan how to help them move further.

At the other end we find the least response, 3%, representing Jesus as a misled man. Ninety-seven percent of the responses to Jesus are highly positive. Thus, if Jesus was not a misled man, He must have been correct as to what He claimed for Himself. Indeed, 6.5% have come to that conclusion. If we add to this the 8% who consider Jesus the greatest religious leader of all time, we come to three-fourths of the Madras City population who can easily recognise Jesus as their personal Lord within their existing Christology.

I am sure the Madras City Hindu and Muslim population is more orthodox in their Christian belief than most of our so-called "Christian population" in cities of the west.

The very small response incorporating Jesus into the orthodox Hindu framework as an avatar, i.e., an incarnation of the Lord *Vishnu* like *Krishnan*, shows that the hold of Indian philosophy on the population is restricted to a small minority. The responses of the more thoughtful orthodox Hindu respondents view Jesus primarily from a more historical perspective as a reformer, leader, or misled man. This historical perspective also is much more in line with the Christian starting point than Hindu philosophical or mythological interpretations. We have another confirmation that the Hindu attitudes toward Christ are on the right track.

Table Four: What Learned from Jesus

Table Four gives us information on what Hindus, Muslims and others feel they have gained from learning about Jesus. At this point we are able to gain an impression as to how deeply they have been confronted by Him and in what ways their religious thinking has been changed. First of all, we note that almost half (45%) testify that they have indeed learned from Jesus. Of these the vast majority speak of learning ethical values: love toward others, help toward the needy and sacrifice for the sake of society. Prayer and peace of mind have been learned to a considerably less extent. Forgiveness of sin is less yet, and the attainment of heaven least.

We have already seen in our study of the rural non-baptised believers that this is the spiritual and moral quest which the Hindu mentality finds fulfilled in Christ. The difference from the "Christian interpretation" of Christ can be elucidated through a comparison of these figures with those of the Christian population. For example, 91% of the Hindus and Muslims who have learned from Christ say they have learned to love others (combining the responses on "much" and "little") The same statistic among Christians is 89%, so Hindus, Muslims and Christians are alike on this point. However, if we compare the figures on learning how to attain heaven, we find that it is 23% for the Hindus and Muslims who have learned from Christ and 74% for the Christians. Christians also participate in this cultural background to some extent, it may be noted here, for with them also gaining peace of mind (85%) and moral strength (91% on all three questions) through Christ is considerably more important than forgiveness of sin (77%) and attainment of heaven.

Table Five: Beliefs About Jesus

In the question no. 35 on the nature of Jesus we have tested the evaluation of Hindus, Muslims and others about Jesus. In Table Five, we test what facts they actually know and believe about Him. In their Christological thinking and in their learning from Christ, we found the popular view-point quite orthodox, but does this thinking have a solid grounding in the facts of Jesus' life, resurrection and ascension? Unless people can express why they believe what they profess, we may suspect that their profession of faith is only an empty repetition of correct words with no real foundation beneath.

In question no. 35 we found a good three-fourths of the Hindu and Muslim respondents professing at least a semi-orthodox belief in Christ. In Table Four, we found 45% expressing that they had been helped in their spiritual growth through learning from Christ. In Table Five, we find from fifty to seventy-nine percent of all respondents professing knowledge and belief in the basic facts about Jesus.

Furthermore, if we eliminate from the Hindu and Muslim percentage those who stated that they simply do not know, we find that the figure jumps to 67% minimum and 92% maximum. Thus, we can conclude that most Hindus and Muslims already know and believe, and the vast majority who know, also believe. Once again, one is tempted to compare these figures with any comparable study of the knowledge and beliefs about Christ in some other city in the West. The statistics show a fairly orthodox Christian belief among many Hindus and Muslims in Madras City and much receptivity.

Table Six: Practices of Prayer to Jesus

In Table Six we move on to the practice of the Christian faith among Hindus and Muslims. The first statistic tells us that 38% of this population has prayed to Jesus. It is striking for any Christian in Madras to walk down the streets of the city, see the masses of people with external marks of other religions, and to realise that every other person he passes has prayed to Jesus (the 38% plus 10% Christians).

Seventy-nine percent of those who prayed to Jesus said that Jesus answered their prayer (the relation of 30% to 7.85% in frame 3). Apparently those who did not experience the help they sought ceased to pray to Jesus, as we see in the last frame. However, 19% of the Hindus and Muslims, who have experienced Jesus' help through prayer once, now continue to pray to him when they are in need. Including the adjoining areas of the city, the total of Hindus and Muslims is approximately four million. Thus, there are approximately 800,000 people outside the church who pray to Jesus when in need.

Those who also pray regularly, whether in particular need or not, are somewhat less in number than those who confessed Jesus as the "one and only true incarnation" in question no. 35. We might at first feel disappointed that those who pray regularly are so few compared to those who pray when in need. However, we see the same tendency in the Christian population, where the percentage decreases from 83% when in need to 66% regularly. By fallen nature we are self-centered rather than God-centered beings, whether of Christian or of other faith.

Table Seven: Experiences in Prayer to Jesus

In Table Seven we can see what the needs were concerning which the Hindus and Muslims turned to Jesus in prayer, and what they experienced in this prayer. The most common need in which the person turned to Jesus was for forgiveness of sin. Fully 25% of the Hindu and Muslim population experienced relief from guilt through prayer to Jesus. The experience of peace of mind and freedom from bad habits is considerably less.

This experience in prayer contrasts sharply with what people testified that they learned from Jesus (Table Four) and with what the rural NBBCs described as their spiritual experience. This is a point in the statistics which may require some further analysis and re-study. However, my explanation would be that the experience of relief from guilt is an immediate experience whenever one prays to Jesus in such a need, while learning and changing is a much longer and deeper process. The struggle for freedom from bad habits and for peace of mind in troubles is not achieved through an occasional prayer, but through a disciplined life of worship and meditation, as we saw among the NBBCs in the last chapter.

Once again in these statistics we find the importance of physical healing. Relief from guilt is a less tangible and evident experience through prayer. Healing of one's body is an obvious answer to one's prayer. Ten percent of the Hindu and Muslim population have experienced important healing through prayer to Jesus, and totally twenty-one percent know something of Jesus' healing power through prayer. In the West, even among sincere Christians, the figures would not be much different, I suspect. Jesus cares for His "other sheep", and they know it.

Prayer for others is higher than I expected, for intercession is a special emphasis in Christian practice (87% in the statistics on Christians). Hindu and Muslim piety emphasises more of one's individual accountability and presence before God in prayer. However, in relation to Jesus, people seem to feel motivated to pray for more than their own needs. Ten to fifteen percent of the Hindus and Muslims relate to Jesus as the Lord who loves and helps all. Perhaps they realise that His love is for all, not only for those who take Him as their "ishta deva" not only for those who are "His People".

Table Eight: Worship of Jesus

In Table Six, we saw how Hindus and Muslims related to Jesus through prayer when in need. In Table Eight we see how Jesus fits into their regular worship practices. The portraits drawn for us here are familiar by now.

We find that this same twenty percent worships Jesus privately at home, perhaps using a picture of Jesus as our rural NBBCs. It is a private affair, not with family members, as we noted in the previous chapter. It also is frequently along with other gods, but we also have this same hard core who remain faithful only to Jesus even while living in an unsupportive and perhaps hostile environment.

Almost one-third of the Hindus and Muslims also come to church worship. We have noted this fact previously at the end of Table Two, and we will see it again in the next table. Lakhs and lakhs of Hindus and Muslims come to the Christian church to learn and to worship. They have experienced the love and power of our Lord and they want to deepen this relationship in mind and in heart. These "other sheep" hear the voice of their shepherd and respond to His call. In the company of family and relations, they commonly worship Jesus among their traditional deities. However, they also come to church where they are free to hear His voice alone.

Table Nine: Preferred Ways to Learn More about Jesus

Along with Table Two, our next table gives us important information as to how we should plan to spread and strengthen the faith in Jesus among Hindus and Muslims in Madras City. It is most enlightening to compare these two tables. In Table Nine the evangelistic method most welcomed is one the church has utilised the least according to Table Two: the professional churchworker, the evangelist. Fully twenty-four percent of the Hindus and Muslims would welcome with great interest an opportunity to sit and talk with one of our pastors or Bible women, and another seventeen percent are open to the idea. However, to date only five percent have had opportunity in any way. One-fourth of the Hindus and Muslims are even ready to enter a process of group discussions.

These statistics are highly revealing, both about Jesus' "other sheep" and about Jesus' "fold sheep". We have already reflected upon our failure to use city pastors for this outreach work. What we must begin to reflect on more seriously, both theologically and practically, is this open door to deep conversation about Christ and His call.

These statistics clearly reveal to us that Jesus' "other sheep" want to be as close to the fold as possible. They want the guidance and enrichment of Jesus' under-shepherds. They already come anonymously to our church services to hear and to worship. They are willing to discuss personally also in order that their faith might be clarified and deepened. What more can we realistically expect of them at this point? If they are a "churchless Christianity" is it not primarily because we have refused to bring the church to them? We will be thinking further along these lines in later chapters.

We have already discussed the interest of Hindu and Muslim believers to "plug into" our church services as much as possible. They seek the nurture of the church, though anonymously for the most part. We see this desire expressed also by their interest in Bible reading and Christian magazines. Fifty-eight percent of the Hindus and Muslims in this survey have had at least an elementary school education, and most of them would like to have a Bible and other Christian literature to read. In Table Two, only five percent had learned much from Bible reading and only three percent from Christian literature; however the interest seems to be there, so we should not be discouraged.

The literary media fit into the dual desire of Jesus' "other sheep" for nurture and for privacy. It is a medium to be developed and implemented properly to reach these people with the kind of material they need. The same is evidently true about our radio ministries, according to these statistics. The need is for nurture in existing faith. The comforting and encouraging call of the Shepherd must reach beyond the confines of the fold to the crags and thistles where the "other sheep" struggle.

However, eighty-three percent are not interested in going out of their house to a mass rally in order to get this nurture.

In Table Two we saw that eighty-five percent had never gone either. Unlike the other unutilised media in Table Two, this medium does not attract interest in Table Nine. The respondents indicate that they either want to have a face-to-face dialogue or they want to have the freedom to think things through leisurely on their own. The general population of Hindus and Muslims apparently do not feel comfortable with the format and content of the big public meetings we conduct. However, these rallies show strong popularity among Christians (60%). They reflect the style and values of the "Christian culture", so Christians feel comfortable at them.

Table Ten: Relation to NBBCs

Table Ten brings us to the end of the questionnaire. This table contains another of the key questions for determining the presence of non-baptised believers in Christ, question no. 77. If we combine all those who agree, we come to a figure of 7% in Madras City. The question is a very strong statement ("Jesus. . . the only true way") so it is significant that only 13.5% strongly disagreed with the statement. There is a spirit of toleration even toward such exclusivistic views.

We gain an impression of similar accepting attitudes in the opinion of half the population that it is permissible to remain within the community while devoted solely to Jesus (question 76). On this item it is significant that so many stated that they "Can't Say." These would probably be those who have not confronted the phenomenon among their family or friends. We see in the final frame that 20.6% do have such NBBCs among their relations.

The impression we gain from this set of statistics is that the NBBC will certainly face opposition from some of his relations (greater or stronger, depending on the family background) but there also will be a strong general environment of acceptance and toleration. No doubt, the personal contacts with Christians through inter-marriage (17%) have facilitated these more appreciative and accepting views toward the worship of Christ in the home, for the survey shows that their Christian relatives hold strongly to the exclusivistic view (84%).

The figure on question no. 76 among Christians shows that this open attitude toward worship of Christ without baptism also prevails among the Christian population (only 24% opposed, with 59% in favour and 17% unsure). The "churchless Christianity" in Madras City is a generally known and recognised phenomenon. Few are trying to fight it, for it is too big and spontaneous. The question we must ask is if it should be intentionally encouraged.

Cross-Table Data on Hindus, Muslims, and Others

We shall now move on to the cross-tables. With the use of the Indian Institute of Technology computer in Guindy, Madras, we were able to collate the information about the general Hindu and Muslim population also specifically in regard to the bio-data of age, sex, occupation, caste, religion, education and income group. We chose four areas for cross-table analysis (How People Learned, What People Accept, How People Worship, and How People Prefer to Learn More) because these covered the crucial areas of understanding people's faith and how to plan effectively for the future. The objective of this information is to determine if certain age groups for example, reveal significantly different responses to certain evangelistic methods.

These cross-tables cover 140 pages of computer print-out material. The material is intended for more scientific study than I am capable of and than most readers are interested in. Therefore I will take only the highlights from these statistics, as they help us understand better the "churchless Christianity" around us. Only a few cross-tables, for the sake of illustration, are included in the appendices.

In Appendix III the cross-table on the age-wise responses to learning in a Christian school is given in Table One. These tables can be somewhat difficult to read, so I will use this table to illustrate once again how it should be used. Along the top of the cross-table are the seven age-wise categories given in the questionnaire.

Along the left side are the five possible responses. The numbers directly opposite "much," "little," etc. are the actual numbers of respondents under each age category. For each response there is listed also a "row percentage" and a "column percentage." Thus, the number in the row percentage gives the percentage for each response within the particular age group. For example, 18 respondents aged 15-20 years stated that they had learned "much" about

Christ in a Christian school. That number of respondents is 16.98% of all those who responded "much" and it is 14.06% of the responses made by those aged 15-20.

At the end of the row or column are the total figures, giving the total number of respondents for each category and the average response in that row or column. One should look for significant differences from the average within each row or column. The cross-tables for each set of bio-data run the same way, and we shall turn to these statistics now.

Cross-Tables according to Age

We will first look into the cross-tables for the different age groups of Hindus, Muslims and others. I will point out some significant facts from the cross-tables.:

In regard to learning about Jesus in a Christian school, there is a clear increase with age. It is evident that the older generation studied more frequently in a Christian school, but now many more government and private schools have come up in the city.

In regard to Christian social work, the population under thirty years of age shows considerably more learning about Jesus through this means than older people.

As would be expected in the physical and mental difficulties of middle age, the greatest influence of Velankanni is found between thirty and fifty years of age.

The influence of radio programmes increases with age. Perhaps the older one gets the more time one has to listen. We should, then plan our radio programmes to meet the needs and interests of these older people.

The influence of TV and movies is quite similar across all age groups. These are, indeed, media which reach the whole population effectively.

Reading of the Bible and of tracts increases steadily with age. Probably, as with listening to the radio, older people find more leisure time to do these things; and we should plan our Bible correspondence courses and tracts with these people also in mind.

The big meetings seem to lack appeal with all age groups.

In regard to street preaching, the reactions are similar across all age groups, except in that half of those who reacted negatively were aged sixty-one or over.

The influence of personal contacts with individual Christians and with Christian family life is equally high across all ages.

As one might expect, the influence of Christian weddings and funerals increase with age, for the Hindu and Muslim friends of Christians would have attended more such occasions as the years go along.

The influence of attending Christian worship is equal across all age groups.

We now move on to the cross-tables relating the different age groups to the statistics on beliefs about Jesus. The significant information for us to consider from these cross-tables is as follows:

Those over sixty-one years of age show much more skepticism about Jesus' resurrection (42% disagree that he rose), while among the teenagers only 12.5% disagree.

In general, one observes significantly more acceptance of Christian truths about Jesus among the younger population. As another example, only 7% of the teenagers disagree that Jesus has power today to help those who worship Him, while 28.5% of the aged disagree.

The next set of cross-tables related age to worship practices. The only significant data I gather from these tables is that the elderly do not go out to worship Jesus at church (14%) while the youth do (39%). Also, eleven percent of those between 15 and 20 years of age say that they worship only Jesus, while the general average is only 4.4%. Obviously, there is a significant attraction for Jesus among the youth, which we certainly should take into consideration as we plan our church worship and outreach programmes.

The final set of cross-tables is that on how Hindus and Muslims prefer to learn more about Jesus. Those below twenty-five years show considerable interest in coming to church worship and in discussing as a group or with an evangelist. Almost fifty percent of those interested in learning about Christ in these ways are the youth. Once again, the elderly are least interested. We may recall here that most re-thinking on basic issues of life is done during youth. Re-thinking in old age requires a willingness to reject and change all that one has stood for throughout life.

Thus, in summary of what we have seen in the cross-tables in reference to age differences, we find that different approaches are needed to reach different age groups. Youth can be reached through the professional services of the church. They already show more acceptance of the Christian faith, and they are open to participate and discuss. The middle aged and elderly prefer to learn more about Jesus at home privately, either through reading or through the radio. Christian institutions of education and service have some impact on those they reach, but in the urban context their influence is limited.

Cross-Tables according to Sex

There are not many differences among men and women in the cross-tables, which is an interesting discovery in itself. In regard to how they have learned about Jesus, men indicate more learning through tracts, big meetings, radio, street preaching, Christian families and individuals, funerals and weddings. They testify to more ways of learning about Jesus, probably because they are able to get out more into society and do what they want.

However, when it comes to actually believing in the facts about Jesus, there is little difference between men and women respondents in the figures of assent. In fact, there is a slight tendency for more women to believe, and about half as many say they disagree. More say that they simply don't know, which is attributable to the less exposure they might have had to Christian evangelistic media.

Men seemed to show more interest in getting to know about Jesus, but when it comes to actually worshipping Him, the women testify more to such practices. Twenty-four percent of the women worship Jesus at home privately and thirty-six percent at church. Among men the figures are 15.6% at home and 28.7% at church.

In regard to preferred ways to learn more, men (among whom there is a higher literacy rate) are more interested than women in reading the Bible and other Christian literature. Although the women are not interested in a discussion group, it is striking that they are as open as men to a private discussion with an evangelist.

Our statistics on men and women show, then, that most media reach both sexes similarly. Men of course, can get out more to public occasions, but women do come to church and they welcome a visit by a pastor or Bible woman. Women also seem to respond better than men to what they have learned about Jesus; they believe and put into practice.

Cross-Tables according to Occupation

As we go through the cross-tables relating "Occupation" to opportunities for learning about Christ, we find that the non-gazetted officers (middle level government workers) and teachers generally tell of more experiences with Christ. Therefore, among those over 25 years of age it will be these middle-level professionals who are most interested to learn about our Lord.

We find that the NGO's also believe the most consistently concerning the facts of Jesus. However, the teachers (though we must keep in mind that the sample here is only eleven persons so not very reliable statistically) state more doubt about Jesus being alive today and able to help his worshippers. The category of occupation which expressed the great doubts throughout these questions was that of other professionals.

Teachers, housewives and NGOs exhibit the most worship of Jesus at home and at church. However, when it comes to worshipping Jesus along with other gods, all the occupations come around 25%, with the professionals the highest at 34%. The exclusive worship of Jesus stands at 4.2% among housewives, while the NGOs who previously showed more interest in Christ have no one who responds to Him to the extent of worshipping Him only.

The inconsistencies in this category continue when we analyse how people of different occupations would like to learn more about Christ. In this category suddenly the "executive" class shows the greatest interest in almost all respects, although the NGOs are most interested to meet an evangelist and learn more. (We should note again, however, that there are only sixteen executives in the sample, so the statistical indications cannot be considered reliable.)

In summary, in regard to occupations there does not seem to be any consistent pattern, except that middle-level workers show interest and housewives practice more. Occupation apparently is not a determining factor in responding to Christ.

Cross-Tables according to Caste

Our next category from the bio-data is "caste". These statistics confirm our earlier discussion on the relation of Harijans to the church. Those of the "Scheduled Caste" category have learned much more than the rest through the organised ministries of the church: big meetings, street preaching, evangelistic, and various church services (funerals, weddings, worship). Obviously, they attend church and participate in its activities much more than Hindus and Muslims of other castes. Thus, in Madras City our regular church ministries are reaching primarily twelve percent of the population, the Harijan community.

The ranking of learning opportunities is similar between the scheduled caste and other caste respondents, except that the scheduled caste ranks street preaching much higher. No doubt, street preaching takes place primarily in their neighbourhoods. Although the ranking is similar, the other caste group indicates generally less learning on each item.

Almost half of the city population is "high caste". What are the evangelistic approaches which have proven helpful among them? I will provide the two lists as I did earlier for all Hindus and Muslims. First, combining the "much" and "little" responses, we find the general impact of various evangelistic media on high caste Hindus.:

1.	Movies	67%
2.	Tracts	52%
3.	Radio	52%
4.	Individual Christian	49%
5.	Christian family	46%
6.	Television	43%
7.	Street Preaching	39%
8.	Church Worship	35%
9.	Christian School	33%

The second list gives only the "much" responses, so we can determine through which media the high caste Hindus have learned the most about Jesus:

1.	Individual Christian	27%
2.	Christian Family	24%
3.	Movies	18%
4.	Christian School	16%
5.	Radio	14%
6.	Church Worship	14%
7.	Christian Wedding	10%

If we compare these lists with the general population of Hindus and Muslims as listed previously, we find the following significant differences. Under general influence, radio is more and street preaching is less. Under deeper influence, the list is about the same with Christian schools slightly higher. Therefore, we see that the most impact on high-caste Hindus has come through personal experiences of Christian lives and from the mass media of cinema and radio. The regular ministries of the church do not touch them, except when they attend an occasional church worship or wedding service or if they happen to enroll in one of our schools.

The fact that our organised ministries do not reach the higher caste people is further illustrated in the cross-tables on beliefs about Jesus. In Appendix III, two of these cross-tables are included as illustrations. Except on the statements that Jesus was a historical person, that He healed the sick and that He has power to help his worshippers, the high-caste respondents indicate more frequently (sometimes more than one-third) that they do not know. Since 81% of the high-caste Hindus accept that Jesus was historical, 71% can easily accept that he would have healed the sick; for all divine men have such abilities. Furthermore, since they accept Jesus as one of the "ishta devata", they would also accept (73%) that He has power to help His worshippers. Only 8.4% of the high-caste respondents doubt this, compared to 10.4% of the Scheduled Caste and 15% of the other castes.

Thus, there is an openness among high-caste Hindus also to accept Jesus' Incarnation, His humanity and His divinity. It needs to be "fleshed out" with more awareness of the facts of His life and status, but the skeleton of belief is there even among those most sociologically alienated from the church.

The other tendency in these figures is that the Scheduled Caste respondents believe more and the Other Caste respondents doubt more. Thus, the high-caste people seem to be less informed, while the people of middle castes know but do not accept. For example, on the important question of Jesus being alive today (cf. Appendix III) 35% of the high-caste respondents say they don't know, compared to 28.6% and 26.6% ignorance among Scheduled Castes and Other Castes; 60% of the Scheduled Caste believe and only 11.7% doubt, while 54% of the Other Castes believe and 20.3% doubt.

The contrast between the responses to Christ among the different caste groups continues in relation to the worship practices (cf. Table Three). More than one-third of the Scheduled Caste Hindus worship Jesus at home (36.4%), mostly together with other gods. However, 14.3% of the Harijan Hindus testify that they worship only Jesus. More than half the Harijan Hindus (53.3%) will also worship Jesus by going to church.

On the other hand, only 16.5% of the high-caste Hindus will worship Jesus at home privately, but more will worship Him together with their other gods (24.4%), and even more will worship Jesus at church (29%). The exclusive worship of Jesus among these people is very small: two percent. The other castes' percentages fall in between these two extremes, generally closer to the high-caste Hindu percentages.

It is clear, therefore, that the worship of Jesus is much less frequent among the higher castes. However, if one takes the actual numbers represented by these percentages, we also realise that the number of high-caste people worshipping Jesus is actually about three times the number of Scheduled Caste people. Furthermore, if we compare this number with that of the total Christian population worshipping Christ in the City, we find that there are approximately as many high-caste people worshipping Christ as there are Christians doing so. (Please recall that high-caste Hindus are 48% of the City population, while Christians are only 10%). Therefore, the "churchless Christianity" among high-caste Hindus alone is as great in number as the "churched Christianity" in the City.

The correct description of the religious reality, at least in Madras City, is not that Christianity is a Harijan religion but a Harijan Church. The high-caste and other-caste worshippers of Christ are doing so primarily privately and anonymously. If we put all nonbaptised worshippers of Christ together, we find that the number of people practicing "churchless Christianity" at home privately in the City is double that of the church membership.

Even if we take the "hard-core" figures of those who worship only Jesus, in terms of numbers the Hindu Harijan worshippers are only one-half of the total. The two percent worshippers of Jesus alone from the high-caste community would come to about thirty thousand; the 4.9% from the middle-caste community would come to about seventy thousand; and the fourteen percent from the Scheduled Caste community would come to fifty-six thousand. There are as many Protestants wholly devoted to the worship of Christ as there are people of all castes outside the church. The "churchless Christianity" is a diverse group but certainly united in firm devotion to Christ under most difficult circumstances.

Therefore, it is important for our evangelistic and nurture planning to discover how different caste groups would like us to serve them. Because of the importance of these tables, I have included all of them in Table Four of Appendix III. I would invite the reader to go through them in some detail. Here I will mention only a few points.

The cross-table statistics show that there is considerably more interest among Scheduled Caste respondents to learn about Jesus in all the methods suggested. However, even among them, there is a sizeable group of 43% who are not interested even in discussing with an evangelist. More than one-third are willing to come to church to learn more.

The percentage of high-caste and other-caste Hindus interested in learning at church is less; however, the numbers are more than five times that of the Scheduled Caste Hindus. They generally prefer more private methods of learning about Jesus, including a clear preference for discussing with an evangelist. Once again, there is a solid sixty percent of this population who indicate no interest to learn more about Jesus in any of the suggested ways.

This should not discourage us, though, for we would have our work cut out just starting to reach the third of the population (more than one million people) who are asking for our ministry in various ways just in Madras City.

Cross-Tables Giving Responses of Muslims

In the cross-tables on the basis of religion, the information in relation to Muslims is of prime interest to us. The analysis we already did in relation to castes covers the Hindu population. Therefore, in Table Five is provided an extract of the statistics covering Muslims in the four areas where cross-tables were computerised.

At first glance the results among Muslims seem quite disappointing. However, if we look more closely, I think we will find points of meaningful contact. Our primary problem seems to be lack of effort rather than lack of results. Once again, the sociological differences between the Christian community and the Muslim community are the major barrier.

It is instructive to follow our previous pattern and identify which evangelistic media have had some general effect and which considerable effect. The figures combining "much" and "little" learning are as follows:

1.	Radio	45%
2.	Movies	39%
3.	Individual Christian	39%
4.	Christian family	34%
5.	Television	36%
6	Street preaching	31%
7.	Christian wedding	15%
8.	Tracts	12%
9.	Christian School	20%

The figures on much" learning are as follows:

1.	Christian family	27%
2.	Individual Christian	25%
3.	Movies	21%
4.	Radio	20%
5.	Christian wedding	15%
6.	Television	12%
7.	Christian School	12%

These statistics show us once again the importance of witnessing through practical living, as the contacts with individual Christians and Christian families are the most important. The general statistics for all Hindus and Muslims on "much" learning from individuals and families are 29% and 26% Even though the Muslim and Christian communities generally do not have close intermingling, such as family connections through marriage, they do respond to the witness of Christian living just like anybody else.

Furthermore, we note that Muslims are as in touch with the mass media as anybody else. In particular, radio programmes have had a significant impact. Perhaps Muslim women, who may not go out to see a movie, will listen to the radio while at home. In general, the Muslims show greater influence than the general population through the mass media. They do not have contact with the Christian religion through any other means, so what they learn through the mass media is heard eagerly.

The statistics, therefore, also give an impression of deeper learning than ordinary. The general population figures tend to have a large gap between the combined "much" and "little" as contrasted with the "much" alone. The gap is anywhere from twenty to forty percent. Thus, there was much superficial learning in the general population. However, in the statistics on learning about Christ among Muslims the gap between the figures on the two lists is much less. The gap runs only from ten to twenty percent. Thus, when the Muslim has an opportunity to learn about Christ, he learns well.

This impression about the impact of Christian witness on the Muslim population of Madras City is confirmed by the next set of cross-table statistics. About one-fourth of the Muslim respondents did not know what to respond to the statements about Jesus' life and power. When they did respond, generally more than half accepted the statement as true.

In the crucial matter of Jesus' resurrection, for example, the Koranic teaching is contrary to the Biblical teaching, for the Koran says that Jesus did not die on the cross. Nonetheless, more Muslims accept the Christian teaching that Jesus rose than accept the Koranic teaching. This is also the statement on which the Muslim respondents showed the most uncertainty. Those who rejected the Christian teaching were only one-third.

However, the strong hold of the Muslim community over its members is revealed in the third set of cross-table statistics. Only five percent worship Jesus at home privately, and there are none who testify that they worship Jesus alone (although the researchers reported one fervent believer in Christ among the Muslims in the pre-test survey, a Muslim girl attending a Christian high school). Knowing the tight control the Muslim community maintains, even this five to eight percent worshippers of Jesus reveals response to the Gospel.

Finally, the statistics on how Muslims desire to learn return us once again to the difficulties before us. Except the opportunity of discussing personally with an evangelist, none of the suggested methods has significant attraction. Surprisingly, even the use of radio, which stood high as a previously useful method, is not welcomed here. Nonetheless, we note a solid ten percent of the Muslim population which is open to all these methods, and we have noted that they use methods well even if they do not ask for them. We do not find the "churchless Christianity" among the Muslims that we find among the Hindus, but the possibilities for the future are not altogether discouraging.

Cross-Tables according to Education

Another important cross-table of information is that dealing with differences due to education levels in the Hindu and Muslim population's response to Jesus. The cross-tables on learning in a Christian school, through Bible reading, and at Church worship are in Table Six of the Appendix. As we did with the differences of age groups, it will be helpful to look at some of the various opportunities to learn about Christ in terms of education levels:

More than half of those who have studied to post-graduate level and almost forty percent of those at SSLC-Graduate levels express that they have learned about Jesus while studying in a Christian school in Madras City. Thus, it appears that our schools have a significant contact with the educated populace of the City.

The greatest impact of radio programmes has been among those of 1-8 years of education. Among those of higher education levels, the impact is more superficial. Thus radio seems to be a medium which meets the needs primarily of those who cannot read so easily.

Movies, however, seem to have a similar impact on all education levels. Only those with no education express little learning about Jesus from movies. (This statistic makes one wonder if the English-language epics, rather than the recent Tamil and Telugu films, have been the most influential.) Otherwise, the medium has reached roughly two-thirds of the Hindu and Muslim populace with some favourable impression about Jesus.

As one might expect, the use of the Bible, tracts, and other Christian literature increases with the level of education. The literary media are geared towards those of higher education.

The large public meetings have attracted no education group in particular.

It is striking to note that street preaching has attracted favourable reception from two-thirds of 9-11 Standard respondents and of post-graduate education, while the uneducated respondents express the least experience of it (56%).

Influence through the individual Christian or a Christian family rises with education level. It goes from 19.3% among the uneducated to 66.7% among the post-graduates in regard to families and from 24.5% to 76% in regard to Christian individuals. Perhaps the educated Christian individuals and their families in the city communicate Christ better, or perhaps the more educated pay more attention to the lifestyles of people around them. At any rate, it is a challenge we must place before our educated Christians.

Learning about Jesus through children in a Christian school is another item which shows a steady difference with education level. Only 7% of the uneducated have learned through their school-going children, while the figure climbs steadily until it reaches 38% among the post-graduates. It seems, then, that the more educated families send their children to our schools. This fact, combined with their personal experience in Christian schools, confronts our schools with a major role in reaching the more educated Hindus and Muslims in the city.

With more education it appears from the statistics on weddings, funerals and church services that people learn more. Perhaps the more educated have gained a level of perceptiveness and curiosity which enables them to learn simply by observing carefully what is said and done. It is certainly encouraging that they are favourably impressed with what they have seen in our various church worship services. Our worship itself is a clear and powerful witness to what we stand for, so we should invite any and all, especially the more educated, to join and learn.

We now move on to the cross-tables on beliefs about Jesus among the different education levels:

In the statistics on beliefs about Jesus the first fact we note is that one-third to a half of the uneducated and around one-fourth of those educated from 1-8 years often express that they simply do not know. We have not developed proper media in the city to bring this information to them.

Major disagreement (around 25%) comes from the graduates in regard to beliefs about Jesus. Perhaps they have learned to be skeptical in their education. The post-graduates, on the other hand, seem to have moved beyond skepticism to a renewed acceptance of these religious truths.

In the cross-tables on worship of Jesus according to education levels, we find that those of 9-11 years education worship Jesus significantly more than others. More than half go to church to worship, and more than a third carry on such worship at home privately. The other education groups stay quite close to the average response throughout. The consistently least response whether at home or at church, is among the non-educated.

One of the standard criticisms of Christianity is that it does not meet the needs of the less educated. Our doctrines and demands are so many that it requires a good deal of background and education to make sense of it all. The less response among the non-educated and the minimum educated should make us rethink our approach to these levels of the society. Do we present the simple Gospel of God's redeeming love in Christ, or do we present a complex system of rules and doctrines quite foreign to these people's way of life? We may have here another gap created by the strong Christian ethos which the church has evolved over the years.

Finally, in regard to these cross-tables it is not worthy that none of those who worship Jesus exclusively are to be found among the graduates or post-graduates. It would seem that some deep discussion is needed at these levels of education, and, as we shall see in the next cross-tables, these well-educated people in the city are ready for such intense dialogue.

In the education cross-tables on how Hindus and Muslims of Madras City would like to learn more about Jesus, we find the same pattern continued. In Table seven of Appendix III the cross-tables for Bible reading, church worship, and discussion with an evangelist are provided. The most interest to learn more, across the spectrum, is shown by those of high school-level education. The least interest in any way of learning is shown by the non-educated, except in regard to discussion with an evangelist where 35% show interest.

It is instructive to compare at this point with the responses to the cross-tables on how people of different education levels learned about Christ previously. Do they want to learn in new ways, or do they want more opportunity like they had previously? For example, we noted previously that well-educated Hindus and Muslims learned much from observing church services. However, when we compare their interest to learn more in this way, it is less than half the percentage on the previous cross-table. They seem to feel that they have learned what they can in this manner, so they want some new experiences.

What do they prefer then? They show an increase of "much interest" in Bible reading and discussion with an evangelist, as well as the new suggestion of an open discussion group. Their interest in radio and literature has not increased. Thus, we find that the reading of the Bible among well-educated Hindus and Muslims in the City has stimulated an interest to read and discuss further.

We had also noted previously that those of less education had found Christian radio programmes useful. However, when we compared with the present cross-tables on ways to learn in the future we find that one-third less of those educated 1-8 years are interested in this medium. They apparently feel that they are not gaining anything new from these programmes. A comparison of the figures on learning through church worship reveals the same lack of increased interest. The literary media also do not meet this situation, neither do big meetings or open discussion groups attract them. Their one real interest also (44%) is in discussing with an evangelist.

What about those of high school-level education? These are the ones we found responding the best in the previous cross-tables. Their interest in learning through church worship also has waned though it still is more than other groups (around 30% show interest). Along with others of good education, these Hindus and Muslims are quite interested in discussing with an evangelist (around one-fourth show "much interest"). However, their real thirst is for Christian literature and Bible reading. Only 9% (of the 9-11 educated) and 5% (of the SSLC/PUC educated) said they had learned "much" through Bible reading, but 33% and 21% say they are "much interested" to learn more in this way. Bible distribution among the educated is a clear need.

Cross-Tables according to Income Group

Our final set of cross-tables is that relating to income groupings in the city. As usual, we will begin with the tables relating income groups to opportunities of learning about Jesus:

In the cross-table on learning about Jesus in a Christian school it is immediately apparent that this opportunity has primarily been experienced by the upper-income group. No doubt, this statistic reflects the prevalence of "elite" convent schools in the city. This figure of "much" learning (25%) is the highest response to any of the organised church activities among the high-income group, and even learning through their children at our schools comes to a total of 26%. It is clear that these city schools must assume most of the burden for reaching this income group.

In the city context at least the poor expressed little learning about Jesus from seeing Christian social work, less even than the upper income group expressed. Only 3% say they learned "much" and 14% "a little". The poor have not seen the love of Christ in their life struggles through us.

The radio ministry reaches all income groups rather equally (around 52%), but mostly in a superficial way.

The television reaches the upper-income group much more than the other levels, no doubt because they can afford a television in the home. It indeed has significant impact on this group, for "much" learning comes to almost twenty percent. This is the level of "much" learning achieved by the cinema among all groups.

The literary media of Bible, tracts and other literature have had superficial impact on all income groups. Obviously, income is not the determining factor in regard to the effectiveness of this medium.

The lower-income group indicates learning from street preaching at a level higher than the other groups and at a level higher than any other organised church activity listed. Therefore in street preaching we have one method which has been found helpful to this category of people. Probably the response comes from the more educated poor, since the uneducated indicated little response, according to the cross-table on education.

The influence of individual Christians and Christian families is strong among all income groups; however, the upper-income group reveals the strongest attraction through this means. In regard to learning about Jesus through a Christian family, for example, 35% of upper income respondents said that they learned "much" along with another 19% who said they learned a "little."

The learning from church services, including funerals and weddings is less among the low-income group. For example, the "much" learning through church worship comes to 10% among the low-income group, 18.7% among the middle-income group and 21% among the high-income group. The city church seems to be a more middle class church as far as its outreach into the community.

We now move on to the cross-tables on beliefs about Jesus. The lower-income group responses reveal once again that our evangelistic media have not been reaching them properly, for (except in regard to belief that Jesus has power to help his worshippers) more than one-third express that they simply do not know about Jesus' life. The most disagreement with statements about Jesus' life comes from the upper income group, especially in regard to Jesus' resurrection, Jesus being alive today, and Jesus raising the dead (about 22%). However, on these statements both the middle-income and the upper-income groups also state a good deal of uncertainty (about 25%). The one point where there is the least doubt and disagreement is on whether Jesus has power to help those who worship Him. Other points may be disputed from historical records, but this last point is known by conviction among two-thirds to three-fourths of all income groups.

In spite of all the poor contact with the ministries of the church, the lower-income group shows the most worship of Jesus according to the cross-tables on worship practices (cf. Table Eight). On the average one-fourth of these people worship Jesus at home and with their other gods, and 7.3% (compared to 3.8% and 1.3% with the middle and upper income groups) worship Jesus alone. Clearly there is a great interest and response to Jesus among the poorer people of the Madras City community. They have had the least opportunity to learn of Him; yet, they are the ones who have used their opportunities the best and responded with the most faith. We have a real obligation and opportunity here in our future evangelistic planning.

As one can see from the cross-table on worship at church, all income groups do come to church. Madras City has congregations of all kinds, as well as several fine cathedrals which are open all day, so the needs and backgrounds of all different groups can be met rather effectively. In this respect rural worshippers of Christ are put at a considerable disadvantage, for they cannot come to church anonymously nor do they have a selection of worship facilities to choose from. Usually it is the one Harijan or Backward Caste congregation which has a church building, and all will know if they attend. In the city different congregations cater to different classes of people. Should we have similar varieties of congregations to cater to the different castes in rural areas?

The responsiveness of the low-income group in Madras City is confirmed when we study the cross-tables showing interest in future learning opportunities. Across all seven tables the low-income group expresses more interest, surprisingly even in the literary media which had not been helpful to them previously. Their interest is especially greater than the other income groups when it comes to discussing with an evangelist (27% compared to 24% and 18% and listening to the radio (22% compared to 17.5% and 14.6%).

These members of the "culture of silence" even show more interest in the suggestion of an open discussion group than others. The poor of Madras City are out to improve their lot in life, and they are eager to see how faith in Christ and the ministry of the church can serve their purpose.

The upper-income group expresses minimal interest in learning about Jesus either at church or at a rally. Although their interest is consistently less than other income groups, around thirty percent of the wealthier people of the city are more or less interested in reading the Bible, discussing with an evangelist, listening to the radio and reading Christian literature. Only twenty-two percent state interest in an open discussion group. The middle-income group shows considerably more interest than the upper-income people.

"Churchless Christianity" in the City

In conclusion, then, what have we found to be the general place of Jesus in the faith and practice of Hindus, Muslims and others in Madras City? What is the nature of the "Churchless Christianity" then which we have found in the city? Is Madras a "Christian city"?

Our statistics have shown that there is a solid twenty-five percent of the Hindu and Muslim population in Madras City which has integrated Jesus deeply into their spiritual life. Half of the population have attempted spiritual relationships with Jesus and had satisfying and learning experiences through it. Three-fourths speak very highly of Jesus and could easily relate to Him as their personal Lord if so motivated. In addition to this population we have the ten percent who are "of the fold," formally Christian. It would be fair, then, to say that a good one-third of the Madras City population relate to Jesus fairly regularly and fairly deeply in their spiritual life.

Madras has been spoken of as the "most Christian" city in India, since it has the largest Christian population in the country at 300,000. However, this Christian population is hardly one-third of the "Churchless Christianity" surrounding it – and occasionally relating to it. Adding all these believers in Christ together, one might almost say that Madras is a "Christian city".

What is the general nature of this "Churchless Christianity" in the city? Most of the time, these believers in Christ relate to Him only in their private prayers and meditations. Occasionally they go to church anonymously, but for the most part they are on their own to nurture their faith. Thus, they easily fall away from a disciplined worship life and into a syncretistic way of thinking. When some need or anxiety arises in their life, they will again turn to Lord Jesus for help, strength and guidance.

These "weaker brothers" in the faith desire to draw upon the strength of the church in their spiritual pilgrimage of life. Especially they desire to meet with the pastors or Bible women. Those of more education welcome Bible study and other Christian literature. Many use the Christian radio programmes also. When they have nowhere else to turn, they even rely on the movies and TV programmes of Christian themes to inform and refresh their faith.

A large number of these people came to the faith through the influence of Christians living around them. Christian school teachers have been a significant influence on those who have gone to a Christian school. However, for the most part it has been their informal contacts with sincere Christian individuals and families which have attracted them to seek and find Christ for their own lives. The confirmation of Jesus' place in their lives, often came through experiences of physical healing, moral growth, and forgiveness of sin.

Although the strongest response to Jesus is found among the Harijan community in the city, in terms of numbers the believers of other Hindu castes are many more. Typically the follower of Jesus will be a poorer member of the society, young and high school educated. The response among women also is greater than among men. The most dedicated followers of our Lord, then, among the "other sheep" are to be found among the teenagers, the housewives, the high school educated and the poor, from all caste communities.

Our Lord truly has sheep in every human flock around the city of Madras. We will now seek to find them out and understand them in more detail through our next set of statistics.

CHAPTER FOUR

"Who Are These 'Churchless Christians'?"

Outline:

Cross-Table on Two Types of NBBCs

General Statistics on NBBCs
(Bio-Data and Sections of Questionnaire)

Cross-Tables Statistics on NBBCs
(Statistics according to Age, Sex, Caste, Education, Income Group & Native Place)

"Who Are These 'Churchless Christians'?"

By now it can come as no surprise that there are true believers in Jesus Christ among the Hindu and Muslim population of Madras City. In Section One, we personally met such non-baptised believers in Christ around rural Tamil Nadu. In the previous chapter we studied the statistics which revealed the pervasive worship of Jesus around the city. In this chapter we want to go through the specific statistics on those whom we might legitimately call non-baptised believers in Christ according to the survey results.

It will not be necessary to go through the statistics in the same detail as in chapter three. We now know the general background of response to Christ, out of which the non-baptised believer is one highlight. Nonetheless, there are some significant differences between the NBBCs and their Hindu and Muslim neighbours, and we should note them. We will also compare the faith and practice of these "other sheep" with the statistics on the Christian community, where helpful.

Cross-Table on Two Types of NBBCs

As we went through the general statistics in the previous chapter we observed in passing the two questions which were used as keys for determining a non-baptised believer in Christ among the general population. One response was no. 35e, stating one's conviction that Jesus was "the one and only true Incarnation of God". The other was assent to the statement no. 77 that "The only true way to worship God is to worship Jesus Christ". We also noted that the question about worship of Jesus alone could be used as a third criterion.

In the results of the questionnaire we learned that these three criteria closely identify the same phenomenon. Beforehand, we had considered the possibility that there would be significant differences on these three questions. Therefore, for example, we prepared cross-tables for each of the key questions, rather than one cross-table for those who responded to both questions correctly. As it has turned out, there is very little difference between the cross-tables for the NBBCs according to question no. 35e and according to question no. 77. Because the respondents to question no. 77 were slightly more than to 35e (52 and 47), I have chosen the former for our detailed analysis in the cross-tables here. Where there are significant differences between these two tables, I will mention it.

We will begin, therefore, with the table which interrelates the responses to the two key questions: 35e and 77. Since it is an important cross-table, it is provided as Appendix IV. From this table we see that 28 of the 47 Hindus and Muslims who responded to 35e also "wholeheartedly agree" that one should worship only Jesus (i.e. 59.6%). Another 13 of this 47 indicate simple agreement; thus, the total percentage of agreement on prayer among those who say Jesus is the only true incarnation comes to 87.2%.

There is strong conviction on both points among these respondents of the Hindu and Muslim population. This segment of agreement on both questions is 5.6% of the total, or in terms of numbers about 200,000 people in Madras City. These are the ones we have chosen to identify as non-baptised believers in Christ.

In the next concentric circle of agreement are those who responded to one of the two key questions but not to the other. Five of those who confessed Jesus as the true incarnation responded with disagreement that one should only pray to Him, and one had no comment. These six respondents evidently agreed with the theology of 35e but not with the implication drawn in 77. They have said that it is not improper to pray in other ways, even though Jesus is the only true incarnation. In this approach the NBBC respondents are not dissimilar to the Christian population, for 15.7% of the Christians also responded negatively or with no comment to question no. 77 (although 86% confess him as the only true incarnation.)

What, then, are the theological convictions of the other eleven respondents who agreed that only Jesus should be worshipped but who did not identify him as the only true incarnation? As one might guess from the prevalent "ista devata" principle, nine of these respondents identified Jesus as "a god like Murugan and Ganesh". One respondent saw Jesus as "a prophet" and one had left this question on the nature of Jesus unanswered. The latter is probably one who practices worship of Jesus alone, but who has not thought out the theological rationale for it.

Finally, it is instructive to locate where the strong opposition to the exclusive worship of Jesus lies. The opposition seems to lie among those who gave a more intellectual response on the nature of Jesus: 13% of those who saw him as a great reformer, 40.7% of those who saw him as the greatest religious leader, and 78.3% of those who saw him as a misled man. (We don't have the cross-tables on these questions according to education, so we are unable to confirm this interpretation.) At any rate, the fact that only 13.5% expressed strong disagreement with such a strongly exclusivistic statement, as pointed out earlier, indicates a spirit of acceptance for NBBC convictions in the general community.

General Statistics on Non-baptised Believers in Christ

Now let us move on to the general statistics about the non-baptised believers in Christ in Madras City (cf Appendix V.) As mentioned above, we will use the statistics on the fifty-two Hindu respondents who said that only Jesus should be worshipped. These respondents come to 7.2% (or approximately 250,000 people) in the city, but we will use the combined percentage of five percent in order to maintain a more conservative estimate of the figures involved.

The Bio-Data

We will first look at the general characteristics of this NBBC population. Their youth is striking. 38.4% are within the five-year span of 15-20 years. The next five-year span contains another 21%, and then it drops off. (The rise between 51-60 years is contrasted with the continued decrease at this age among the NBBCs on the "nature of Jesus" table, so these elderly NBBCs seem to practice worship of Jesus without having a solid theological foundation for their practice.) The contrast with the general Hindu/Muslim population (17.6%) is especially great during the teenage years, but the percentage from 20-25 years also is higher.

The two possible explanations for this statistical fact might be suggested. One explanation would be that there has been a significant rise in belief in Christ among Hindus in recent years. Such a development would be wonderful, especially in view of the post-Independence initiatives by government and private organisations undercutting, opposing, and restricting Christian evangelistic activities. One would hope that this explanation is the correct one.

However, the second explanation seems to be the more plausible one, especially in view of the witness given by our rural non-baptised believers in Chapter One. The response to Christ has probably been one feature of youth all through mission history in India, as young people re-consider their direction and values of life in the natural maturation process. However, once the conflicts of marriage and the responsibilities for children come into the person's life, spiritual convictions give way to social realities.

Several of the rural NBBCs specifically said that they "lost the chance of taking baptism" once they got married. They chose marriage over baptism, and by marriage they were cut off from the nurture structures of the church. They could not practice or hold the faith and often fell into the enervating inner contradiction of living "against conscience". From these statistics it would seem that at least half the earlier NBBCs eventually regress into the state of the Martandam Panikkar quoted above.

A good majority (60%) of the NBBCs are women, most of these being housewives (18 of 31). Sixty percent of the NBBCs are young people, as we saw above, and sixty percent are also under "Others" in regard to occupation in the tables. Thus, we may conclude that almost all of the NBBCs in this survey are in a dependent position socially and economically. The younger people may be students or unemployed. The housewives are not independently employed. Many non-baptised believers cannot afford the risk and conflict of taking baptism.

The contrast of the NBBC population with both the general population and the Christian population comes most prominently in the statistics on caste. Of course, we have seen all along that this sociological issue is the most dominant, so we should not be surprised to find differences here. I will place the statistics side by side here for easy reference:

	H.C.	S.C.	Others	Blank
Hindu/Muslim/Other:	382	77	266	1
	52.62	10.61	36.64	0.14
Christian	9	22	52	0
	10.84	26.51	62.65	0
NIBBCs:	17	14	21	0
	32.69	26.92	40.38	0

The statistics show clearly the awkward position the high-caste NBBCs are placed in. They are a small percentage (4.5%) within their own community. Their social partners are a small percentage within the church. Yet, they are one-third of the NBBC population. One-fourth of their fellow high-caste Hindus will worship Jesus, as we saw in the previous chapter, but only the NBBCs do so with theological conviction and disciplined persistence. They do not fit into the church sociologically, and they do not fit into their own community spiritually. Only one-third of the high-caste people who believe completely in Christ have taken baptism.

We note that the percentage of Scheduled Caste NBBCs is similar to that in the church. More than one-third of the people of Scheduled Caste in the city are believers in Christ, either baptised or unbaptised, and almost one-fourth of those of other castes. Conversion to Christianity through baptism is not a big sociological problem for these two groups. They have many friends in the faith within their own community.

It is the high-caste people that are only 6%, inclusive of baptised and non-baptised, within their home community. It is no wonder that they compromise their faith more and resist conversion more. We should also remind ourselves that this situation persists even in a cosmopolitan setting like Madras City. The situation in the tight social network of the villages where eighty percent of the Indian population lives is even more formidable for them.

As we noted earlier, there were no Muslim NBBCs in our sample population. There is one of "other religion," perhaps Parsi or Jam.

A further distinctive characteristic of the NBBC population is that 88.5% of them have had a high school education. The coinparable figure for the whole city population is 77%.

In the figures on the educational background of the NBBCs we note that they are similar to the city norm in all areas except under the categories 1-8 standards and post-high school education. The percentage of NBBCs is considerably above the 1-8 standards figure for the general population, and considerably below the percentage of graduates and post-graduates. Thus, we can see that the NBBCs are generally of lower education, though of some education. Most will be fairly literate.

In terms of income grouping, once again, the NBBCs are more in the low-income group (50% to 31%) and fewer in the high-income group (6% to 20%) among their fellow Hindus and Muslims. The "middle income" percentage is about the same. Therefore, we get an impression once again of dependence and lack of freedom, a fact we had also noted among the rural non-baptised believers.

As mentioned in the explanation of the questionnaire, we had postulated that there might be a corrolary between geographical background and openness to Christian faith. However, only a slight increase in Kerala and southern Tamil Nadu origins is to be noted among the NBBCs. Therefore, contact with the Christian faith outside of Madras City is not a significant factor.

The total picture we can draw from the bio-data of the non-baptised believers is similar to that found among rural NBBCs and worshippers of Jesus among the general population. Most are women, generally housewives. Most are fairly well educated but of low-income financial standing. Most are young, probably unemployed or studying. Very few might be Muslim. The distribution among high-caste, Scheduled Caste, and other-caste backgrounds is about equal. They are generally in a situation of dependence upon others, either financially or socially – or, as in the case of housewives, both.

Learning Experiences

We now move on to an analysis of how these non-baptised believers in Christ have learned about Him. I will point out only those areas where the NB.BCs are significantly different from the general Hindu and Muslim population. We will also compare with the Christian population where relevant.

We will begin this comparison by listing the most influential experiences for the NBBCs, compared to the general Hindu/Muslim population and the Christian population. I will restrict these figures to the "much" responses, as these influences will be the most important in achieving the level of commitment which the NBBCs have made:

General Hindu/Muslims

1.	Individual Christian	29%
2.	Christian family	26%
3.	Movies	19%
4.	Radio programmes	18%
5.	Church worship	16%
6.	Christian school	15%

NBBCs

1.	Individual Christian	40%
2.	Christian family	36.5%
3.	Church worship	36.5%
4.	Radio programmes	35%
5.	Movies	33%
6.	Christian school	25%

Christian

1.	Church worship	85.5%
2.	Christian family	77%
3.	Sunday School	73.5%
4.	Individual Christian	71%
5.	Bible Reading	72%
6.	Individual Christian	71%
7.	Radio programmes	69%

It is evident that the non-baptised believers in Christ provide an amalgamation of Hindu and Christian experiences of Christ. They share with their Hindu and Muslim brothers a prime influence by individual Christians and families. (In the case of the Christian family influence one would assume that it is one's own family.) The top six influences are the same, but church worship moves up considerably among the NBBCs. In this influence they share experience with the Christian community, where church worship is well above the rest. Reading of the Bible and going to Sunday School are of great importance among Christians, but does not come on either of the other lists. Furthermore, among all those of Hindu or

Muslim background, movies have been a significant learning experience, while Christians do not mention movies significantly. Radio and Christian school have had significant influence on all three groups.

Therefore, we find that the non-baptised believers share a reliance on the informal evangelistic media with the general Hindu and Muslim population. No doubt, their use of church worship also is at more of a distance, except among those of the same caste group as the local congregation. They pick up what they can on their own initiative.

Now let us look at the various media, as previously, to see how the non-baptised believers' have learned differently from others in more detail. We begin with the Sunday School. Previously we had not much to say about learning in a Sunday School, for so few Hindus and Muslims had such an opportunity 3%. Among the NBBCs this opportunity rises sharply to 11.5%. In fact, six of the twenty-one Hindu and Muslim respondents who had been to Sunday School and learned "much" are now non-baptised believers in Christ. Of the seven who had the opportunity of attending Sunday School, six learned "much" there. We have in our Sunday Schools a potentially powerful medium of sharing Christ with others, as it has been highly powerful in the Christian community (73.5%).

The Christian school continues to show its significant impact. Thirteen out of the twenty-one NBBC respondents testify that they learned "much". Four out of seven whose children attend a Christian school also have learned "much".

Christian hospitals and social work in Madras City continue to show little learning about Christ, even among the NBBCs.

More than one-third of the non-baptised believers say that they have learned something about Jesus by visiting Velankanni. However, another 13.5% say they went but learned nothing. Velankanni apparently has its role, but it could be more.

Radio, however, has played a significant role among the non-baptised believers. Almost half of those who have used the medium have learned "much" through it. The influence of TV is less, and the total influence of movies is more. Only seven out of fifty-two NBBC respondents say that they have not had the opportunity to learn through movies about Jesus. The mass media provide the forum which they prefer and which they eagerly use. Christians also use these media even more than the NBBCs (except the movies which are stereotyped as sinful among some Protestant groups). Nonetheless, almost two-thirds of the Christian respondents said they learned about Jesus through the cinema.

However, in reading the Bible the non-baptised believers are much less diligent than the Christians. Their reading is more superficial, as with the general Hindu/Muslim population. The Bible does not seem to have the devotional and edifying role among the NBBCs as it has among the Christians. The same seems to be the case with the other literary media like tracts and magazines.

Mass public meetings have played a big role in the spiritual life of the Christian community. Almost eighty percent of the Christians speak of what they learned; only twenty percent have not gone. The NBBCs also have used this medium almost three times more than the general population. However, the figure for the NBBCs is still only one third. These meetings evidently serve a need for some of them, as we saw among the rural non-baptised believers, but the real community served is the Christian community. At any rate, the meetings are not really evangelistic opportunities as much as nurture opportunities, for the vast majority of those in attendance are people of faith already.

Street preaching has been much more effective among the NBBCs — as among the general population — than the big meetings. More than two-thirds testify to the effect this medium has had upon them. This medium comes to them as one of the mass media; they do not have to go to it and face the public notice of attending.

More than two-thirds also speak of the influence of Christian individuals and families upon them, and the effect is deeper than the street preaching or any of the mass media. There is nothing to compare with the living proclamation of the Gospel, even for those born into the Christian community (cf. the list above.)

Bible & Picture Distribution, Learning from and Belief in Jesus

As one would expect, the non-baptised believers in Christ strongly support the distribution of the Bible and of pictures of Jesus by 89% and 83%. They want others to come to Christ as they have. They want Christ to be a part of their community so that they can worship and respond to Him in freedom and fellowship. Significantly, in regard to the Hindu mode of religious commitment, the picture of Jesus, the NBBCs express more agreement and less opposition than the Christians.

In regard to learning from Jesus also the non-baptised believers reveal an absorption of Christian teaching into their Hindu framework. The first thing which is striking in the statistics is that so many (almost one-third) say that they have learned nothing from Jesus. Their relation to Jesus obviously is not at an intellectual or even moral level. He is the object of their devotion their "ishta deva" who represents the power and love of God to them. Their contact with Jesus has not yet brought them into a transformation of mind and heart. The same figure is only 23.4% among the NBBCs identified through question no. 35e. Question no. 77 brings out those who emphasise the worship of Jesus, as we noted earlier.

In this section we are once again impressed by the moral dimensions of the non-baptised believers response to Jesus. On all the moral issues, among those who say they have learned from Jesus, only around fifteen percent say they have not learned to love others, or to help the needy or to serve society. The highest responses to "much" also (around 60% among those who have learned anything at all) are in these ethical spheres. At this level they are about 25% above the general Hindu/Muslim response and about 15% less than the Christian response. Considering the less access the NBBCs have had to Christian nurture, this level of ethical response is indeed remarkable. It betokens a searching and fertile heart.

The pattern of responding at levels between the general response and the Christian response continues in the other categories as well. Almost double the percentage of Christians testify to having learned "much" from Jesus in spiritual ways (such as peace and joy, forgiveness, heaven), but the NBBC response is almost five times that of the general population. It is also striking, to note that the percentage of Christians who say they have not learned from Jesus in these various areas is almost the same as the NBBCs in each case. Once again, we note that the NBBCs response to Jesus is considerably above that of the Hindu and Muslim population and quite close to the Christian response — in spite of all the disadvantages the NBBCs suffer.

When it comes to belief in Christ, the similarity to the Christian community is particularly evident. If we eliminate from the NBBC percentages those few who state they do not know (apparently because they have had so little nurture experience), we find that the percentage of belief in the facts of Jesus' life and ministry is almost exactly that of the Christians. All the percentages are well over ninety percent, and the highest have to do with Jesus' power today: His healing, His being alive, His ability to help His worshippers. This level of knowledge and belief is all the more remarkable when one recalls the scant opportunities for learning which the NBBCs have had. The doctrinal orthodoxy of the two lakhs "Churchless Christians" in Madras City certainly is impressive.

Practices of Prayer and Worship

In the figures about prayer to Jesus, we have some disparity which calls for some adjustment in the first percentages on whether one has prayed to Jesus or not. On this question seventeen respondents have indicated that they never prayed to Jesus. However, as one looks down the line of respondents to other questions, one finds that only fifteen and thirteen respondents leave the question blank. My interpretation on this disparity is that a few respondents took the initial question in terms of regular prayer or worship and responded negatively, but then corrected themselves in subsequent questions. I think we are justified to take the lower figure of thirteen as the ones who actually never prayed to Jesus. (It is eleven in the figures according to the NBBCs based on question no: 35e.)

Be this as it may it is amazing that at least one-fourth of the NBBC respondents (that, too, based on question no. 77) state that they have never prayed to Jesus. They must be individuals who have an intellectual knowledge and belief in Jesus, but no real prayer experience or personal relationship. Might we call them "nominal NBBCs"? The human tendency to place God in a religious corner of our life and not let Him pervade every nook and corner of our existence is found among these NBBCs as well.

As we noted previously among the general Hindu and Muslim population a strong percentage (79%) of those who prayed to Jesus witness that they experienced help. The witness among the non-baptised believers rises to eighty-nine percent. No doubt, it is this experience in prayer which has prompted them to recognise Jesus as their Lord and Master, to whom they continue to turn when in need. Probably those who did not experience the help they sought are those two respondents who say they no longer pray to Him.

(For some more information please refer to the Foot Notes on page 144.)

In the previous chapter we discussed the lack of emphasis on freedom from bad habits and attainment of peace of mind in these experiences of prayer. Among the NBBCs this moral and spiritual growth is there to the level of forty percent, but it is still only half that stated by the Christian population. The NBBCs need the nurture of the church. The number who have reached beyond their personal needs to pray for others is encouraging, especially that forty-four percent testify that they do this "much".

As we had noted in the prayer life among the NBBCs, we note in their practices of worship that one-third testify to no disciplined spiritual practice, either at home or at church. However, we also note that more than half say they worship only Jesus, which is admirable when one considers the family and social pressures under which so many suffer.

It is interesting to compare that ten respondents among the NBBCs state that they worship Jesus along with their family members while twenty state the same in the sample of the general Hindu/Muslim population. On the one band, it is encouraging that nineteen percent of the NBBCs can have fellowship in their worship of Jesus, even while remaining in their own society. On the other hand, we note that there are an equal number who worship Christ as a family but who did not respond to our key questions. Such worshippers of Jesus would not speak of Him as exclusively as we did in our key questions. It may be that Jesus is worshipped in their families along with the other family gods, for the statistics on these two statements are the same. Nonetheless, the family has accepted the NBBC and his Jesus into their family worship circle.

Our churches remain the most popular way for people to worship Jesus. More than two-thirds of these NBBCs (about 200,000 people in the city) frequent our churches. They want a worshipful atmosphere devoted to Christ, which they cannot achieve in freedom and concentration in their home setting. We have around us a "Churchless Christianity" in an organisational sense, but not in the sense of desiring no place to worship Jesus. As the Mylapore pastor witnessed concerning his "watchnight" service, thousands of non-baptised believers and other worshippers of Christ eagerly desire that there be "Jesus temples" in the city available and convenient for their use. Are our churches organised and available as a "house of prayer for all people?"

The desire for the "living water" which will really quench their thirst is evident in the largest percentage who prefer to meet an evangelist personally to discuss. 61.5% are much interested. Another 56% express a willingness to try to open discussion groups (although here we also have the largest hesitation).

Those who are comfortable with reading the Bible express much interest in doing so. 56% express "much" interest, and only 4% "little" interest. In the first section on previous learning opportunities approximately the same percentage expressed some experience but not much learning (17.3%). However, they seem to have experienced enough to know that there is much more to learn from the Bible, and they are eager to learn. No doubt, they only need some guidance and encouragement.

Radio has been a tried and tested medium of learning about Christ. The non-baptised believers continue to look for help from the church in this way. What they need is real edification, not more evangelisation.

Interest in mass meetings has more than doubled over what the NBBCs have experienced so far. Perhaps what is needed is an announcement of nurture meetings which will meet their need more specifically.

Finally, we come to the section of the questionnaire which enables us to understand how non-baptised believers reflect on their own situation. The vast majority (81%) feel quite confident that they are correct in remaining unbaptised, though worshipping only Jesus. Only six percent feel it is wrong, while the other 13.5% have not thought it through to a conclusion. Obviously, most plan to remain part of the "Churchless Christianity" for the foreseeable future.

Also, they are quite aware of the fellowship of faith which they have already in their situation. Half speak of the Christian relatives which they have, and forty-four percent speak of NBBCs among their own relations. They know they are part of a greater fellowship in Christ, even though there are real conflicts and pressures which they must face. They need not seek spiritual fellowship in Christ only in the church, for most of them can find it also within their own family circles.

Therefore, as we look over the total situation of the non-baptised believers in Madras City we have reason to feel encouraged and confident about them. Although they desire to have much more personal and deeper opportunities to learn about Christ, they evidently have also made the best use of the more impersonal, mass media opportunities which are already available to them. Their faith in Christ is strong and orthodox, but a solid one-fourth of them are not deep enough in the faith so that they can mature in moral. spiritual, and devotional practice. However, most have had a very personal experience of the reality of Christ's power and love, and a faithful relationship has grown out of this beginning.

These believers evidently desire further nurture in this faith, and they look to the church for help. At the same time, however, they feel they are correct in remaining within their community as non-baptised believers in Christ. Even within their community there are Christian relations and other non-baptised believers to support and guide them in the faith.

Cross-Table Statistics on Non-baptised Believers in Christ

We will now look at the cross-tables on the non-baptised believers in Christ as identified through question no. 77. A similar set of cross-tables for question 35e are also available at Gurukul, but as explained earlier, the differences between the two tables is not significant so only one is used for our purposes. Since the information is quite similar to that collected through the general cross-tables, I have not included any of these cross-tables in the appendices.

Cross-Tables according to Age

As usual, we will first take up the age-wise cross-tables in regard to opportunities for learning about Jesus. We will be especially interested in the learning experiences of the young people, since they are the predominant group among the non-baptised believers in Christ and since the numbers in some of the other categories are so few as to make conclusions quite tentative.

The first opportunity which comes out strongly among the young is the Christian school. Half of the NBBCs between 15-20 years of age indicate that they have learned about Christ in a Christian school. Some of them probably are still studying in Christian high school or college in the city, and they represent several thousand young people in our institutions.

The next significant influence we find among the young non-baptised believers—as well as all the other age groups—is the radio. Three-fourths of those between 5-25 years of age indicate learning through Christian radio programmes. That number represents almost half of the NBBCs, so radio programmes for NBBCs should have a youth orientation.

The other mass media of television and movies show predominantly a superficial impact on the young NBBCs. While three-fourths of the 5-20 age group, for example, indicate learning through these media, only one-fourth indicate "much" learning. It takes more than a mass media impact to create the faith of a nonbaptised believer. The impact of the literary mass media (Bible, tracts, literature and street preaching) show the same pattern.

Where, then, has the deeper influence come? The personal contacts with Christian families and individuals show "much" learning at a higher level, especially among the 21-25 and 26-30 age groups. The only item on which the youngest group of NBBCs show "much" learning higher than "little" learning is worship at church. Even among teenagers, then, our worship and our churches have played major role in bringing them to the faith. Otherwise, it seems that the process has been an accumulation of smaller influences.

In regard to worship practices, we find in the cross-tables some significantly different patterns among the younger and older non-baptised believers in Christ. Firstly, we note that the younger NBBCs affirm worship of Christ more, whether at home or in church. The teenage NBBCs show the most exclusive worship of Christ (65%) whereas the 51-60 age group shows the least (28.5%). This elderly group also comes to church the least (28.5%).

They, together with the others over thirty years of age, have the least fellowship in Christ also at home, for thirteen of the fourteen older NBBC respondents say they do not worship Jesus with their family members. One-third of this older grouping also worship Jesus along with their other gods. The younger people can apparently get out to learn and worship independently. These older non-baptised believers need a more home-based ministry, especially when a sizeable number are housewives.

In the cross-tables on preferred learning opportunities, we find no significant differences between the different age groups. Therefore the general comments made above on the one-way tables will hold good for all age groups.

A new set of cross-tables which we computerised specifically for the non-baptised believers in Christ is that dealing with their home situation, the final section of the questionnaire. In the first cross-table on whether one is convinced that it is proper to worship only Jesus and still not convert into a Christian, we find little difference between the age groups. On question no. 77 (the one from which this set of NBBCs is drawn) it is the teenagers who express the highest "wholeheartedly agree" to the statement. Those with Christian relatives are approximately the same percentage in all groups. No definite pattern is evident among the age groupings in regard to the final question of the questionnaire as to their awareness of other NBBCs among their relations; therefore, I have provided this table in Appendix V for separate study.

A summary look at the age-wise statistics confirms that the younger group is the more receptive one. Previously we noted the influence of the Sunday School and the Christian school. Here we noted in addition that especially the teenaged NBBCs were thirsty to learn more and dedicated to apply more what they learned in worship. Clearly, the older NBBCs faced many more social and personal difficulties in carrying out their spiritual pilgrimage, but the youth are still eager to test out the path on which Jesus might lead for their life. However, when it comes to desire to learn more, all ages showed interest.

Cross-Tables according to Sex

The next set of cross-tables we will study is for the non-baptised believers in Christ according to sex. Throughout the statistics we find that women speak of learning about twice what men report. Although women's access to outside learning will be less, as we noted in the previous chapter, they obviously use these opportunities more intensely.

The statistics on learning through a Christian school experience show that the impact on girls in Madras City has been much more than on boys. Twelve female respondents say that they learned "much" about Christ in a Christian school, while only one male respondent says so. 55% of the women have learned through a Christian school, and only 19% of the men. Clearly, our girls schools are doing a good job of sharing Christ. It may also be that girls take the matter more seriously than boys at that stage of life.

We find a similar increase of impact on women NBBCs from visiting Velankanni. Eight women indicate "much" learning at Velankanni, and only one man. Almost half of the women but only nineteen percent of the men have learned about Christ at Velankanni. Velankanni is a healing centre devoted to Mary; thus, healing in such a context may be more meaningful to women.

Throughout the cross-tables on mass media, whether literary or non-literary, women indicate twice as much learning as men. Only when we come to the more "outdoor" mass media like big meetings and street preaching do we find the response of men and women similar.

Learning through contact with Christian families and individuals, as well as through church services, is once again double for women. Women use well the variety of learning opportunities available to them.

We are not surprised, therefore, to find in the cross-tables on worship practices that women also are more faithful in worship of Jesus. In all the tables half of the NBBC men do not worship Jesus, whether at home or at church or with other gods. On the other hand, three-fourths of the women indicate that they worship both alone and with family members (their children?) as well as at church. The two points where both men and women non-baptised believers come fairly close together are in giving Jesus the primacy in worship. With both men and women eighty percent avoid worshipping Jesus together with other gods, and with both more than half testify that they worship only Jesus.

As with the age-wise cross-tables on preferred opportunities for learning more about Jesus, we find no differences among men and women. Therefore, the comments made in reflection upon the one-way tables will apply equally for men and women.

In the cross-tables on their family situation, we observe firstly that both men and women agree overwhelmingly that it is legitimate to remain unbaptised while worshipping Jesus alone They also equally divide between "wholeheartedly agree" and simply "agree" on the statement that one must worship only Jesus, and in both cases about forty percent have non-baptised believers in Christ among their relatives.

However, there is a striking difference on the question of whether one has Christian relatives. Almost two-thirds of the women do, while this is true of only 28.6% of the men. Twenty-three women had said earlier that they learned about Jesus from a Christian family, and here twenty women say they have Christian relatives. Perhaps the close family ties of women prompt them to learn more readily from Christian relatives than men.

In summary, then, we had seen under the NBBC bio-data that women are 50% more in number than men in Madras City. Now we have noticed that the women also indicate a far greater interest to learn about Jesus and to worship Him regularly. The large number of NBBC women who say they have Christian relatives makes one wonder if they have been reached in this way. At any rate, the women have made it clear that they are as ready as men to learn about Jesus in whatever way the church may try to nurture their faith.

Cross-Tables according to Occupation

The cross-tables according to occupation are not very helpful to us. We had seen in the general statistics that no correlation could be found. Now we find in the NBBC statistics that the only category which has a significant number of respondents (besides "Others" at thirty–one) is "housewife" at eighteen. The statistics under "housewife" are almost identical with those of women, and these we have studied in the section above.

Nonetheless, if we venture to operate on the guess made previously that many under "Others" are students and unemployed youth, we can attempt a few conclusions. The first thing we note is that this group is somewhat more attracted by the mass media of radio, TV, and cinema than the average. Three-fourths have learned about Jesus on the radio, almost half on TV, and almost all at the cinema. Their exposure to the literary media has been more superficial but, nonetheless, quite pervasive (Bible 55%, tracts 71%, literature 48%.) This is the group which has shown the most interest in the big meetings 39%), compared to only 21% among housewives. Otherwise, their statistics are not remarkable. (We may note here that the nil influence recorded under the "Other" group in regard to learning through marriage and the ninety-percent from this group which record no learning through school-going children would be further supporting indications that this "Other" category are young people).

Thus, we may venture a conclusion that the students and unemployed youth have the time and interest to go out investigating about Jesus. They use all the mass media, whether by the church or by the general society, to learn more.

The cross-tables on worship practices, preferred learning opportunities and family situation show no significant differences. Housewives practice the same as other women, and the "Others" category is identical with the general statistics; therefore, what has been said already in regard to these other statistics would apply for housewives and unemployed youth as well.

Cross-Tables according to Caste

We now proceed on to the cross-tables describing the non-baptised believers, according to castes. It is instructive once again to compare the "much" learning experienced. This time we will compare each caste with the others) since the differences are considerable:

High Caste

1.	Radio programmes	47%
2.	Movies	47%
3.	Xn individual	47%
4.	Church worship	41%
5.	Xn weddings	38%
6.	Xn family	35%
7.	Xn school	35%

Scheduled Caste

1.	Christian family	50%
2.	Xn individual	43%
3.	Radio programmes	36%
4.	Street preaching	36%
5.	Church worship	36%
6.	Christian school	29%
7.	Big Meetings	29%

Other Castes

1.	Xn individual	33%
2.	Church worship	33%
3.	Xn family	29%
4.	Movies	29%
5.	Radio	24%
6.	Xn School	19%
7.	Street preaching	14%

Some of the characteristics we noted in the general caste-wise cross-tables are to be found again. The "Other Castes" (really "middle caste") group indicates considerably less learning than other groups. Their list is similar to the Scheduled Caste list except that the Scheduled Castes again have street preaching much higher and have included big meetings, while movies have had significant influence on the middle caste respondents but not on the Scheduled Caste respondents.

In regard to the strong influence of the Christian family among many Scheduled Caste non-baptised believers, one might wonder if some of these respondents are actually born of Christian parents. We have noticed in Chapter Two the temptation for Christian parents not to baptise their children. However, many of these children grow up in the Christian faith, nonetheless, and often keep a close relationship with the church because of sociological ties. Many also keep the Christian faith, though remaining unbaptised because of the desire for government privileges as a Hindu Scheduled Caste member.

Because of the sharp sociological separation from the church, we find the greatest contrast in relation to the high-caste NBBC list. First of all, we note that these respondents record significantly greater learning about Jesus than those of other caste groups. We also note once again the importance of the mass media for these people. They share the ability of others to be influenced by a Christian individual or family or by attending a Christian school, but otherwise they have had to rely on more distant contacts with the church as in observing marriage ceremonies and worship services. The high-caste NBBCs are more isolated from the structures of church nurture.

We will now proceed to point out any significant details in the caste-wise statistics on opportunities for learning about Jesus. The percentages on Sunday School influence are not high, but we have already noted the strong influence this medium has. We also noted previously that the strongest influence was on women. Here we note that most of those influenced were also high-caste. Later in life the high-caste person may not feel free to join in church activities, but in childhood it is possible and highly fruitful.

Among those non-baptised believers who attended a Christian school two–thirds learned "much" about Jesus, no matter which caste. The high-caste NBBCs learned willingly from Christian teachers of any caste.

Half of the NBBCs have been to Velankanni, and the high-caste respondents indicate the most positive learning (29.5% say "much").

The strongest mass medium over all (inclusive of literary and non-literary media) was the cinema among the non-baptised believers, especially among the high-caste (69.5%) and middle-caste (18%) respondents. Except for the outdoor mass media like street preaching and big meetings, the non-Scheduled Caste people indicate much more learning.

The three worship media (weddings, funerals, church) show much more learning by the high-caste NBBCs. Although the Scheduled Caste respondents indicate more learning at church than at weddings or funerals, it still is less than high-caste respondents. This is surprising since there should be little sociological barrier for Scheduled Caste NBBCs to get deeply involved in church life. Perhaps worship life is more important to those of high-caste background.

If worship life is more important to high-caste NBBCs, they must feel quite frustrated and confused in their spiritual life. For when we read the statistics caste-wise on worship practices, we find that the high-caste non-baptised believers are the least consistent in carrying out their espoused conviction that only Jesus should be worshipped. The Scheduled Caste NBBCs are much more disciplined and consistent in their worship practices (cf. Table Two in Appendix V). The only question on which the high-caste NBBCs show more consistency than the others is - surprisingly enough - in that only 12% worship Jesus with their other gods.

The NBBCs of all caste backgrounds show considerable interest in all the suggested means of learning more about Jesus. However there are some interesting differences between them, which can best be illustrated by listing the seven opportunities side-by-side in comparative ranking in regard to "much" interest:

High Caste

1.	Radio	59%
2.	Evangelist	59%
3.	Rallies	47%
4.	Church worship	47%
5.	Discussion	41%
6.	Literature	35%
7.	Bible reading	35%

Scheduled Caste

1.	Evangelist	79%
2.	Bible reading	71%
3.	Radio	64%
4.	Rallies	64%
5.	Literature	64%
6.	Church worship	42%
7.	Discussion	21%

Middle Caste

1.	Bible reading	62%
2.	Radio	57%
3.	Evangelist	52%
4.	Rallies	47%
5.	Church worship	47%
6.	Literature	43%
7.	Discussion	29%

The most eagerness to learn overall is shown by the Scheduled Caste NBBCs (average of 52%, compared to 48% among middle-caste people and 46% among high-caste). The form of ministry toward which they are most receptive overall would seem to be a combination of mass media like radio programmes and big rallies with personal discussions with a pastor, evangelist or Bible woman. The interest among Scheduled Caste and middle-caste respondents in Bible reading could be included in such a nurture strategy. These points will be taken up for further consideration in Section III.

In caste-wise statistics on the NBBCs' description of their situation, we note once again the isolation of the high-caste believers in Christ. The high-caste non-baptised believers are as adamant as anyone else that they do not need to be baptised, but they have the spiritual fellowship in Christ in their family circle -whether baptised or non-baptised — than that reported by the Scheduled Caste believers (cf. Table Three in Appendix V). The high-caste respondents also reflect their less consistent worship of Christ - probably because of this lack of family support - by the fact that more merely agreed with statement no. 77 than wholeheartedly agreed.

In summary, we find considerable differences among the different caste groups in all respects. We found the high-caste non-baptised believers in Christ highly responsive to the mass media opportunities they had to learn about Christ, and they continue to prefer this way of learning for the future. They have the least fellowship in Christ within their family circle, and this may account for the lack of disciplined worship of Christ which we found among them. The high-caste NBBCs show increased interest in learning through church media, although a good half of them seem to be reluctant to expose themselves any further and will probably continue to rely on the mass media which they can find from time to time.

The middle-caste NBBC respondents showed the most (almost double) increase between previous learning opportunities and future learning opportunities. They, too, have been relying primarily on the mass media, but now express even more interest than the high-caste respondents in church media. Some of the middle-caste community have sizeable converts in the church (e.g., the Nadar community). However, others of this caste will face much the same sociological problems that the high-caste people face. Their decreased hesitation to come to church media to learn more shows that their family and caste situation is not so tight, and they would be quite responsive if approached properly.

The Scheduled Caste respondents have already relied heavily on church media for learning about Christ, and their close sociological relation to the church has enabled them to move closely with Christian families and individuals. They, too, show a considerable increase of interest in learning, especially through church media. This group has revealed the most disciplined worship life, probably because of the spiritual support which they speak of in their family and community. They have the most contact with the church and are the most responsive to faith in Christ.

Cross-Tables according to Education

In the cross-tables according to education levels we find, first of all, that the impact in Christian schools increases with the education level. Only 11.5% of those educated 1-8 years indicate much learning but 28.5% at 9-11 level and 46% at SSLC/PUC level, plus one of the two graduate NBBCs. It may be that these more educated NBBCs have had more years in Christian schools, or it may be that their experience of Christ in a Christian high school or college came at a time of life when they were seeking spiritual truth. At any rate, it seems that learning about Christ at a higher level of education probably in teenage years is more effective in bringing about deeper commitment.

The influence of visiting Velankanni is about fifty percent for all education levels, and the radio is about seventy percent. The other mass media of television and movies have had primarily a superficial impact of about fifty percent and ninety percent, likewise across all education levels. Therefore, we find that these media attract and affect all education levels quite equally.

When we come to the literary media, we find, however, that education does make a noticeable difference. As was mentioned in the introduction to the questionnaire (chapter 3), those of less than high school education often end up functionally illiterate, especially after a few years. We find, therefore, that only eight percent of the 1-8 level NBBC respondents learned much from Bible reading and tracts and none learned "much" from other Christian literature. When we consider that this education level accounts for half of the NBBCs in the city, we recognise that we cannot rely on these traditional media to nurture most of the non-baptised believers. Even among those of higher education the figures do not rise above thirty percent for "much" learning.

The other traditional church mass media of rallies and street preaching also show mostly "a little" learning among the Madras City non-baptised believers in Christ. The only items on which the lower education NBBCs show some significant "much" response is on individual Christians, Christian families, and church worship. However, even in these cases the figures come to only one-third. It is only the SSLC/PUC level respondents who indicate more than fifty percent "much" learning on any item, namely from Christian individuals and from church worship. Otherwise, the picture we get once again is that the relationship to Christ has come in various ways and through various influences across all education levels. (The cross-table on church worship is included in Appendix V).

However, when we come to worship practices, we find that education level does make a significant difference at several points. Those of at least high school-level education show much more consistency in faithfulness to Jesus in worship. Those of lesser education prefer worshipping Jesus at church (77%); for only 58% worship Jesus at home, only 11.5% with family members, 27% along with their other gods, and only one-half Jesus alone. Evidently they do not feel strong enough in their home situation to practice what they have espoused as correct in question no. 77.

On the other hand, more than one-fourth of those of higher education are able to worship Jesus with their family members. More than two-thirds worship Him privately and exclusively, and only one NBBC over eighth-standard education worships Jesus along with other gods. More than half of these NBBCs also worship Jesus in church, but they do not rely on this medium like those of lesser education do. Therefore, we see that the majority of non-baptised believers in Christ lack stability in the faith through lack of nurture. Those of higher education seems to have found various means, both literary and non-literary, to nurture themselves enough to stand firm in Christian practice.

It then becomes important to find out how the 1-8 level group would like to be nurtured in the faith. The three media to which this group responded with highest "much" interest are reading the Bible (58%), discussing with an evangelist (58%), and listening to the radio (65%). However, it is noteworthy that there is a solid core of 30-40% in this group who express no interest in any of the ways of learning suggested. They perhaps feel too insecure to venture further in any way. We must meet people of this education-level group and find out how best we can serve their needs.

Of course, the literary media are more attractive to the more educated non-baptised believers. Eighty-six percent of the high school-level NBBCs express interest in Bible study, and about half of the SSLC/PUC group in both the Bible and other literature. Discussing with an evangelist and listening to the radio also strongly interest them. The number of graduates in the sample is only two, so one cannot generalise on the basis of their statistics; however, it is striking that neither of the graduate NBBCs expressed interest in learning through any of the suggested ways. Perhaps they - as well as a good one-third of the others of higher education - feel they can manage well enough on their own without help from the church.

The statistics on the family situation of the non-baptised believers do not reveal anything significant in regard to education-level differences. As one might expect from the description of the statistics above, the agreement of the lesser educated NBBCs to worship of Jesus alone was less wholehearted than those of higher education; however, it still was more than half.

In summary on the situation of our urban NBBCs according to education level, we have not found anything particularly surprising. As one might expect, the less educated are more vulnerable and less reachable - as well as larger in number.

Those of high school-level education are the other large population, and they express interest in literary media. Therefore, our nurture materials should be oriented toward their capabilities and interests. In all cases, however, it is the more personal approach of the evangelist which would be the most appreciated.

Cross-Tables According to Income Group

We have analysed the background of the non-baptised believers of Madras City according to caste, and now we will do so according to class. The number of respondents in the "high income group" was only three, so we cannot make any confident generalisations about this group - though I will indicate where these three give a strong indication.

The low-income group has had the least opportunity to learn in one of our city Sunday Schools. Only one of the twenty-six NBBC respondents of this group indicates learning in a Sunday School;

whereas five of the middle-income group do and one of the high-income group. Remembering the high learning which has been achieved through this medium and the attraction Christ has had for the low-income group, we must discover why our Sunday Schools have not been more effective among the poorer people of the city.

Similarly, we find that our urban schools have had less effect on the low-income NBBCs. Only 11.5% (as contrasted with 39% for the middle-income and 33% for the high-income groups) express that they learned "much" in a Christian school.

None of the respondents learned much about Jesus through our social work in the city. Twenty-seven percent of the low-income group did learn "a little".

Visiting Velankanni, as well as the literary and non-literary mass media, indicate a similar effect on both the lower and middle income, groups. With the upper-income group we find that two-thirds of them regularly express that they have used these media meaningfully. Thus, we may anticipate that the upper income group will use the more distant, more secular media, rather than the regular church media.

The two types of learning experiences on which the low-income group indicates significantly more "much" learning than the other groups are the mass rallies (19%) and street preaching (27%). They have learned slightly more than the others through Christian family (totally 69%).

The church worship media were used most by the middle income group in the city, especially worship at church which came to the highest "much" response (56.5%) for them. These media show response from the high-income group as well, but not so consistently. Thus, it seems that the middle-income NBBCs feel more comfortable with the ministry of the church in Madras City than either the rich or the poor.

The figures on worship practices show no significant differences between the income groups.

It is impressive to note in the statistics on preferred learning opportunities that the low-income NBBCs consistently indicate the most interest to learn about Jesus, while the high-income respondents indicate some interest only in reading Christian literature and listening to the radio (cf. Table Five, Appendix VI). It is clear that the church has a neglected and responsive group among the poor NBBCs. Among the middle-income group somewhat less than half show no interest on the various items. Among the poor the negative responses average a little above one-fourth. Thus, we find that among all income groups there is a sizeable proportion of non-baptised believers in the city which is uninterested in the ministries of the church. The percentage of this proportion increases with income level.

In the cross-tables on the family situation of the urban NBBCs according to income group, we find that more than half of the low and middle income groups have Christian relatives, while none of the three high income respondents speak of it. These high-income respondents, however, all speak of having relations who are non-baptised believers in Christ, while only 31% of the low-income group do and only 52% of the middle-income group. Thus, we see that the high-income NBBCs are fewer and more isolated, which would also account for their greater hesitation to practice a disciplined worship of Jesus and to avail themselves of opportunities to learn more. The other income groups have more support within their family circles and therefore feel more confident to proceed according to the leadings of their heart.

Cross-Tables According to Native Place

Because of our initial expectation that the geographical background of the non-baptised believers in Christ may play a significant role we also arranged cross-tables according to native place as well. However, as I mentioned earlier, we found this bio-data to be insignificant in forming the background of the NBBCs. In the cross-tables we note only that those whose native place is in southern Tamil Nadu worship Jesus significantly less than those from the city itself 45.5% vs. 77%). We expected that people from southern Tamil Nadu and Kerala would have more influence through Christian relatives and other NBBC family members, but we find that approximately half, whether from the city or not, testify to such family spiritual fellowship. Geographical background of the non-baptised believers is not important in their spiritual development.

Summary of Cross-Table Statistics

The overall picture we get of the non-baptised believers in Christ in Madras City is consistent with the general spiritual background from which they come. They are only five percent of the total Hindu and Muslim population in the city, and they are scattered in various caste, class, and age groups. Therefore, they are quite unrelated to each other.

Nonetheless, we have found that they have much in common. Their practice of the Christian faith is largely orthodox, even though they lack the nurture and support of a steady Christian fellowship. They have drawn from the Christian community both through individual contacts as well as through public Christian ministries such as radio and worship services. Most show considerable interest in developing these contacts with the ministry of the church, especially in discussing with an evangelist and in attending mass rallies. Many also have Christian relatives and NBBC relations, so they can be nurtured through these natural family lines as well, especially the women and the scheduled caste believers.

Furthermore, within the general population of non-baptised believers we have discerned certain groups which are characteristically more responsive: teenagers, women, the poor, the Scheduled Caste, the high-school educated. Generally these are the same groups which have had a stronger relationship with the organised church. Thus, the core of the "Churchless Christianity" is much the same as the general population we identified previously. What marks them from the general population is a greater zeal to learn about Jesus and a greater determination to be faithful to Him. These are the ones who are willing to come to church ministries and gain the spiritual support they desire, and through them many more can be reached.

We noted other groups, however, who are more hesitant: high-caste people, upper-income people, older people, well-educated people. People in these categories are generally less responsive and less faithful. They are less interested in relating closely to the church. The high-caste people indicate a strong interest in learning more about the Christian faith, but primarily through mass media. These categories of people are the most isolated and the weakest. They are the "other sheep" caught in the thickest thorns and crevasses of the society.

Therefore, the population of non-baptised believers in Madras City we have found to be a diverse and generally isolated group, yet of considerable numbers. It is spread over all caste and class communities of the city as a kind of leaven in the lump. Its fermentation potential is dependent upon the right environment being provided. The spiritual forces within the general environment are warm and encouraging. However, the spiritual force of the church remains distant and cold for most of the non-baptised believers.

There is not much we in the church can do to change the general social structures in which the non-baptised believers live and move. The church also has little effective access to people within those structures. Yet, we can seek to develop lines of communication and encouragement to those seeking to draw on our strengths. Through them a spiritual growth from within might be effected and our Lord's reign might spread even more. The church will be a resource for these "other sheep" living in other folds though responsive to the one shepherd. It is this possibility which we must now reflect upon theologically and practically.

SECTION THREE

Theological and Practical Implications

CHAPTER FIVE

"What Does All This Mean?"

Outline:

"What Does All This Mean?"

What does all of this mean? What are the implications of this "Churchless Christianity" for the church? Must we expand and revise our traditional theology in order to accommodate the facts of this broader work of God? What practical responsibilities does this phenomenon of Christian faith outside the church lay upon our ministerial planning and ecclesiastical structures? What are the implications for our whole strategy and goal of mission?

No doubt, these questions have arisen in the minds of every reader, as they have arisen in my mind throughout this research. As I mentioned in the Introduction, the main objective of this book is to present the facts of the "Churchless Christianity" around us so that more people can reflect missiologically about it. In this section, I will offer my reflections; however, I do not feel at all that I have the answers to the many theological and practical questions which this extra-ecclesial activity of God raises for us. As one noted missiologist advised me: "Do not try to develop a theology too soon. Important matters like this must be reflected on for a long time by many people."

The most we can do at this point is reflect on the phenomena from the standpoint of the church. In due time the implications will coalesce into a systematic consensus, an indigenous theology on "Churchless Christianity" in India The pages of these two chapters are simply part of that larger thoughtful process which will take place throughout the church in India. I see my role at this point to stimulate this larger process of reflection, rather than to attempt any arguments toward conclusive reformulations.

A SOCIOLOGICAL PROBLEM

It seems to me that the first discernment we must come to is that the problem we are faced with in regard to these non-baptized believers in Christ is a sociological one rather than a theological one. The issue is not our theology of baptism or our theology of the church, as we shall see. It is not a change in our traditional theology but a clarification and expansion of it which is required. The issue is the sociological distortion of theology in practice.

The non-baptised believers we have met, both personally and through the statistics, have respected baptism and desired to receive it. They have honoured and utilised the ministry of the church. If baptism and the church were carried out in practice as our theology conceives them, there would be no problem and there would be no non-baptised believers.

It is clear, furthermore, that the communalised nature of the church exists quite apart from baptism. Even among the non-sacremental churches where baptism is considered unnecessary (as among the Salvation Army) or merely symbolic (as among the Baptists) the church is just as exclusively communal as among those churches who emphasise the necessity of baptism. The Subba Rao movement of thousands of non-baptised believers in Christ in Andhra Pradesh is a popular preaction of the upper castes and classes in a Baptist church area.[1] The Salvation Army church is just as exclusively Harijan and Backward Caste as the CS1 in southern Tamil Nadu and as the Baptists, in Andhra Pradesh. The Sattur Nadar didn't join the church even after taking baptism because the sociological realities remained. The character of the church is formed by the structure of the society irrespective of the theology or practice of baptism.

Therefore, the primary questions raised for us by the phenomenon of non-baptised believers in Christ around us are not about their authenticity but about ours. The questions are about our recognition of sociological realities in ecclesiastical structures and mission planning. The questions are about developing a style of church fellowship and ministry which make the call of Christ and gift of His Spirit available to all in the fullest possible freedom and power.

Cross-Cultural Evangelism in Scripture and History

The issues around the question of non-baptised believers are issues of cross-cultural evangelism. Any evangelism across new frontiers faces these issues. We find the dangers and distortions involved in cross-cultural evangelism throughout the history of God's mission. The caste system in India has not produced a new problem of mission. It has produced an Indian form of an old problem.

Throughout the Scriptures we find these same problems of sociology distorting theology, especially in areas of cross-cultural evangelism. The Old Testament People of God were called from the time of Abraham to be a "light among the nations." Yet, the morality of the patriarchs throughout the history of Genesis rises little above the morality of the nations around them. Their religious understanding also is close to the Hindu "ishta devata" principle, for they quickly conclude that Jehovah is the God who is obliged to protect and bless them "for the glory of His Name" (cf. Joshua 7:8-9). The people of Israel are a small, insecure nation among the nations, and they call upon their God to assert His power on their behalf among the gods.

Circumcision, which was begun as a sign of spiritual commitment to the historic covenant of God with His People, is soon distorted into a communal rite of sociological identity. To be circumcised is to be a Jew sociologically, rather than to be an obedient servant of God theologically. As the prophets always tried to remind the people, the physical circumcision's only intention was to be an inauguration into and a continual reminder of the real spiritual circumcision "of the heart" (Dt. 10:16, Jer. 4:4, Rom. 2:28-29). However, as far as the general mentality of the people was concerned, circumcision is what set them apart ethnically from the despised "uncircumcised Philistines" around them. The laws were given to Israel to arouse the admiration of the nations and to attract them to the light (cf. Dt. 4:5-8). However, they were reconstructed by the Israelites into sociological barriers which preserved their identity and reduced their religion and their God to one of the many ethnic religions around them.

The geographical boundaries of Israel became the limits of "the presence of the Lord" (I Sam. 26:20). The Creator of the universe became the "God of Abraham, Isaac and Jacob." Jehovah's dwelling was brought from the highest heavens to Mount Zion, the "citadel of God" to be found on "His holy mountain" for ever and ever (Ps. 48). Jehovah was understood by the Jews and acknowledged by the nations as "the God of the Jews."

To be circumcised was to become a Jew. Throughout the nations to which the Jews had been scattered by their Assyrian and Babylonian conquerors, many spiritual seekers came to know of the Lord. They desired to enter into covenant with Him, but not through circumcision. They did not want to become Jews. For generation upon generation every synagogue had its attachment of "God-fearers" who worshipped the only true God and revered His laws. They came to Jerusalem occasionally for the great festivals. However, they desired to remain as a Persian, as a Babylonian, as a Parthian, as a Roman. They desired to marry among their own people and remain identified with their own society.

Many of Peter's and Paul's first converts were from among these "God-fearers" (cf. Acts 2:5-11, 10:1-2, 14:1, 17:4, 12, 17, 18:4,7)[2]. They were expecting the Messiah and they acknowledged the revelation of the Old Testament. They desired to enter into the covenant. It was the communalised circumcision which prevented them. When St. Paul offered them a way of entering into covenant with Jehovah outside of circumcision, they quickly and enthusiastically responded. They could become Christians without becoming Jews. They could form into the People of God in Galatia and in Rome as members of their own society and culture. Through baptism they could enter into a transcultural spiritual unity of faith which broke down the sociological barriers which the Jews' distorted religiosity had erected (Eph. 2:11-22, Gal. 3:23-29).

Paul was determined that faith in Christ should raise the new believers above sociological barriers. He pleaded with them not to "submit again to a yoke of slavery". He threatened them that they will "have fallen from grace" and be "severed from Christ" if they insist on circumcision in the new convenant (Gal. 5:1-4).

Baptism was the new rite of entrance. It was a purely spiritual rite, practiced by Gnostics in their initiation ceremonies, by Jews in their proselyte ceremonies, by Essenes in their purification ceremonies, and by John the Baptist in his repentance ceremonies. Baptism was a pan-cultural rite for entrance into a pan-cultural religion.

Baptism was a sacrament of liberating Gospel, uniting the devotee of Christ with God and with neighbour.

> In so far as through baptism one is united with Christ and Christ gives himself in love for the salvation of all, the baptised person also understands himself as no longer belonging to himself or to a narrow inward-looking community but to the whole community.[3]

The parallel issues of cross-cultural evangelism which we see between circumcision in first-century Asia Minor and baptism in twentieth century India raises the missiological question about the place of baptism in our evangelistic work. Baptism was clearly not intended by Paul to separate people from their homes and societies. Rather, Baptism was intended solely to communicate the freeing and regenerating and transcending Gospel.

> The separation that is called for is only in the realm of commitment to God, and as such only from sin and all that is carnal and contrary to the purpose of God in Christ. If baptism in the N.T. has the strong motif of breaking down all natural barriers and keeping the community always as open-ended, one wonders whether making baptism the water-rite — the criterion for membership in the Body of Christ, the community of new creation, is in accordance with the divine purpose for baptism.[4]

Throughout the mission history of the church, baptism has been intended for this uplifting, freeing expression of the Gospel. Throughout the evangelisation of Europe acceptance of the Gospel was acceptance of a liberation from the fears and oppressions of animism. Although the Germanic tribes conquered the Roman armies, they were soon absorbed into the Roman civilization. The Germans "felt for it all the respect of the Barbarian for civilisation. No sooner did they enter it than they adopted its language, and also its religion"[5]. Thus, throughout the evangelisation of Europe, Baptism was an up lifting, freeing expression of the Gospel.

However, in the process of evangelisation in Asia and Africa during recent centuries, the cross-cultural situation has been often quite different. As a consequence, people's attitudes toward conversion and toward baptism have been different. Where the Christian mission has reached into animistic societies like those of early Europe, baptism has generally been viewed as uplifting and liberating. However, in many other parts of Asia and Africa, people have not admired the Western civilization which came along with the Christian missions. When baptism was presented to them as a call to separate themselves from their traditional cultures, the people hesitated-like the God-fearers hesitating before circumcision.

Many peoples of Asia and Africa highly valued their traditional way of life, and they did not feel it was the call of God in Christ to disrupt it, As the Brahmins resisted disruption of traditional caste distinctions, so the Chinese resisted disruption of traditional ancestor worship. In Madurai, de Nobili tried to separate the call of Christ from these social traditions, and in China Rizzi tried to do the same. However, in general Christian missionaries failed to allow a new form of Christianity to develop on the new soils of Asia and Africa.

As a result, Christian mission work in Asia and Africa had to swim against the mainstream of the culture, rather than with it. Primarily those who were already strong individualists or social rebels found in baptism an affirmation of their aspirations. Many others from the mainstream of society rejected baptism, rather than reject their culture.

In Japan a "no-church" movement developed among the more educated and more well-to-do in society, and it continues to this day quite separate from church life. In government statistical surveys 3% of the Japanese population state their religion as Christian but only 1% are on the church rolls. In Africa thousands of Christian cults have arisen in recent decades, once again quite separate from and often in opposition to the church. They emphasise tribal traditions, polygamy, the use of local drums, dance, and women's leadership. They are developing a form of Christianity which reflects their own cultural traditions and values. New forms of Jewish Christianity have developed in Israel and in the United States of America and new forms of Muslim Christianity have developed in Bangla Desh.[6]

Cross-Cultural Evangelism in India

In all these diverse developments the common thread we find is the attempt to adapt the Christian faith to local culture. Throughout mission history in India we find the same reaction. This history has been detailed by many others.[7] I would simply bring to recollection here the Church of "New Dispensation" under Keshub Chander Sen, the "Hindu Christianity" of Bramabandhab Upadhyaya, the "Hindu Church of Christ" of Kandasami Chettiar, and the "Churchless Christ" of Subba Rao—all just during this century.[8]

Today the worst abuses, such as insistence on eating beef for high-caste Hindu converts and eating pork for Muslim converts, are no longer defended. However, the general cultural alienation from the mainstream of Indian spirituality and values continues. The early missionaries ignorantly accepted the title of "Firangi" given to them by the Hindu community thus accepting the description as "barbarian and irreligious" because of their alcohol-drinking, beef-eating, and anti-Hindu habits. Even today Christians are typically portrayed in films and stories as prostitutes, drunkards, stumbling in speaking the local languages and of Western dress.[9]

Christian congregational organisation, modes of worship, names, customs of dress (especially among women), styles of church art and architecture, religious language, eating habits, selection of religious leadership, approaches to religious nurture and propagation, attitudes toward Indian history, and expectations on personal habits often differ significantly from the mainstream of the society. Yet, few will today attempt to defend these differences on the grounds of theological necessity. These practices are simply the developments of the Western missionary tradition over the past several centuries. The effect, however, is the same as that of insistence on beef and pork-eating, and on circumcision and Sabbath observance: change of cultural habits along with change of faith.

In North India this movement out of the mainstream of social life progressed farther than in the South. Converts to the Christian faith in the North have been more isolated and individual. These scattered families and individuals could not survive economically and socially in their village communities, so most of them moved to the cities and towns, where the mission compounds were. They came from various caste communities, but now they have consolidated into a "caste-less" community - or, one might say, a new "Christian" caste — in urban areas. In the South, where conversions were more through mass movements of caste groups, caste identity and social customs are more intact. However, both in the North and South the basic caste characteristic of endogomy is socially expected and organisationally enforced within the Christian community. We will discuss the question of caste in more detail later, at this point I simply want to illustrate the process of social alienation in this regard as it has developed in Indian mission history.

What we must recognise is that conversion to the Christian faith in a situation like this implies much more than a recognition of the truth of Christ's claims about Himself. In our survey of the rural non-baptised believers in Christ we found that baptism was a problem not because of a lack of faith-commitment but because of consequent social and cultural implications. Baptism for these non-baptised believers did not mean the uplifting, freeing Gospel it meant in the New Testament period or in Europe or among the Harijans of last century. It meant a self-removal from social, family and cultural ties about which they are justly proud and happy. Long before Christian missions appeared on the scene it was established in the Laws of Many that the disruption caused by a spouse converting to another religion was so grave that he/she should be divorced with no maintenance responsibilities.

This cultural objection to conversion has been raised and pressed all through our century by the greatest leaders of the nation, from Ram Mohan Roy to Mahatma Gandhi.[10] However, it is good that we are reminded once again, this time through a noted non-baptised believer of fifty years ago in Madras, Mr. Kandasamy Chettiar:

> I have never felt any inward call such as I could recognize as divine in its inspiration to join the Christian church in the narrow sense in which some use the term. For I believe such a step as this can be justified on no less an authority than the constraining power of God such as compelled Abraham to leave his. . . I have no feeling but one of reverence toward those, and they are many, who shift their tents under orders from above. I look upon them as more blessed than myself. But I have nothing but contempt for those, and they are also many, who, yielding to the very human influence and to a call from unworthy quarters cut themselves off from those whom it is their duty to be in touch with, if for nothing else, at least in the interests of the Lord whom they profess to follow. Nor do I believe that while every believer is called upon to let his light shine before all the world, he is also called upon to join the Christian Church in the narrower sense of the term. There is nothing essentially pure in Christian society for that is what the Christian church amounts to so that one should hasten from the one to the other like a Pilgrim from the city of Destruction to the Heavenly City."

Several sociologists have combined to document the cultural character of Christianity within the Indian society. Their research, published under the title "The Church as Christian Community," covers rural, town and urban Christian communities in North India. The studies demonstrate how the Christian community is understood both by the Christians and by their neighbours as another "*qaum*", or caste-community, within the overall social fabric. The

Christians share with other *qaums* the general attitudes toward religion and morality, and they also share the general attitudes toward their *qaum:* membership through birth, group-serving loyalty, and accommodation as one community among many other even though such a self-understanding is quite contrary to the Biblical understanding of the church.[12] Although neither the Christian community nor anyone else would actually define or describe the Christian church in these terms, "there is a 'visceral' instrument of church perception" which lies much deeper than any theological descriptions or organisational structures.[13]

Because of these sociological realities, conversion of a member of another *qaum* to the Christian faith involves serious sociological consequences both for him and for the Christian community. These sociological consequences account for the hesitation and resistance to conversion on both sides:

> With the appearance of the convert, theology suddenly becomes embedded in sociology, and a different set of concepts and concerns becomes operative. The average convert in India must find a new family, a new community, a new social and economic life along with the new spiritual life he has adopted. His own people force him to this by completely ostracizing him. The local church or Christian community must not only make a place in its spiritual fellowship to include the new believer but, if it is to see him survive, must open its homes, intimate associations, channels of communication, and means of livelihood to him. . . Because of the differences of custom, attitude and behaviour between sub-cultures in India - separated so thoroughly by caste - the behaviour patterns and home life of one group is quite foreign and even repugnant to other groups.[14]

Therefore, the emotional adjustment, patience and understanding involved in these new social inter-relationships demand extraordinary effort on the part of all concerned. Only the extraordinary individual and the extraordinary community can face this prospect with courage and open-heartedness.

As I have been presenting this research to various groups of pastors, evangelists and lay leaders over the past years it was interesting to note the reaction when I asked the group if there is such a thing as a Christian culture. Most did not know what to answer, for a culture is so close to one's very way of thinking and living that one can hardly notice it. Some asserted that there definitely is and must be: others insisted that there is not and must not be. Certainly from the perspective of the non-baptised believers we have met, the Christian community is not only a culture but a caste.

To change faith through baptism involves practically the change of one's whole social identity.[15] One identifies with a new history and a new group of people. One must learn new habits and new customs. One is even expected generally to take a new name. If one is comfortable in his traditional society and culture, baptism is truly a "coming down", as the R.S. Mangalam evangelist said it must be. Baptism is not uplifting and freeing. The theological intention of baptism is contradicted and undercut by its social effects. Sociology has completely distorted theology.

This point was illustrated to me in a surprising way through a small drama I witnessed at a Christian elementary school orphanage.

The group of boys acted out the life of David Livingstone, missionary to interior Africa. The concluding scene in which a tribe of cannibals comes to accept Jesus reaches its climax when missionary Livingstone dramatically announces to the tribal chief, "Now that you have accepted Christ, you must learn to kneel and pray." All the actors then knelt and prayed together, and Livingstone confirmed that they were now Christians.

Obviously, things never happened so crassly even among the most culturally insensitive missionaries. However, it is clear that among these Christian boys customs of worship and change of faith are inseparable. Christians may not acknowledge that they have a strong cultural identity built up over the years (although it would certainly be helpful if Christians objectively reckoned with it), but it is highly obvious to those outside the Christian fold.

A THEOLOGICAL QUESTION

In this situation it is incumbent upon us to develop theological tools for discerning faith-culture issues. In this regard Protestant theology has been the most naive and insensitive. Throughout the mission history of the Roman Catholic Church and the Orthodox churches, issues of faith and culture in cross-cultural evangelism have been recognised and resolved more responsibly.[16] We Protestants have tended to be much more blind and "imperialistic". The debate over indigenisation began from the beginning of the Orthodox and Roman Catholic missions in India (e.g. the indigenous customs of the Syrian Orthodox in Kerala and the officially sponsored experiments in indigenous worship in the Roman Catholic Church even until today). However in Protestant circles the matter can hardly be spoken of outside of a seminary classroom.

In two other articles I have tried to approach the faith-culture issues raised by these non-baptised believers by utilising the traditional Lutheran theological principles of the Two- Kingdom distinction and of Luther's conservative approach to the Reformation.[18] In this chapter I will take the matter up utilising another Lutheran theological principle, the adiaphora principle. None of these approaches solves the dilemmas involved. However, we are able to think through the alternatives in terms of categories which have proven helpful in previous dilemmas of church history. Hopefully, in due course more theologians of other traditions will take up this issue and provide their insights from their particular perspectives.

Adiaphora Principle in Justifying Faith

The "adiaphora–principle" was a theological tool developed during the controversies of the Reformation period. The principle intends to discern between matters which must be considered essential to salvation and matters which are peripheral. In usage it is a reductionist principle, attempting to isolate the bare minimum which must be insisted upon for true Christian faith. For example, in defining the essential marks of the church, the Lutheran Confessions (Augsburg Confession, Article VII) identify only the preaching of the Gospel and the administration of the two Sacraments. Everything else in regard to church order and customs is considered areas of human freedom, or matters of "adiaphora".

Thus, in regard to the faith-culture dilemmas presented to us by the facts of non-baptised believers around us, we must try to identify which traditional practices of the church actually are adiaphora. These non-essential - though perhaps salutary - traditions need not be insisted upon. In fact, if they are insisted upon, we seriously mix Law and Gospel and make people "submit again to a yoke of slavery" (Gal. 5:1).

Of course, the first theological question we must confront is if we can consider baptism an adiaphoron. Is the administration of baptism an essential function of the Gospel? Is baptism necessary for salvation? Is baptising a clear command of our Lord to be followed without fail by the church in carrying out its mission mandate? These questions came up whenever I discussed this research about non-baptised believers with different groups. The matter has been debated for many years by the most eminent scholars.[19] I would encourage the reader to make his own study into these questions.

At this point, I would only apply the perspective of the adiaphora principle for consideration in the debate. Dr. Bergquist, in his thoughtful article referred to above, points out that baptism is "a window to the central meaning of the Christian faith", clearly demonstrating the basic Christian doctrines of man's need for repentance and forgiveness, of the necessity for God's gracious initiative, of man's necessary response in a life of disciplined love, and of the call of God for a new community in mission to the world.[20] There is no doubt that baptism clearly teaches these basic doctrines of the faith, and in the sacramental traditions of the church (making up eighty percent of Christendom) baptism also effectively conveys this reality. However, the adiaphora principle makes us ask the question if baptism is essential to the teaching and conveying of this faith. Is baptism, like Holy Communion, useful and effective as a means of grace, but not essential? If so, to require it absolutely would open us to Jesus' fierce condemnation of the Pharisees as blind guides of the blind vainly "teaching as doctrines the precepts of men" (Mt. 15:1-14).

The aim of the adiaphora principle is to maintain the freedom and purity of the Gospel. Baptism, as a sacrament instituted by Christ, is intended as a communication of the Gospel. It is to communicate the forgiving and renewing love of God in Christ, the rebirth in the Spirit (Jn. 3:5), the dying and rising with Christ to walk in newness of life (Rom. 6:3-4). The adiaphora principle insists that whatever does not lead us directly into this Gospel-gift is not to be required. When the Jews distorted the Gospel-gift of circumcision into a legalistic, self-justifying, social rite, Paul had to insist that "neither circumcision, nor uncircumcision counts for anything, but a new creation" (Gal. 6:15, 5:6).

Has the Gospel-gift of baptism been distorted into a legalistic, self-justifying, social rite which believers in Christ have every justification to refuse? Manilal Parekh's sense of this adiaphora principle is quoted by Richard Taylor: "In our cultural context baptism has tended to become a social rite which in a fundamentally Christian sense is as objectionable as it is unnecessary"[21] Kai Baago quotes our contemporary non-baptised leader, Subba Rao in the same vein in one of his lyrics: "Come out of those jungles of religion. If you once enter there, you can no more find the way. Look for Christ, who by-passed the jungles, who pointed out the direction, who over ruled the ceremonials, and who showed us how to live always for others".[22] These believers in Christ are convinced that baptism is obscuring, not conveying, the Gospel in the way it is now popularly understood and used by the church.

We should be clear here that the point at issue is much more than the exceptional case. The traditional theology of the church has accepted the exceptions to "outside the church no salvation" through the principles of "the baptism of desire" and "the baptism of blood". However, what we are confronted with here is more than the isolated individual who may desire baptism but cannot get it before his death or the rare case of one who is martyred before getting baptised. We are also talking about a phenomenon quite different from non-sacramental traditions like the Salvation Army and Quakers, which arose as reform movements within Christendom and theologically reject the meaning and practice of baptism. Nor is the issue the many groups of new converts (like the leper colony outside Madras) who are growing in the faith nor the many groups in remote villages where churches have pulled out mission workers for financial reasons (like the Methodists and CNI in Uttar Pradesh) who still cling precariously to vestiges of the faith through the passing down of Christian lyrics.

We are talking about millions of believers in Christ in India and around the world who decide against baptism even though it is acknowledged by them and available to them. Do they fall under the stricture of Bernard that "it is not the lack of baptism but the contempt of baptism which damns"? Accepting Bernard's sound principle, must we look upon such people as pollutors and deniers of the Gospel from whom we must separate ourselves in order to be true to our Lord (cf. Ezra 10:11)? Or is it possible that these believers have not rejected the true baptism of our Lord but actually desire it? Many missiologists are convinced that the latter statement is the case, and it is our responsibility in the church to restore the true baptism of grace which has become obscured in practice.

The approach to recapturing the Gospel-character and intention of baptism proposed by several missiologists has been to emphasise baptism as a privilege rather than as an obligation.[23] M. M.

Thomas suggests that we bring non-baptised believers into the full fellowship and ministry of the church, including Holy Communion, and present baptism as a Gospel-gift which one "may ask for some time in the process of his growth in Christ."[24] McGavran creatively suggests that people, who because of caste constraints find baptism a threat and a burden rather than a joy and release, might make a public covenant to take baptism when they can do so happily with three thousand of their fellow caste people.[25] Therefore, it is not because of disrespect or demeaning of the nature of baptism that its implementation is being rethought, but out of a conviction that:

> If baptism is to be retained in Indian Christianity, the churches that retain it should be constrained to find in it (or for it) a meaning that is strongly supportive of Christian life and faith. Otherwise its liability to the Gospel in India can hardly justify its continued practice.[26]

The theology and practice of baptism in a mission context like India is being rethought not in terms of conservative preservation of historical traditions and congregational piety. The criteria of reflection are determined by missiological impact. The concern is the extension of the Kingdom of Christ, not the maintenance of church structures. Where ninety-seven percent of the population is looking at baptism from the outside, we must be sure that baptism clearly presents the Gospel-gift of God's uplifting, freeing, redeeming love in Christ.

Theology reflects upon this missiological requirement, and restructuring of God's good gifts may be necessary. What is a clear presentation of the Gospel in one period of history and in one social context (e.g. a largely Christian society) may be twisted into an obscuring of the Gospel in another context. It is a highly sensitive and dangerous task, but also highly necessary.

It is God's clear will that all people be baptised into Christ, but it is also His will that we make disciples of all nations (Mt. 28:19). We have seen how the whole social and cultural situation has set these two good commandments of God against each other in many cases. In the quotation from Kandasamy Chettiar and in the rural survey we saw how people were expecting a direct word from God to relieve them from the conflict of these contradicting divine commands. They know it is God's good will that they be baptised, but they also know that it is His good will that they affirm their family traditions, serve their family needs, get an education and a good job to support their family and serve society, and so on. Soren Kierkegaard developed a whole theology on his analysis of Abraham being placed into this contradictory situation of having to disobey a clear traditional commandment of God not to kill in order to obey a more pressing, immediate command of God. Are the non-baptised believers the contemporary "Abrahams" who must leap by faith into the darkness of "the theological suspension of the ethical," as Kierkagaard put it?

Baptism is a clear commandment of our Lord, but the intention of our Lord's Word is always renewing and uplifting Gospel. "The commandment is holy and just and good", but Satan is always at work to find "opportunity in the commandment" itself to deceive humankind and kill the Gospel. Sin can work "death in me through what is good" when baptism becomes a source of pride, self-righteousness, social exclusion, spiritual apathy, communalism, legalism and caste rivalry in popular Christian thinking. "Sin, finding opportunity in the commandment, wrought in me all kinds of covetousness," and "the very commandment which promised life, proved to be death to me" (Rom. 6:8-13).

However, can we go to the extreme of saving that baptism is an adiaphoron, an optional practice in the church? In answering this question it is important to distinguish between the role of baptism in justification and in sanctification. Scripture is clear that we are justified solely by grace through faith, not through anything which we do and present to God as making us worthy before Him (cf. Rom. 1:17, 3:19-22, Gal. 2:16). Scripture also is clear that it is the "living and active" Word of God (Heb. 4:12) whether active through the water of Baptism or through preaching or through any of the other means of grace, which is grasped by faith and converts us into children of God (cf. I Jn. 5:6-10, I Peter 1:23, II Thes. 1:10, Heb. 10:30). Paul places faith and baptism side by side as ways to "put on Christ" and become "Sons of God" (Gal 3:26-27). The Spirit thus makes His dwelling within us, and we are renewed for a life of good works (Eph. 2:8-10, Ph. 3:3, Ti. 2:14).

This gift of justifying grace in Christ certainly can be received outside of baptism, as the very examples of Cornelius, the thief on the cross, and perhaps even the disciples demonstrate. Therefore, we dare not erect any legalistic restrictions on how God may reach out to draw people unto Himself. We dare not suggest any other foundation "than that which is laid, namely Jesus Christ" (1 Cor. 3:11.) As Peter at the first Council of Jerusalem courageously acknowledged in the same kind of faith-culture problem:

> God who knows the heart bore witness to them, giving them the Holy Spirit just as he did to us; and he made no distinction between us and them, but cleansed their hearts by faith. Now therefore why do you make trial of God putting a yoke upon the neck of the disciples which neither our fathers nor we have been able to bear? But we believe that we shall be saved through the grace of the Lord Jesus, just as they will. Acts 15 :8-11.

Our Lord has assured us that "the Father will love whoever loves me" (Jn. 14:2; 6:37, Eph. 3:16, I Cor. 8:1-3).

Adiaphora Principle in Sanctifying Grace

The real issue in regard to the necessity of baptism is that of sanctifying grace. A person may come to faith in many ways, but he is also called to live in that faith and grow into mature humanhood, "to the measure of the stature of the fullness of Christ" (Eph. 4:13). The warning of eternal condemnation is never linked with baptism in Scripture (also not in Mk. 16:16), but it is most clearly linked with sinful living (Ph. 3:19, Gal. 5:21, II Thes. 1:8, 2:12, Heb. 10:29, etc). The new life of love in the believer is the evidence of the saving gift of the Holy Spirit (I Jn. 2:5-6, 3:23-24, Gal. 5:23-24, Mt. 7:15-27).

By our faith in Christ and by the gift of the Holy Spirit in our life, we know that by God's grace we are in Christ and He is in us. We rest assured that God "has chosen us in him before the foundation of the world that we should be holy and blameless before him" (Eph 1:4-5, 11:14, Rom. 8:29-30, II Thes. 2:13, II Tim. 1:9, I Peter 1:5.) Those who are in Him through faith and love are in His Body both now and forever.[27]

Christopher Duraisingh has pointed out that the New Testament Greek word for baptism is not the ritual word "baptism" but the active word "baptisma". The real meaning of "baptism" then, is immersion even unto death (Mk. 1:9-13, Lk. 4:16-17, Mk. 10:39).[28] Whether "baptisma" in the Spirit comes through water or without (cf. I Jn. 5:6-8, I Cor. 10:2, 12:13), it is an immersion into the life, death and resurrection of Christ (Rom. 6:3-4) (Col.

2:11-12). It is being sent as He was sent in the power of the Holy Spirit (Jn. 20:21-22), or it is not baptism.

What Paul says about "real circumcision" as a matter of the heart is true also of baptism. "He is a Jew (or a baptised Christian) who is one inwardly. . . His praise is not from men but from God" (Rom. 2:29). He fulfills the very purpose of the Gospel-gift: "the obedience of faith for the sake of his name among the nations (Rom. 1:5). The ones who lived the "baptisma" life of self-sacrificing love are the ones to whom it will be said at the last day by their Lord: "Come, O blessed of my Father, inherit the Kingdom prepared for you from the foundation of the world" (Mt. 25:31ff, Jn. 3:35, I Jn. 2:5-6, 3:23-24).

The question, then, becomes if "baptismos" is the one graciously ordained way of God to bring believers into saving "baptisma". Our Lord made it very clear that belief in Him meant release to newness of life only through radical discipleship. We must decide for life solely in the Kingdom of God's love and power, or we will never experience the freedom and upliftment of the Gospel (Mt. 6:19-34). The warning to leave all and follow Him is a Gospel-Word, for it enables the believer to set his priorities right and his goals clear, thus freeing him for the joy of fellowship with Christ and the satisfaction of useful service in His Kingdom: "If any one serves me, he must follow me; and where I am, there shall my servant be also; if any one serves me, the Father will honor him" (Jn. 12:26).

For the non-baptised believers we have met in the previous pages, the "baptisma" call of Christ is clear. Neither material benefits of this world (Heb. 12:16, Mt. 13:45-46) nor fear of suffering and persecution (Jn. 15:18-21, 16:1-4, Heb. 10:32-35) nor concern for family obligations (Mr. 8:18-22, 19:29, 10:34-39) nor social standing (Jn. 12:42-43, 19:38) must be allowed, to deter one from the joy of committed discipleship and the certainty of eternal reward (Lk. 12:13-31, 6:49, Mt. 5:11-12, 10:22, 7:13-14). For many non-baptised believers the rite of baptism presents them with the opportunity for entering into the fullness of the Kingdom with its Gospel-gifts of peace, joy and power.

Especially in our Indian missiological context, the step of baptism can free the non-baptised believer from all the compromises of consciences, involvement with fearful family deities, and tendencies toward self-serving worship of God which sap and misdirect the energies of his spiritual life. The refusal of baptism may well be a sign of refusal to repent and thus enter the new life of the Kingdom to which our Lord calls (Mk. 1:15). Hear the joyful witness of one non-baptised believer who received the "baptisma" of the Kingdom through taking "baptismos".

> Though I didn't see heavens opened, I knew the Spirit of God had sealed a covenant with me and a deep conviction that I belonged to Christ got implanted in my heart. Although none of my Hindu relatives were around me then to witness my baptism, I knew that after baptism I could boldly declare to them and to others that I had identified with Christ. It meant sanctified separation from my old Hindu ritualistic tradition and superstition. I was prepared to be dead to self and the world I feel within me an urge to partake of the suffering of Christ by labouring for Him and for the blessing of many others. I experience also the resurrection power of the Lord Jesus Christ. . . . The power of the Holy Spirit has been enabling me to refuse to yield to unrighteous gain and deceit. . . . I can say boldly that they (my Hindu relatives) respect me more now than ever before. . . . I am not ashamed of this great name of Jesus.[29]

There is no doubt that every spiritual person must rejoice with Dr. Rajendran. Even the great Hindu scholar Dr. T. M. P. Mahadevan affirms that "conversion (to Christianity) from within is certainly to be welcomed. . . . and I would adore such a convert".[30] There can be no lesser goal for the Christian faith than such truly deep conversion and commitment to Christ. This is the whole point of the Gospel-gift of baptism.

Now the adiaphora principle raises for us the crucial question once again: Is such conversion and commitment to Christ possible only through baptism? If so, baptism is absolutely indispensable in the life and mission of the church.

There are few who would press the necessity to such an extent. Scripturally it is clear that reception of the renewing Holy Spirit through faith in Christ is the key to the new life in Christ, or "life in the Spirit". When the seed of the Word is received gladly in receptive soil, it will produce even a hundred fold (Mt. 13:23). It is the power of this divine Word which "cleanses" and empowers us like a vine feeding strength into all its branches grafted in through faith (Jn. 15:1ff). The promise of Christ to those who receive Him is that He will dwell in them (Jn. 6:52ff) and unite them through faith in God (I Jn. 4:15), bringing upon them all the gifts of eternal life even now (I Jn. 5:17, Jn. 3:16, 5:24, 6:40).

These gifts are "the gift of the Spirit" in our heart, for where the Spirit is at work His fruit will be seen in attitudes and actions of love, patience, kindness, etc. (Gal. 5:23-24, Mt. 7:15ff, 12:35). Similarly, wherever Christ is affirmed as Lord and Saviour; there too we know the Spirit dwells (I Cor. 12:3,1 Jn. 4:2, Rom. 8:15-16). Therefore, as baptism relates us to God in Christ through the Spirit, so in an even more fundamental sense does faith. For without a living faith, i.e. an on-going relationship with God in Christ, the branch must whither and fruit disappear.

Nonetheless, the matter is not resolved so easily. Even though baptism cannot be made theologically necessary in an absolute sense for sanctifying grace, it may still be practically necessary. Baptism grafts one into the Body of Christ and into the flow of the Spirit through its ministry, its sacraments, its gifts, and its fellowship (I Cor. 12:13), building up the Body's members for spiritual growth and ministry (Eph. 4:11-16). Great figures like Kandasami Chettiar, Subba Rao, and the Uttamapalayam Gounder may be able to stand strong without the regular ministry and fellowship of the Church - although even they gathered their own fellowship groups eventually. However, ninety-nine percent of humanity must draw on the resources of the church in order to gain the strength, perseverance and power for meaningful and useful Christian life.

A PRACTICAL RESPONSIBILITY

Therefore, a fundamental practical problem in the spiritual progress of the non-baptised believer is access to the on going means of renewing and strengthening grace in their lives. The goal of justification is sanctification. Without receiving the Word in the first place there is no justification (Rom. 10:14ff) and without receiving the Word continually there is no possibility of sanctification (Jn. 15:1ff, 17:17). Herein lies the solemn responsibility of the church over against the non-baptised believers in Christ: "Feed my lambs."

Theologically and practically we have no choice but to consider the non-baptised believers in Christ our pastoral responsibility. At issue is not their salvation, for we know that any who confess Christ before the world will be confessed by Christ before the Father (Lk. 12:8, Rom. 10:9-10). At issue is their strength and direction in the faith. We have seen how easily believers in Christ living in a Hindu context can drift into a thoughtless "ishta devata" mentality and into a self-seeking religiosity. If they are to be powerful and clear witnesses to the Gospel call of Christ in their own societies (as we must consider them missiologically), they must be fed on the solid food of the Word and equipped with all the weapons of faith for the strategic battle they must wage "against the principalities and powers" around them on all sides (Eph. 6:10ff, Heb. 5:14).

A Responsibility to Affirm them in their Faith

The non-baptised believers cannot be considered members of the church (nor, I feel, can they be called "Christians", for that is a title ascribed to any who take baptism). Yet, they certainly are part of our fellowship in Christ through faith. They are the sheep of Jesus' flock who are not in our fold, but they are fellow-sheep responding to the voice of the same Master and entering in by the same gate (Jn. 10:9ff). We know they will share our reward even though they are not with us, for they bear our Lord's Name with us and share in His power (Mk. 9:38-41). They are the "believers added to the Lord" but who do not dare to join the apostles' public gathering at Solomon's portico in the temple (Acts 5:12-14). They are the priests who "were obedient to the Faith", but perhaps not to be numbered among the disciples (Acts 6:7).

The lakhs of non-baptised believers in Christ in Madras City, as well as all over rural Tamil Nadu (and, no doubt, all over India, Asia, Africa, Communist countries), are those addressed by Paul when he wrote:

> to the church of God which is at Corinth, to those sanctified in Christ Jesus, called to be saints together with all those who in every place call on the name of our Lord Jesus Christ, both their Lord and ours. (Cor. 1:2)

Our Lord clearly considers us one with them. How can we do anything less?

Our temptation is always that of the disciples, who quickly came to consider themselves as the "in-group" with our Lord and everybody else really had no right to Him. These close disciples tried to stop the Syro-Phoenician woman, the little children, the two blind men, those who healed in Jesus' name, the Samaritan woman, the repentant woman, and so many others. It was all well-intentioned, but badly misguided. We see now that their own pride and self-righteousness and selfishness were limiting the mission of their Lord. They were obstacles rather than instruments of His open-hearted love.

There is no doubt that the same condemnation must come upon us as upon anyone of Jesus' time who might cause "one of these who believes in me to stumble" in his faith: "It would be better for him to have a great millstone fastened round his neck and to be drowned in the depth of the sea" (Mt. 18:6). If we insist upon baptism among people who are in such a precarious spiritual position, are we placing a great stumbling-block in their path as they venture on their lonely, treacherous pilgrimage of faith?

Has baptism become the "stone of stumbling" rather than Christ Himself (I Cor. 1:23, Lk. 2:34), thus obscuring Christ's loving call for them and frightening people prematurely away? Are those who refuse baptism denying Christ even when they boldly and publicly witness to Him, as we observed in so many examples, in our survey (cf. II Tim. 1:8; 2:12)? Is it not the standing for right in society that the Scriptures set before us as the point of joyful acceptance of persecution (Mt. 5:9-12, I Peter 3:13ff) rather than baptism? Has baptism, therefore, in our social context been distorted into death-giving Law rather than life-giving Gospel (Rom. 7:9-lI, Gal. 3:21ff)? We must certainly be careful how we deal with baptism in our missiological situation, for it is a life-and death matter for millions.

How quickly we might slip into the "elder brother" attitude which Jesus condemns so strongly in His parables. If our Lord's love extends to those who fall into the degradation of pig-tending (Lk. 15:11-32), or if our younger brother says "no" publicly but then obeys privately (Mt. 21:28-31), or if we lead an exemplary life of self-sacrifice and all another does is repent wholeheartedly of the sin he is caught up in (Lk. 18:9-14), or if we sweat in the heat of the day without government privileges and without social status and yet our Lord rewards us equally with others whom we despised (Mt. 20:1ff), will we be offended at His generosity? Will we try to keep Jesus close to us and crowd out those seeking just to touch the edge of His cloak and be healed (Mt. 9:1-21)? Will we place burden on new converts so heavy that we ourselves could not bear them (Mt. 23:4, 13)[31]? Will we be the zealous "Judaizers" of the present age, unthinkingly imposing the tradition and culture of the mother church on the new converts (Gal. 31:1-7)?

Our Lord warns us in the church clearly and strongly that our role is not to judge. For when we judge, we really only "justify ourselves" before men, "but God knows your hearts; for what is exalted among men is an abomination in the sight of God" (Lk. 16:15). The Pharisees were the protectors of the letter of the Law, and our Lord fiercely condemned them for making their own "divine traditions" more sacred than the fundamental law of love from which every divine law must come (Mk. 7:9, Mt. 12:1-3, 23:23, Jn. 7:21-24.) If our evangelistic goal is only to make more church members, then Jesus' woe also is upon us; for we may make the convert only a new child of the law and "twice as much a child of hell" as ourselves (Mt. 23:14).

In such a situation our Lord must assure the non-baptised believers of today in the face of the church just as He assured His disciples in the face of the Pharisees:

> If they have called the master of the house Beelzebul, how much more will they malign those of his household. So have no fear of them; for nothing is covered that will not be revealed, or hidden that will not be known. What I tell you in the dark, utter in the light; and what you hear whispered proclaim upon the housetops (Mt. 10:25-26).

Will we judge unacceptable whom our Lord has accepted (Mk. 2:15-17)? If we in the safety and security of our Christian community judge harshly those outside the fold struggling in the thorns and brambles, it is almost certain that we in turn will be judged one day by them and by our common Lord.

Our Lord has said, "He to whom much has been given, of him shall much be required" (Lk. 12:48). To us in the church has been given all the riches of the Kingdom: the Word, Sacraments, fellowship, the assurance of baptism. To others in our fellowship of faith has been given temptation, opposition, oppression, ridicule, deprivation of spiritual nurture, misunderstanding within the faith and outside, and on and on. Would we add to their burden by arrogantly and self-righteously demanding that they vicariously demonstrate to us and to the world the superiority of our religion by leaving all to follow Christ (Mt. 19:27)?

A Responsibility to Serve Them in their Mission

Clearly our responsibility before our Lord is not to add to the burden of our brothers and sisters but to bring them all the support and strength that we possibly can. Doubtless, the expectation and judgement of our Lord is much greater upon us than upon them. He knows the conflict of their hearts, as He knew it in his first disciples during their hour of temptation: "The Spirit indeed is willing, but the flesh is weak" (Mt. 26.41). The call of the church is to bring the ministry of the Lord into the lives and hearts of His needy people. Let the non-baptised believers find in the priestly ministry of the church what Scripture affirms they will find in their Lord:

> We have not a high priest who is unable to sympathize with our weaknesses, but one who in every respect has been tempted as we are, yet without sinning. Let us then with confidence draw near to the throne of grace, that we may receive mercy and find grace to help in time of need. (Heb. 4:15-16)

Therefore, the call of the church is not to stand in judgement over against the non-baptised believers but to serve them. It may be that the non-baptised believer in some situations is considered a weaker, less committed, less informed person in the faith. Yet, he/she must be considered a brother/sister and treated as such:

> As for the man who is weak in faith, welcome him, but not for disputes over opinions. . . . for God has welcomed him. Who are you to pass judgement on the servant of another? It is before his own master that he stands or falls. And he will be upheld, for the Master is able to make him stand. (Rom. 14:1,3,4)

Our Lord has called us to receive those of child-like faith for "whoever receives one such child in my name, receives me" (Mt. 18:1-5).

Thus, we do not put any kind of "stumbling block of hindrance in the way of the brother" in his chosen path of faithfulness. In mutual respect and love we pursue only "what makes for peace and mutual upbuilding", concentrating on the essentials of "baptisma": that is, "peace and joy in the Holy Spirit," for "he who thus serves Christ is acceptable to God and approved by men"

(Rom. 14:13 17:19, cf. 15:4-7, II Cor. 1:24, Mt. 7:1-5, Gal. 6:4-5, I Cor. 4:4-5). Even though it may not be according to our traditional norms and customs, we humbly and joyfully acknowledge that "with men this is impossible, but for God nothing is impossible", that in the last analysis "many of the first will be last and the last first" (Mt. 19:23-30).

Our attitude also is not to compel all non-baptised believers to join the church. Joining the fellowship of the church is a Gospel privilege and blessing which is to be desired and sought. It may be that even after baptism they will feel called by God to remain aloof from the organisational life of the church. Their fellowship and responsibility may be primarily outside the church, like the Ethiopian eunuch who returned alone (Acts 8:39) and the formerly demon possessed man who was turned back by our Lord to rejoin his family and witness to God's deeds in his own community (Mk. 5:18-19).

However, even when non-baptised believers are outside the church, they are not outside our fellowship. A physical family will feel close bonds of love and concern and mutual help even though separated by miles and years, looking forward eagerly for the happy day when they can be reunited beyond all obstacles of human existence. Just so the church members feel unbreakable bonds of fellowship with their brothers and sisters in Christ in the spiritual family of God. We don't even have to see each other to be strengthened by each other's love, prayers, and faith.

Rather, we may even be proud and admiring toward our non-baptised brothers and sisters in Christ. We may rejoice in humility and repentance that God has been "able from these stones to raise up children to Abraham" because we have been unable to bear fruit (Mt. 3:9-10). He is harvesting where we could not sow (Mt.25:26), bringing growth where we don't even know (Mk. 3:26-29), sending His Spirit where we never could imagine (Jn. 3:6-8).

We may see these non-baptised believers as the forward troops in the battle for whose work all our resources in the church are actually intended. Our Lord did not take us from the world when he called us to Himself but to be with Him in the world (Jn. 17:15). In the families and communities of the non-baptised believers He wills to work with His "other sheep" to sanctify the children and husbands/wives (I Cor. 7:14), to convert them by words and deeds of exemplary love (I Peter 3:1-2), to go along the restricted highways and byways of society telling all along the path about the feast to which they are invited (Mt. 22:8-10). "So, brethren, in whatever state each was called, there let him remain with God" and present the Gospel-call (I Cor. 7:24). To the thousands of lonely "Naamans" among the non-baptised believers we also are called to affirm and send them in their difficult witness situations as Elisha did, saying "God in peace" (II Kings 5:19).

The attitude of the church is crucial to the missiological strength of the non-baptised believers. It is a basic psychological principle that we become what others say we are. If the church says the non-baptised believers are quasi-Christians or even deniers of Christ the expected missiological effect can only be uncertainty and discouragement among the front-line troops, If, on the other hand, the church affirms them in their faith and in their mission situation, they will rise to the occasion.

One pastor of the *Ezhava* caste told me how he started two new congregations by pastorally following up girls from his congregation who had to marry Hindus because of caste considerations. According to the church rules, he should have excommunicated them automatically; and we can be quite sure what would have become of these girls - and of this opportunity - as a consequence. However, when he affirmed them in their strategic location, they rose to the occasion and the Lord blessed their efforts, as He has always promised He would.

A MISSIOLOGICAL VIEW OF CASTE

Correcting the Caste Systems

Is it proper, like the pastor mentioned above, to foster and use caste ties in order to extend the reign of Christ? Or is caste to be rejected and bypassed as a diabolical work of Satan through and through?[32] To me, this issue is not primarily a strategic one but a theological one. Our approach to it must derive from our entire understanding of the purposes of God in history, as we shall see in the next chapter. It is a fundamental issue of faith-culture relationships in the Indian context which must be approached from a broader sociological perspective than the feelings of the Harijan and backward-caste Christian community.

When people loosely talk about working toward a "casteless society" in India, I wonder if they have conceived of the implications. As T. S. Eliot has pointed out, such social distinctions in a nation are the fertile milieu out of which its culture develops and perpetuates over the centuries.[33] The destruction of caste in India is the destruction of the well-springs of India's magnificent culture. Certainly that cannot be our Christian objective — or our national policy.

We must be clear, however, that the caste system is quite distinct from the oppression of the outcastes. As hard as Mahatma Gandhi fought against untouchability he also never rejected the basic caste social system but strained to gain a change of heart within the system. Untouchability certainly is diabolical. Even the hierarchizing of castes by birth rather than by talent and attainment is a corruption of the caste system which the most conservative Hindu leaders accept. Those who strive the hardest for the cultural rejuvenation of Hinduism, like the Arya Samaj and the RSS and the Sankaracharya of Kancheepuram are the ones who attack untouchability and caste-hierarchizing most vehemently. Certainly we must be one with them on this.

We must also be one with the government in seeking liberation from the social oppression of the caste system for Harijans through educational and economic advancement. The Nadar caste is an example of how economic advancement brings social prestige. Our cities also have gained a cosmopolitan character in regard to caste distinctions especially among the upper classes. Cross-caste marriages among people of higher education and income are increasingly common.

The other way out for the Harijan is through conversion to another religion. There is no doubt that the Harijan community in India is on the move today. Through education or economic advancement or conversion or just violent revolt they will set themselves free from the caste system in coming years, and we must certainly be with them in this God-willed struggle for dignity. However, the other point we must not lose sight of is that for eighty percent of India the caste system is not a source of oppression and dehumanisation but a foundation of security and self-respect.

We must also stand firmly against caste distinctions in our church organizational activities. High-caste and low-caste must not be seated on opposite sides of the church, enter by separate doors, or join at the Lord's Table separately, as is practiced in some Roman Catholic churches in village areas even today. I also do not agree with "reserved constituencies" for membership on the elders' council in congregations of mixed caste composition. Any pastor of whatever caste background must be acceptable to any congregation. We all know that what I am describing is not a conflict between Brahmin Christians and Harijan Christians but primarily between low-caste Christians of varied stripes, between Nadars and Harijans in southern Tamil Nadu and between Malas and Madigas in Andhra Pradesh and so on.

It has often been cited that the most caste-conscious society in India is the Christian community, so we have no reason to throw stones at anybody else. The church is called to be the community of the Kingdom, reflecting even now the glorious day when all peoples will sit together at the one Table of our Lord's Feast. Our firm self-expectation is that "in Christ there is no Jew or Greek." At the same time we are ready "to be a Jew to a Jew" in order that we might bring him to Christ.

Thus the missiological issue here is that of being "all things to all men". We must begin where people are at and work with them through the power of the Word where our Lord wants to take us. Because we are "free from all men" and all social distinctions in Christ we are also free to make ourselves "slave to all" becoming even as one under the law" that we "might win those under the law" (I Cor. 9:9-23). Our freedom from caste-feelings in Christ is exactly what enables us to deal sympathetically and evangelically with those under the law". If we ourselves are still "under the law" of caste-feelings, we will psychologically condemn in others the demon which we fear to confront in ourselves (Mt. 7:1). Our lack of charity and perspective on this issue is a sign of our lack of love and maturity in the mind of Christ.

Appreciating the Caste System

We have already seen how Paul approached these differences in ethical opinions on religio-social matters with an open mind. He felt that such matters should not be made a stumbling-block or point of offense in the church. Rather, all were to strive for a unity in the Spirit which enabled every member of the Body to "do nothing in selfishness or conceit, but in humility count others better than yourselves" (Ph. 2:1-3). Thus, there will be differences of opinions and background on these social issues as there are on political issues, and economic issues. No one is to be compelled against his conscience to accept another's or the majority's opinion. If he does he has violated the fundamental freedom and responsibility he has before God and, therefore, "is condemned", for "he does not act from faith; for whatever does not proceed from faith is sin" (Rom. 14:23).

It is striking how we in the church of India allow open debate and freedom of dissent on so many political and social issues but not on this one. We make no insistence, for example, that a wealthy convert give up his possessions in order to free himself from the grave social sin of perpetuating the gap between the rich and the poor in our society. Certainly such a church policy would have much more biblical precedent than making an issue of cultural matters (of Acts 4:32ff, Lk. 18:18ff. ev. 25). What is the difference between one being born into the social sin of caste hierarchy or the social sin of class hierarchy?

The answer, it seems to me, is that we in the church have viewed this matter from the perspective of the Harijan community. For those who have suffered centuries of social indignity, E.V.R. Periyar is right that "a person can endure an empty stomach, but he cannot endure the loss of his dignity." However, we must not forget that this is only one perspective on the caste issue.

Eighty-five percent of the society, including the tribals are quite content to maintain the caste system, even with its hierarchisation. The system provides everyone in it a basic self-identity, social group and economic security. Even in urban areas where class has become much more important in hierarchizing people than caste, marriages still follow caste lines to a great extent, as do political and economic groupings.[34] The basic lines of mutual trust and responsibility remain among fellow caste members, which is as true among those in the castes as it is among the tribals, the Harijans, the Muslims, and the Christian *quam*.

This strong, inviolable sense of family and social identity is what has provided the amazing resiliance and happiness of the Indian people throughout the fearsome turmoil and inequities they have faced in their national history, past and present, in my opinion[35]. How else can one account for the smiles on the faces of the hungry poor, the feeble elderly, the unemployed youth, the house-confined women? Everyone who has visited India leaves with the deep impression that this caste-ridden poverty-stricken country is actually happier than any egalitarian, wealthy Western country. Even the opponents of caste agree that the caste structure is the bedrock of the society. Is this all to be given up, or is it to be enriched and improved with the presence of Christ?

In addition, we must frankly recognise that when we speak of correcting social sins it involves more than a personal self-sacrifice. There is a qualitative difference between repenting of bad personal habits and repenting of caste or wealth or the dowry. All of one's family members and one's whole position in society are involved. Personal change is within the expectations and values of society, but social change is usually against the desires of those one holds most dear.

It has taken centuries for the church in the West even to recognise social sins (like slavery, racism, prejudice, poverty and status of women) much less to deal effectively with them. The church and the Christian community are fish swimming in the same water as anybody else in the society. History shows that attitudes and practices in the church change only as the total society changes.

It is, therefore, quite unfair to demand that a convert rise above his caste feelings and connections the moment he is baptised or as a qualification for baptism. It is all the more unfair when we recognise that the convert is taking baptism into a community which is as caste-conscious and caste-biased in practice as any other organisation in the country. Certainly we cannot responsibly excommunicate him/her if he/she takes a Hindu or Muslim husband/wife when the Christian community is unwilling to provide a spouse from their own families. When the church itself is struggling - rather unsuccessfully - against the cancer of casteism in its own body dare we judge or exclude those who suffer from the same disease?

The struggle is so difficult that even anti-caste reform movements within Hinduism today have been gradually molded into new caste-wise religious groups (e.g., The Lingayats in Karnataka and the Sri Narayana Guru sect in Kerala).

As every Indian will freely admit, "Caste is in our blood." With political, economic and educational developments in the country caste will certainly take on new forms - as it already has but it will remain the woof and warp of the society. If we want the direction and power of Christ to be an integral part of this development, we must see that He is there in the mind and hearts of all sections of the society.

Using the Caste System

We will never come to a proper missiological understanding of caste, until we distinguish between the social system and its religious context. Certainly the caste system has received a religious rationale under Brahmin influence. However, the system stands on its own sociological legs, irrespective of religious props given to it.[86] If the caste system is a religious system, we cannot use it in church work. If it is merely a social system, we not only may use but we ought to use it.

The early missionary analysis of the caste system was that it is a direct religious expression of Hinduism which must be opposed and removed. If they fought the caste system, they thought they were fighting Hinduism. If they could destroy allegiance to the caste system, they thought they could destroy the foundation of Hinduism. Besides the fact that such an unspiritual strategy of conversion is unchristian in its outlook, it has proven quite misconceived also in its results. The caste system continues in the allegiances and practices of the Indian whether he has rejected Hinduism or not. The system is followed for its social merits not for its religious rationale.[37]

Forrester in his fine historical survey of "Caste and Christianity" has documented how only a thin line of missionary opinion has adopted this more secular appreciation of the caste system. There was only a pocket of Lutheran missionaries in the Thanjavur area in the nineteenth century and later Bishop Heber and Max Mueller in the twentieth century. However, significantly, the national clergy evinced a much less aggressive attitude though they agreed that the caste system was wrong.[38] The western missionaries felt revulsion at the cultural sins they found in India, just as Indians are repulsed at the cultural sins (such as premarital sex, divorce, fragmented family life, materialism, etc) which they find in the West. However we each realise the deep social currents which produce such sinful manifestations in our own cultures, so we are more tolerant and patient. The caste system is a social system to be worked with and improved, not a religious system to be attacked and rejected.

Therefore, we should look upon the caste system positively, as the social system in India with which we are to work. Rather than try vainly to level the mountains, we should follow the river valleys in the society. Caste lines are the natural lines of communication and decision making. If we can affirm the integrity of tribal societies, we can affirm caste societies, for castes are really tribal groupings living side-by-side. This is the whole point of McGavran's detailed analysis in "Understanding the Church in India":

> In only twenty-nine of the more than three thousand ethnic groups of India (castes and tribes) do Christians form any considerable proportion of the total population... In more than 2900 castes and tribes there are practically no Christians at all. What few converts there are have been from any one of these have been forced out of their families and communities and the door locked and barred against normal intercourse... It will take special emissaries of the Cross - missionaries - largely Indian.... to establish congregations among them. Contextually sound evangelism is required. No conceivable amount of conversion by extraction will liberate these castes. Any converts from them will be simply purged out of the caste fabric, forming their tiny part of the existing conglomerate churches and leaving the 2900 people more adamant than ever against the Christian faith.[39]

Indeed, it has been caste lines which have proved the greatest assistance - rather than the greatest resistance - in evangelisation when properly utilised. Forrester points out in relation to the later mass movements to Christianity how the earlier missionaries' religious objection to the caste system had been not only theologically misconceived as well:

> Ironically in the light of later developments, they saw the maintenance of social links between converts and their Hindu caste-fellows as simply a standing invitation to apostasy rather than an evangelistic opportunity "the retention of Caste tends to keep up an intercourse with the heathen which is contrary to the plain Apostolic command, 'Come out from among them, and be ye separate, saith the Lord; and touch not the unclean thing."... A worldly spirit is thus gratified; dissimulation is practically promoted, and the road to apostasy is kept open".[40]

As long as this theologically and missiologically misconceived attitude persists, the church will be only three percent and "Churchless Christianity" much more. We want converts to come as groups, because we want to affirm them in their culture.[41]

What we need is creative, practical planning on how we can affirm the utility of the caste system without at the same time affirming untouchability or hierarchisation. McGavran has made several useful suggestions, one of which I have mentioned earlier. He has also suggested that we encourage house churches and multi-caste use of one church building with occasional joint services.[42] We might also consider a cadre of caste workers similar to the successful Zenana Mission workers among women. From our surveys and from our personal experience we know that truly spiritual evangelists of any caste are welcome in almost all Indian homes. As different denominations had once made geographical comity arrangements, we may want to do the same on a caste-wise basis, especially in rural areas. In towns and cities, nuclear families may come for baptism but in rural areas we can only expect it of caste groupings. We have yet to experiment seriously with secret baptisms.

However, we proceed with our experimental ministries, we should expect a healthy degree of diversity for many years to come. Isolated, private worship of Jesus in one's bedroom will exist side-by-side with house churches and regular church services. Many different approaches towards worshipping the one Lord of all can be encouraged and fostered. We will not judge these various approaches in terms of their relation to the caste system, for the social system is not really our interest. Our interest is that the seed be sown as widely and steadily as possible, and it will bear fruit in its own way.

Footnotes to Chapter Five

1. Subba Rao distinguishes between Christ and Christianity, calling the Christ of Christianity "The God of the untouchables" (similar to the Nayar woman in our survey who spoke of Jesus as "the God of the Nadars"). Subba Rao sees Christianity as just another religion which in fact obscures the radiance of Christ through rituals and "merchants of religion." Thus he feels his distinct call is to make the love and power of Christ available to all, quite separate from anything to do with the church. (cf. Kai Baago, ed., **The Movement around Subba Rao**, pp. 5-9). In this attitude toward the church Subba Rao stands in the company of the greatest Christian saint India has produced, Sadhu Sundar Singh:

   Narrow-minded Christians often do not consider those to be Christians who believe in Christ, if they have not publicly identified themselves with the Christian communities. I do not agree that they are right in not coming out openly, yet I have never been able to feel that they are not Christians. Among them are some whose service for Christ is far greater than any Christian workers. Especially is this so in places where it is difficult for Christian workers to go. (**With or Without Christ**, p. 25)

2. Roland Allen, **Missionary Methods, St. Paul's or Ours?**, pp. 1-21.

3. J. R. Chandran, "Baptism — a Scandal or a Challenge," **Religion and Society** (XIX: 1), p. 58.

4. Christopher Duraisingh, "Some Dominant Motifs in the New Testament Doctrine of Baptism." **Religion and Society**, (XIX: 1), p. 15; cf. T. V. Philip, "The Meaning of Baptism: a Historical Survey," ibid., pp. 19-20.

5. Henri Pirenne, **Muhammed and Charlemagne**, pp. 19-20.

6. cf. Phil Parshall, **New Paths in Muslim Evangelism**.

7. I would refer the reader to J. Paul Rajashekar's article in **Debate on Mission** and M. M. Thomas **"The Acknowledged Christ of the Indian Renaissance."**

8. Kai Baago details several earlier movements of the nineteenth century in Madras and Bengal; however, these organisations were short lived and local in impact. (**Pioneers of Indigenous Christianity**, pp. 1-11; Baago, **The Movement around Subba Rao**, pp. 1-2) These phenomena illustrate both the strength and weakness of the non-baptised response to Christ in Indian mission history. The strength is shown in the perennial development of non-baptised believer movements wherever the Gospel is preached. The weakness is shown in the ephemeral character of the movements because of lack of organisational structure.

9. Julian Saldanha, "Hindu Sensibilities toward Conversion," **NCC Review** (CII: 1), pp. 19—21.

10. Mahatma Gandhi spoke for most of caste-Hindu India when he observed according to Saldanha *(ibid.,* p. 19), that Christian Indians "completely cut themselves a drift from the nation in whose midst they live" and appear "almost ashamed of their birth, certainly of their ancestral religion, and of their ancestral dress;" thus, he "cuts himself off from his own people and begins to fancy himself a limb of the ruling class." Gandhi asks the question many are still asking: "Why should a man, even if he becomes a Christian, be torn from his surroundings?"

11. Quoted by Baago, **Pioneers of Indigenous Christianity**, pp. 82-83 (cf. also the essay by T.A. Kareem "My Experience as a Non-baptised Believer in Christ" in '**Debate on Mission**'. A couple of quotations from Sadhu Sundar Singh's contacts with non-baptised believers from with or without Christ during his evangelistic tours will further illustrate this prevalent attitude toward baptism into the church:

    "It would be better for me (a Muslim in Cairo) to drown myself in the Nile rather than that I should be baptised as a member of the Church, because the life of its members is often little better than that of the members of my old religion. What good would it be if I got out of the thorns to fall into the mud? It seems better that I should keep apart from them all and remain in touch with my Lord, that whenever and however I can, I may bear witness to Him. I fully believe that He will accept my work for him." (pp. 37-38)

    A landlord in the Punjab: "They have become European in all their ways, and are not one whit better morally and spiritually than my people here, but are, indeed, in some ways much worse. Besides this, I do not think that it is the Lord's will that I should move from here and go to them. Some of them are, no doubt, true Christians, but the majority of them are in no way better than non-Christians. It seems to me better to live on here and do what I can for the Lord according to my ability." And with tears in his eyes he added: "I have perfect assurance that if He were to come today, or if I were called at once into His presence, he would in no way cast me out." (p. 44).

12. pp. 126-31.

13. p. 219.

14. p. 197. Julian Saldanha confirms this description of sociological realities; "In India the various religious communities exist, or rather coexist, in watertight compartments, each governed by its own personal laws. Inheritance and succession, marriage, as also what pertains to the maintenance, guardianship and adoption of minors and dependents, are all comprised within the domain of personal law. The Christian community is governed by laws of European origin and inspiration. Conversion results in a switching over from one personal law to another and imports a shifting of one's allegiance from one social group to another. From this point of view, missionary activity appears to Hindus as a mode of communal aggression, a threat to the very existence of the Hindu community. Conversion, therefore, implies a change of one's social community with far reaching legal consequences... However, unlike other religions, Christianity as such does not claim any particular code of social conduct or personal law as being peculiarly its own. This creates the possibility for the Church to rise within Hinduism, without appearing as a rival social unit." (pp. 29-30).

This latter thought about the possibility of Christianity developing within Hinduism will be developed in the next chapter.

15. The radical Hindu RSS makes this point very forcibly and tellingly against the Christian church in arguing that baptism is not, in fact, a spiritual event but a political event, as practiced today (cf. "Dialogue with RSS" **Gurukul Perspective** of July, 1980, p. 5.) Therefore, they have successfully advocated for legal strictures against conversion to Christianity.

16. cf. the instructions of the Pope to all Roman Catholic missionaries in China back in 1659:

"Do not regard it as your task and do not bring any pressure to bear on the peoples, to change their manners, customs, and uses, unless they are evidently contrary to religion and sound morals. What could be more absurd than to transport France, Spain, Italy, or some other European country to China? Do not introduce all that to them, but only the faith, which does not despise or destroy the manners and customs of any people, always supposing that they are not evil, but rather wishes to see them preserved unharmed. It is the nature of men to love and treasure above everything else their own country and that which belongs to it; in consequence there is no stronger cause for alienation and hate than an attack on local customs especially when these go back to a venerable antiquity. This is more especially the case, when an attempt is made to introduce the customs of another people in the place of those which have been abolished. Do not draw invidious contrasts between the customs of the peoples and those of Europe; do your utmost to adapt yourself to them."(quoted by Stephen Neill, **Christian Missions**, p. 179).

17. cf. **Church-State-Society**, pp. 74ff.

18. cf. "Why Baptism after Conversion?" **Indian Missiological Review** (V: 1)

19. In more recent literature I would refer the reader to the articles in the March 1972 issue of **Religion and Society**, on the one hand, and, on the other hand, to the articles by James Bergquist in the July-September 1967 issue of **Indian Journal of Theology**, by Donald McGavran in the October-December 1982 issue of **Indian Church Growth Quarterly**, and by G. Rajendran in **Debate on Mission**.

20. James Bergquist, "Baptism in the Context of Christian Mission", **Indian Journal of Theology** (XVI: 3), p. 187.

21. Richard Taylor, "On Acknowledging the Lordship of Jesus Christ without Shifting Tents," **Religion and Society** (XIX: 1), p. 59.

22. Baago, **The Movement around Subba Rao**, p. 14.

23. cf. Bernard Lucas quoted by T.V. Philip in "The Meaning of Baptism," **Religion and Society** (XIX: 1), p. 28, and M. M. Thomas in his correspondence with Leslie Newbigin (*ibid.*, p. 89); also see Kenneth Cragg in **Call of the Minaret** (pp. 349—50) and Donald McGavran in "Six Door-Opening Actions," **Indian Church Growth Quarterly** (IV: 4), p. 244.)

24. M. M. Thomas, Introduction to **The Movement around Subba Rao**, p. iv.

25. Donald McGavran, "Six Door-Opening Actions," **Indian Church Growth Quarterly** (IV: 4) p. 243.

26. Introductory editorial in **Religion and Society** (XIX: 1), p. 4.

27. Even the most traditional and conservative confessions of the church maintain this same simple and clear definition of the church as the fellowship of those who hold faith in Christ and live in the gift of the Holy Spirit. (cf. Apology to the Augsburg Confession, VII: 5, 13, 20, 22). It is to such clear foundations that the adiaphora principle consistently drives us, as Paul Aithaus summarizes Luther's position:

    "If we can be baptised we should be; for we should not despise the sacrement of baptism. If baptism is, however, not available or if it is denied, we shall still be saved if we only believe the gospel. "For wherever the gospel is, there is also baptism and everything that a Christian man needs." This means, then, that baptism is only a special sealing of the gospel. In its content it is nothing else than the gospel itself and, accordingly, baptism is contained within the gospel. This means that the content of baptism is present and effective for faith even without the actual administration of baptism." (**The Theology of Martin Luther**, pp. 349-50).

28. Duraisingh, op. cit., pp.7-10.

29. "My Decision to Be Baptised," **Debate on Mission**, p. 373.

30. "The Christian Image in India," **Debate on Mission**, p. 302.

31. Donald McGavran in **How Churches Grow** (pp. 93-101) argues in this regard against what he terms the attitude of "perfectionism" in the church over against new converts. He concludes with the plea:

    "What saves? Is it disbelief in evil spirits?... Is it ability to... repeat the Catechism? Is it even obedience to the Christian moral code? Or is it faith in Christ? Is it an affirmation by man after man and community after community that Christ is Lord, a cry, "Lord, I believe, help Thou my unbelief?" The theological answer would be: Must we not accustom ourselves to the thought of very large populations of Christians, real Christians, whose standard of living, degree of belief in primitive science (magic), ability to read the Scriptures, and actual apprehension of the mind of Christ leave much room for improvement? Can we not count on the Holy Spirit to operate in their lives? So let them in. If they believe in Christ, belong to His Church and accept the Bible as their Scriptures, they are His. These are the multitudes God has called from the highways and the byways. That is why they have come. Who are you to deny entrance to those whom God has called? He will give them a new white robe. That is not your task. He will go with them. He will guard them and illumine them. And when it is His gracious pleasure He will call them home and judge them. All five replies warn against permitting the passion for perfection to deflect the church from discipling populations as they become ready for it."

32. cf. Hoefer, "Why Baptism after Conversion?" **in Indian Misslological Review** (V: I) for a theological framework in which this issue might be approached.

33. T. S. Eliot. **Christianity and Culture,** p. 139.

34. Victor E. W. Hayward, ed., **The Church as Christian Community,** p. 63.

35. cf. K. M. Panikkar, **Hindu Society at the Crossroads,** pp. 9ff.

36. *Ibid.,* pp. 128ff.

37. The Christian Nadar community is a good example of the fact of caste living dynamically without Hindu religious support. Our Gurukul Director Rev. J. G. Johnson has brought to my attention a small booklet published in Tamil by the Nadar Christian Welfare Association entitled "Caste and Christianity" in which the author, Mr. K. J. Roberts, attempts to provide Biblical proofs for the practice of the caste system.

38. Duncan B. Forrester, **Caste and Christianity,** p. 118.

39. Donald McGavran, **Understanding the Church In India,** pp. 28—29.

40. Forrester, op. cit., p. 71.

41. Parshall illustrates this approach from his experience with Muslims in Bangla Desh. He points out the familiar problem that a new convert through his baptism "has openly declared himself a traitor to Islamic social structures. political and legal systems, economic patterns; and, worst of all, the religion of his fathers has been profaned and desecrated. He has now become a worshipper of three gods, a follower of a corrupted religious book, an eater of pork, a drinker of wine, and a member of an alien society of war mongers and adulterers. There is, unfortunately, just enough semblance of truth in these accusations to render them almost impregnable. Individual baptisms of Muslim converts have almost always led to exclusion from one's own native society and inclusion in a foreign-influenced Christian community." (p. 190)

42. McGavran, **Understanding the Church in India,** pp. 116-17. The "house church" has a long and illustrious missiological history beginning from the first centuries of the church. Luther also had this to say as he rethought church structures in his day:

    "Those who seriously want to be Christians and to confess the gospel in deed and word ought to write themselves in by name and perhaps gather by themselves in a home for prayer, Scripture reading, Baptism, Holy Communion and other Christian exercises. In this kind of order one can know those who do not behave as Christians, punish them, reform them, cast them out or excommunicate them according to the rule of Christ (Mt. 18:15f). Here one could also impose common aims upon the Christians, which would be contributed willingly and distributed (II Cor. 9:1, 2, 12). One could hear a lot of grand singing there. In sum, once one has the people who seriously desire to be Christians, the orders and procedures could quickly be brought about. However, I cannot and may not yet order or establish such a fellowship, for I do not yet have the people for it. And I do not see many who are urgently seeking it." quoted by J. C. Hoekendijk, **The Church Inside Out,** p. 93, from Luther's Preface to the German Mass.

43. Forrester presents this view of Maynard which coincides well with the missiological approach offered by the non-baptised believers:

"The nature and vocation of the church had been subtly and significantly modified as a consequence of its largely falling victim, like earlier religious protests against caste, to re-absorption into the system". Maynard believes that within the Indian context becoming a Christian need not involve becoming part of an organised church which operates in such a caste-like way; indeed the most effective way of countering the caste-spirit would be to have Christians express Christian notions of brotherhood while remaining within their caste. This, he believes would be a far more effective road to the transformation of Indian society than constantly reiterated denunciations of the caste system. But the presupposition of this policy is a transformation of the church, which would give up its inherited structures and its caste-like organization in order to become "the fresh and living fellowship of those of every race and caste who love Christ and in His Spirit serve their fellow men." (pp. 143-44).

CHAPTER SIX

"Where is all this Leading?"

Outline:

A Missiological understanding of the Church

- New Missiological Church Structure
- New Missiological Church Nurture
- New Missiological Strategy

A Missiological vision for the Church

- Participation in all Cultural Life
- Development toward a "Christ-ized" Hindu Culture
- Integrated Fulfilment of All in Christ
- "Baptism" of Cultures in Christ

"Where is all this Leading?"

In chapter five, we asked some specific practical and theological questions. We tried to see the church's responsibilities over against the specific needs of the non-baptised believers. However, the implications for the church and its missiological thinking also are more far-reaching, I feel.

The facts around us compel us to rethink our whole understanding of the church's mission within the Kingdom. We have been confronted with the fact of God's activity in Christ far beyond the confines of the church, and we are driven back to Holy Scriptures to seek guidance in appreciating the implications. The consequence is that we are lifted above the limits of our institutional thinking to the expanses of the very vision of God for all history. Within this expansive vision and work of God the church must reset its own vision and work.

A Missiological Understanding of the Church

NEW MISSIOLOGICAL CHURCH STRUCTURES:

What is called for, then, is a more missiological understanding of the church and of its ministry. At present our church rules are oriented toward preservation of the flock, rather than toward extension of the flock. The requirement of marriage within the Christian community, the requirement of baptism publicly in a local congregation, the requirement of burial only for the baptised (whether they ever came to church and believed or not), the requirement of church membership for pastoral services, the requirement of church functions being conducted according to traditional (Western) forms, the requirement of participation in Holy Communion only for the baptised, the Protestant requirement of closed, unartistic, symbol-free church buildings, the requirement of Western worship gestures, the requirement of abandoning the use of *tilak* and *kolam,* etc. all should be rethought from the standpoint of facilitating the flow of the Gospel beyond the Christian community.

Theologically we must move away from the conception of the church as a ship intended to shelter its occupants from the temptations and struggles of life so that they can reach the heavenly shores safely (cf. I Peter 3:19-21). Such an image may be appropriate where the Christian faith is strongly rooted in the society. However, where the church is only a weak three percent and where "Churchless Christianity" is a scattering of believers throughout the society, the more common, missiological Scriptural images of yeast leavening the lump (Mt. 13:33), salt (Mt. 5:13), light in the darkness (Mt. 5:16), scattered seed (Mt. 13:3ff), weeds and wheat growing together (Mt. 13:24ff), lost sheep (Mt. 18:12-14, Jn. 10:1ff, Lk. 15:3-7), seed growing in the night (Mk. 4:26-29), uninvited guests to the banquet (Lk. 14:15ff), etc. would seem much more appropriate. On the basis of these images we should frame our theological understanding and organisational practices in the church.

Some rethinking along these lines has already taken place. I will illustrate a few of the ideas merely to stimulate more creative thinking and wider reading on this most-important matter facing the church. M. M. Thomas has suggested "Christ centred fellowships":

> There are independent churches in Africa which have faith in Christ but no sacraments and which have now been accepted into the fellowship of the World Council of Churches, hoping of course that they would grow into fuller plenitude along with other churches. The Church in India can extend into the religious and secular communities of India only if we are prepared to recognize partial formations of Christ-centred fellowships as valid beginnings of the form of church life itself in these communities. It is the only way in which the form of church life in India can be renewed. Otherwise the rigidity in the name of plenitude in a situation which is far from having plenitude will continue to pervert the church into a closed religious community.[1]

In another article Dr. Thomas proposes that the church organise itself as an "open fellowship" in order to express the New Humanity in Christ it is intended to represent.[2]

Richard Taylor has suggested the idea of "non-cultural koinonia". He refers to the historical precedents founded by Stanley Jones, Kagawa, and Kandaswami Chetty, and, he goes on to propose that the celebration of the Eucharist theologically must be established at the heart of such a fellowship in Christ: "I dare say that the Eucharist is the ultimate basis for this koinonia fellowship. Eucharist and fellowship go together, finally, for all of those who confess and believe."[3]

Abhishiktananda proposes in a footnote that a "Christian third order" be established in India along the pattern of those in Sudan and other countries of Africa. The purpose is "to provide spiritually for people who have felt the call of Christ but who are practically unable to abide by the commitments of baptised Christians or even regular catechumens." He bases this proposal on the policy of the Roman Catholic Church established in the "Decree on Missions" at the last Vatican Council:

> If in certain religions, groups of men are to be found who are kept away from embracing the Catholic faith because they cannot adapt themselves to the peculiar form which the church has taken on there, it is the desire of the Council that such a condition be provided for in a special way...[4]

Donald McGavran proposes home Bible study "congregations" who covenant to take baptism only when three thousand of their fellow-caste members accept Christ. In this way he anticipates that people of different castes from the church will feel less threatened in their ethnic identity by people accepting Christ. There will be less opposition and more freedom in the spread of the Gospel.[5]

The National Council of Churches at a consultation on "The Mission of the Church in the Context of India" at Narsapur in March 1966 and again at a consultation on "Baptism and Conversion in the Context of the Mission of the Church in India" at Ban galore in October 1982 took up this issue of more open church structures for serious consideration. The Narsapur Consultation identified the essential elements of the universal Church as Scripture, sacraments, ministry, fellowship of prayer, witness and service. But they also upheld that the church is not "to impose its whole traditional life upon the new convert" nor to demand that all the essential elements be present in order to accept any particular groups. The main point to be expected is that individuals and groups testify to what we understand as the Lord's will.[6]

The Bangalore Consultation in one of its yet-to-be published group reports went on to spell out how the church might relate creatively to such individuals and groups.

> Such people may be called by Christ to discpleship outside the immediate fellowship of the church, and we are not to stand in judgement on their level or style of commitment. Non-baptised believers in Christ may see it as their divine responsibility to maintain solidarity with their family and community in order to serve Christ's purposes there, rather than in the church community.
>
> Therefore, we in the church are called upon to develop new channels of fellowship which will mutually enrich both baptised and non-baptised disciples of Christ. At the level of our local congregations we must strive to establish fellowship and joint action with all who are serving Christ's purposes in the community. We need each other. We need to include all people in our prayers and intercessions. New public liturgies need to be developed which will incorporate all who are committed to Christ. Our Church buildings are to be kept open day and night so that they may truly become "a house of prayer for all people". Christian festivals are to be organised so that the whole community might participate. Christians are to participate in community festivals in all aspects possible. Thus we will both encourage and profit by what God is doing outside the church to bring about His Kingdom on earth, for it is to this that we are called in our baptism.

Finally, I will illustrate from the thinking of theologians of other contemporary cultural contexts that the need for opening church structures is felt not only in India but all over the world. Christianity has become a minority religion in almost every country of the world, and the prospects for the future indicate the same on an increasing basis.

Therefore, J. C. Hoekendijk argues that the church rules framed in the previous age of Christendom must be recast. "Exceptions out of the old books have become common facts of life." He quotes the statement of Lund back in 1952 accepting the need "to reexamine our practice in the light of the exceptions which are already customary". As the church looks forward to the prospect of being only 16% of the world population by the year 2000, "could it not be possible that our churches are 'houses in Egypt' that we must leave?" Even in the West a new, unprecedented situation must be confronted: "Are we ready to accept the dispersion; to accept the fact that so many have already drifted far away from home and can no longer be called back to the stately and static patterns?"[7]

A British missiologist, E. L. Allen, on the basis of his world-wide travels, concludes his study of the future relationship of Christianity to other world religions by proposing that the mission-minded Christian of the future

> be willing to receive into the fellowship of the church all who would confess Christ by name; indeed, he invites them to enter it. But he does not demand that all become Christians. For he knows that Christendom has so sadly misinterpreted Christ that he may draw some to himself within their own religions as he could not do by gaining them for ours.[8]

Similarly, the noted church theologian John Knox concludes his classic study on "The Church and the Reality of Christ" with these observations:

> I must not fail to recognize that the characteristic life of memory and the Spirit, in which to be a Christian is to share, has come down to us from the ancient past within the body of an actual human community which, in its wholeness or as a total body, is marked by certain historically created forms or structures without which it could not be the particular community it is. But I must also recognise that it is possible for an individual or a group to share in this life and to belong to this body without adequately acknowledging, in thought or practice, the structural elements which have actually given the body its character and the institutional forms through which the life has actually been conveyed to us.[9]

Kenneth Cragg, the noted Muslim missiologist, has recommended the formation of separate fellowships for unbaptised "lovers of Jesus". These believers in Christ would participate in "the fullest fellowship of the church" without in any way compromising "the theological truth about the final place and necessity of baptism."[10]

Therefore, we see the trend for radical rethinking on church structures which is being carried out around the world by theologians of all traditions and persuasions. We too must feel the encouragement and compulsion to move forward. What is called for is some boldness of experimentation on the local level, with the official support and evaluation of the church. In fact, we must come to expect such experiments of our pastors and evangelists, for we know that otherwise they can never carry out their God-given task. Let not the colleagues of the "de Nobilis" of our century do what they did to him in the sixteenth century.

NEW MISSIOLOGICAL CHURCH NURTURE

In specific then, what might we be called to do in the days ahead? In our basic self-conception, it seems to me, we are first of all called upon to recognise that we as the church are servants of the Kingdom. We are not the Kingdom of God. We are unworthy, privileged servants of the Kingdom, simply called to do our duty of service (Lk. 17:7-10) and to see that whatever our Master has entrusted to us brings good results (Mt. 25:14ff). As Murray Rogers has expressed it in his introductory summary of Abhishiktananda's appeal to "The Church in India"

> (The Church) is simply the poor and humble servant of the Lord whose witness, radiant with the Spirit, will bring all men to faith in Christ. It is her inner life, her experience of the Spirit of Christ her Lord, which she wants to share with everyone. All the external parts of her life exist simply to participate more deeply in and, I would add, to share more effectively the experience that Christ has himself in the life *of* the Father,[1.]

We are to feel our responsibility to the Kingdom more than our rights and privileges as a church. The proper understanding in our situation of the traditional phrase "Outside the Church no salvation" must be "Without the church no salvation". No doubt, this terminology is actually more correct, as Luther also interpreted it in his Large Catechism (II 45, 56) when he said that no one can come to the Lord Christ" without the church, for "outside this Christian church (that is, where the Gospel is not) there is no forgiveness"." Similarly, where the Gospel is believed and lived, there is forgiveness of sins and there is the church. There are many of Jesus' flock who are not of "this fold". Our responsibility is to affirm and serve them.

Our task is to share that life-giving Gospel, and trust that Christ will reign and form His church. It "exists in the Spirit" ("Es steht im Geist"). The Gospel alone is the "substance" of the Church, which "begets the believers, gathers them, and combines them into a supra-individual unity."[13] Thus, we in the organised church are to take up our divinely-given task "as servants of Christ and stewards of the mysteries of God" (I Cor. 4:1) in seeking all possible means of expressing the unity we have "in the Spirit" with all those "saints... who in every place call on the name of our Lord Jesus Christ, both their Lord and ours" (I Cor. 1:2) and in sharing with them in every possible way the treasures of the Gospel entrusted to us. Luther continues (in the Schwa-bach Articles):

> Such a church is nothing else than the believers in Christ who maintain, believe, and teach the above-mentioned articles and doctrines (i.e., the Trinity, deity of Christ, work of Christ, original sin) and suffer persecution and pain because of them."

It will be important for the church to share its inner experience and "mysteries" in a manner which is acceptable to those it seeks to reach. Most of the eighty percent of India around us feel no need for what we have to offer. They are quite proud of their own spiritual heritage, even if they have never drawn upon it seriously themselves. They know that this treasure is there and available to them whenever they might want to draw upon it. They see their saints and gurus all around who are living evidence of the truth of their religion's claims. Therefore, they can only receive in tolerant pity those who may approach them confident that they are offering a Christian treasure which surpasses anything they might have asked or dreamed of within their own heritage.[15]

Therefore, it is both foolish and beside the point to profess or "prove" the superiority of Christianity to our Hindu and Muslim neighbours. For every characteristic of our faith or of Jesus Christ which we may point out, others will most easily point out similar and even superior characteristics in their traditions and saints. "Superiority" is related to the criteria and examples one chooses to draw upon.

Rather, I would suggest that we boldly follow the lead of our non-baptised believer fellow-saints and accept in practice the "ishta devata" principle. We have illustrious evangelistic precedents for venturing forth in this way, provided by Elijah on Mount Hermon, by Daniel and his three friends in Babylon, and by St. Paul on the Areopagus. If we are truly convinced that the ascended Christ is "far above all rule and authority and power and dominion, and above every name that is named" (Eph. 1:21), then we can throw our Lord into the Hindu pantheon of gods with no hesitation or fear. We know He will emerge victorious if He is just allowed to enter the battle.

In this regard our brothers and sisters of the "Churchless Christianity" have shown much more insight and courage than many of us. They are convinced that Jesus' claims are true, and they are willing to risk their security in life before their relations and before their family gods. They have allowed their Lord to use them as the battlefield on which He will show His might, and almost all testify to the victory He is winning. Those pastors and evangelists who have similar courage to throw our Lord into the fight and to follow up the battles have been able to gather new recruits for our Lord's side. Are we disciples "of little faith" who fear to face the storm even though we know it will subside at a single word from His mouth (Mt. 8 :24ff)?

If we were boldly to take this as our evangelistic approach, we would certainly have to redraft our church structures and rules. I have already listed some of the areas where church rules would have to be rethought. In regard to structures, we would have to get in touch with the troops at the frontlines of the battle, as also suggested earlier, so that we could provide every assistance and encouragement for them, the fifty percent of non-baptised believers in Christ who have Christian relatives and the seventy-five percent who have had meaningful contact already with Christian individuals and families would have to be reached in these informal manners. We would have to develop special literature, broadcast special radio programmes, hold special mass meetings and retreats, widely distribute pictures of Jesus as well as Bibles as the non-baptised believers have already requested of us. Once we decide that this is where the battle must be fought, we will find countless means and opportunities to get our supplies to the battlefront.

We will keep our churches open from early morning to late night so that anyone can come to worship Jesus whenever and however he/she wishes. We will create a stimulating environment of Christian worship through meaningful art, symbols, and Bible verses. We will have a "priest" available at all times, especially in towns and cities, so that special prayers may be offered and inquiries answered at the "Christian temple". We will have festivals and Bible studies conducted as public occasions in public places. We will not object when village caste women want to worship separately like the Uttamapalayam Goundar women. Like one Andhra pastor I know, we will even be willing to pass Holy communion through a window in the house so that we can respect their social customs. The whole organisational structure of the church will be oriented toward the nurture of the much greater number of sheep "outside this fold".

Can we also make the strengthening sacramental life of the church more fully available to these "frontline troops"'? Theologically we must rethink our sacramental practices from a missiological standpoint. We have seen that some pastors are already giving the Lord's Supper to non-baptised believers. They come in sincerity of faith and desirous of spiritual strength, so on what basis are they to be denied from their Lord's Table? Can we leave the decision to local pastoral discretion?

Even if people come into our Lord's House and approach His Table from the back door, can we not welcome them? Even if they cannot participate in the power of the death and resurrection of Christ through the sacrament of baptism (Rom. 6:3-4), can we avail this same blessing to them through the Eucharist (I Cor. 10:16, 11:23ff, Jn. 6:51)? Should we prepare Jesus' "other sheep" for receiving the Lord's Supper first, and use this sacrament as a preparation for the other one? We have a lot of rethinking to do if we start thinking missiologically. We Protestants must also rethink our rejection of the ancient practices of private confession and anointing with oil. These sacramental practices may be of great spiritual strength to those who come to the fold from outside to hear their Master's voice and feel His loving hand.

It is a historical and sociological fact that no movement can survive for long without solidifying into some kind of institutional structure. The "Churchless Christianity" we have identified is so loosely structured that it can hardly even be called a movement. It is a spontaneous phenomenon of the Spirit. Therefore, it can quickly evaporate under intense pressure and heat or be slowly absorbed during years of stagnation, as we clearly saw in our rural interviews and urban statistics. It is the call of the church to protect and strengthen and stimulate this spontaneous development so that it actually becomes a movement. The church is absolutely necessary, as the supply lines are necessary to the front line and as the skeleton is to the flesh. The consolidation of this movement into Christ may be a century in the making. There will be much give and take and stress and strain in the process.

NEW MISSIOLOGICAL STRATEGY:

In addition to recognising where the battle must be fought, we must recognise how the battle is to be fought. Our non-baptised believers have already witnessed to us how they were convinced to join the Lord's side. They had to see His power before they could take the risk. We may wish that the preached Word was enough to be convincing, but we tend to forget that our Hindu and Muslim audience has good reasons for both doubting our claims and for believing the claims of their own leaders. Our Lord also did not only preach. He performed "mighty acts" which were signs of the Kingdom He presented to His contemporaries. Through these signs he "manifested his glory; and his disciples believed on him" (Jn. 2:11, Mk. 16:15ff).

There are those traditions in the church which have taken seriously the use of miracles in evangelism. However, most of us have not accepted the challenge of bringing Christ to our Hindu and Muslim neighbours in such a dramatic way. We have tried to wage the battle on fields where the opponent has not even placed His army. When we claim victory, therefore, they can only laugh at us, thinking that we know our Lord could never win on the same field with their gods. Our fine organisation, our fine institutions of service and education, our fine theological arguments, all are quite beside the point. The point at which we engage battle meaningfully is in the spiritual realm. Our neighbours know, as St. Paul did, that "we are not contending against flesh and blood, but against principalities, against the powers... against the spiritual hosts..." (Eph. 6:12).

For a spiritual battle we must use spiritual weapons. Rather than preach forgiveness of sin and hope of heaven, we can proclaim peace of mind and heart. In spite of the more otherworldly message we proclaimed, we found that our non-baptised believers and other Hindu and Muslim listeners actually heard a different message in their hearts. They heard a message of new spiritual life and strength. They brought Christ on to the battlefield where they wanted Him to win. They found the "peace of Christ" the "Shanti", they were seeking in vain elsewhere.

The non-baptised believers we met personally and through the statistics also brought Jesus' power into the field of their personal needs. They went to Him for healing of mind, emotions and body; and they emerged victorious through His strength. Convincing demonstration of spiritual power is seen in healing. If a god does not heal when appealed to, he either lacks the power or he lacks the love. When someone appeals to Jesus in his need and experiences healing, he knows that Jesus both has the power and cares for him personally. For a god may have the power and yet not care enough for the individual to use it on his behalf. Once a person is convinced through the experience of healing that Jesus has power and love for him personally, he is willing to take the risk and commit himself to his new Lord in spite of the threats and difficulties which may occur.[16]

A third arena of spiritual power is that of moral growth. We found throughout our research that many in "Churchless Christianity" had found in Christ new strength for leading a better moral and ethical life. Such a life is "written on their hearts" (Rom. 2:14), and they seek the spiritual power to fulfill this inner longing. No doubt, the deep impression made on them by Christian individuals and families arose from the living demonstration of this spiritual power. Cleansing of the mind and heart is the first stage in any spiritual progress according to all the schools of Hindu philosophy, so it is not surprising that so many would turn to Christ with this spiritual need first. They can testify that He has won the battle over the evil forces in their inner life.

A fourth place where Jesus' power and love is to be experienced is in miraculous visions and dreams. Much scientific research has been carried on in recent years re-establishing the legitimacy of such spiritual experience. In our Indian context, however, the reality — and almost the necessity — of such spiritual experience has always been popularly heard. Once again, it is through such an experience that one can become convinced that Jesus is God "for me". Even now a movement among Saiva Siddhanta Lingayatsis reported now in Karnataka based almost wholly on a series of visions of Christ.

Finally, we know that the final test for the validity of Christ's claim is if He can lead to true God-realisation. Every Hindu is convinced that such a spiritual victory is not only possible but expected in any real religious life. The popular disgust with Christians and with our clergy arises from the observation that this great and fundamental spiritual goal seems to have no compelling attraction in spite of our claims for the power of Christ. As one RSS member of our Gurukul dialogue put it to us: "If you really had spiritual life in you, you wouldn't have to come after us. We would flock to you".[17] When we show Christ's victorious power in this arena, we will have won the battle.

It is in these areas that we have heard the witness to Christ outside the church throughout mission history in India. This is the testimony throughout the pages of M. M. Thomas' "The Acknowledged Christ of Hinduism". It is the testimony of the great Sadhu Sundar Singh who made clear that his vision of Christ brought not an awareness of forgiveness or heaven into his life, but a realisation of the spiritual and ethical yearning which his pious mother had implanted in his heart: "Even if the Bible were to disappear, no one could take away my peace; I would still have my Christ."[18]

Subba Rao also, more recently, professed to the same spiritual realisation through his vision of Christ. He professed Christ as the one way for man to his vision of Christ. He professed Christ as the one way for man to attain the attitude of selflessness which can unite one with the Eternal Spirit and enable one to "live for others and be a Christ." He himself healed thousands during his life, and he professed that the same gift of spiritual peace and power is available to any who sought it of Jesus with a pure heart.[19]

It is clear that the arena where the victory of Christ is expected is that of demonstrated spiritual power. Therefore, we will direct people to seek Christ in these needs. We will hold evening healing services as a regular part of our monthly schedule, inviting all to come with whatever needs they may have. We will visit the sick and distressed in whatever house they may be in order to pray with them in Christ's name for His spiritual power in their lives. We will train our clergy and evangelists in exorcism. We will choose young men and women of serious spiritual character for greater training, and only such persons will be used for presenting and representing the Gospel in the larger community. They will demonstrate and preach the renewing spiritual power of Christ reigning in our minds and hearts.

We have also seen in the course of our inquiries among non-baptised believers and other Hindus and Muslims that the influence of our school and hospital workers can be considerable. Once again, it depends on the spiritual quality they bring to their ordinary tasks. We have found many people being deeply moved by their contacts with Christian teachers and doctors and nurses. When we appoint and train people for such ministries, we must keep this primary spiritual dimension of their work in mind. They must give their medicine and treatment with prayer.

Similarly, we must encourage our teachers to assume their role as spiritual "gurus" among their students. Many people of high caste and class are reached only through our schools in both rural and urban Tamil Nadu. Many non-baptised believers, no doubt, look back upon some teacher as the representative of Christ in his life. Our teachers must keep up these spiritual ties with their former students. Our schools must organise a follow-up ministry through newsletters, annual functions and class reunions, whereby the experience of Christ among former students is recalled and deepened.

In all these ways we are simply trying to be faithful to the responsibility of sowing and nurturing which our Lord has entrusted to us. One will water the sprout from the seed which another has sown, confident that in His own time and way God will bring the increase and the fruit (I Cor. 3:6). Our situation before the fact of the increase of "Churchless Christianity" all around us is like that of the man who awoke to find in amazement that the seed he had scattered had grown in the night to full fruit, and "he does not know how it happened" (Mk. 4:26-29). The facts around us encourage us all the more to have confidence in the inherent power of the Word of God to bring to life and to keep alive so that God can reap His harvest (Mt. 13:23, 30).

We will continue to encourage individuals and groups to come to Christ and to His church through baptism. However, we will also encourage individuals and groups to come without baptism. Our concern is not to question how the spirit leads them on this point — though we hope and pray that as many as possible can enter the fullness of God's good gifts through the fellowship of the church. Our concern and call is to feed all with the call and strength of God's Word for a life of powerful witness to His Name.

A Missiological Vision for the Church

PARTICIPATION IN ALL CULTURAL LIFE:

This attitude of openness to do battle with the "principalities and powers" will also influence our attitude toward involvement in India's general social life. Rather than seeking to withdraw ourselves in order to avoid temptations, syncretism, and losses we would send our people forth into general society armed "in the strength of His might" and thus "able to stand against the wiles of the devil" (Eph. 6:10-11). Such an approach would change not only our mission strategy but our whole Christian style of life and content of worship.

In regard to our involvement in the religious life of the society, we would take the lead from our non-baptised believers in Christ. We have found that they involve themselves fully in the social aspects of the family and community festivals, but they publicly withdraw when the religious aspects take place. Their attitude is noted and respected. They involve themselves for the sake of showing social solidarity just as we do when attending a Hindu or Muslim wedding, which is also a religious festival.

Why cannot we all show our social solidarity in this way also at Pongal and Deepavali? Once we respectfully involve ourselves in others' religious life, we can respectfully also invite them to join in ours. Confident in the Spirit of Christ among us, we have nothing to lose and everything to gain.

Once we stand in the strength of our own spiritual tradition, we will also not be threatened by the good we find in others. We will not need to highlight the weaknesses and faults in other religions in order to feel confident and proud in our own. We found among many of the non-baptised believers, as well as among many converts, a deep experience of Christ out of which they could relate to others with inner authority. They can share Christ with joy and enthusiasm because they know what they have found in His peace and power. Such believers do not need a command to witness for Christ. Witnessing proceeds from their life naturally and freely. They know of Christ's victory in their personal lives, so they have only a positive witness to give.

Because of this fulfilling experience in Christ, such new believers in Christ do not feel it necessary to reject everything of their past. One missionary in Sri Lanka told about a group of Buddhist converts who were meeting for the last time before they would together take baptism the next day. One of the members of the group told with joy how he planned to go to the Buddhist temple that evening for one last time. When asked why he would do that just before his baptism, he said, "I want to say thanks to God for all I have received through being a Buddhist." He felt that he had been led through the goodness of Buddhism to seek the Source of all goodness in Christ, and for that he could only be thankful.

This is what baptism should be. However, all too often it has been used by the church as a means of cutting a person off from his cultural heritage, not only spiritually but emotionally and socially also. At the same RSS dialogue referred to previously, one participant rightly asked us why it is that someone who has accepted Christ and His love should so often turn with such hatred toward his own family and society.[20] By their hesitation over baptism, our non-baptised fellow believers-in-Christ should be reminding us of the theological meaning this sacrament of fulfillment should have.

Once we regain this sense of spiritual continuity in conversion, we will also be less suspicious of continuity of "Hindu" worship forms. We had noted throughout our study of the non-baptised believers how they tended to carry on with their worship of Christ in the same manner as they had previously worshipped their other gods. If we accept the "ishta devata" are as the proper battlefield for our Lord to gain His victory, we will accept that the puja room and the picture and pilgrimage are the proper forms for this battle to take place. Already the Hindu style of the Syrian Orthodox community around Kottayam and the Muslim style of the new Mappila convert community around Malappuram give us a sign as to how things might eventually develop.

As we have almost unquestioningly taken over many of the superstitious and Hindu worship forms in our wedding ceremonies (e.g., the "rahukalam", "muhurtha nall" wedding months, astrology, noise at tieing of tali, dowry, nagaswara, etc.) why should we not give the freedom for Jesus' other sheep to do the same with their regular Christian worship? Often we church Christians react more emotionally to deviations from our established patterns of worship than to deviations from our traditional theology. We should let the non-baptised believers shave their heads at times of repentance and vows, wear their thread, keep their friends, take cremation at death, and in general maintain every cultural tradition possible.

DEVELOPMENT TOWARD A "CHRIST-IZED" HINDU CULTURE:

We will eventually look to our non-baptised believers to provide leadership in developing a truly indigenous form of Christianity in the country. To us the Western worship forms and organisational structures have become indigenous. However, the NBBCs are still in the old forms and can freely and creatively experiment, even together with their relatives of other religions.

At issue there is really a matter of fundamental mentality, not merely a change of candles to oil lamps. The forms of Christian worship are drawn from the semitic cultural background with its emphasis upon corporate worship, covenant commitment to the group, social ethics, political protest, the prophet and the king. In this basic religious mentality we share, of course, with the Jews and Muslims as well. However, the religious mentality of India and of our non-baptised believers is individualistic, devotion-oriented, monastic, prayerful, and experiential.

Thus, Buddhism, Jainism and Hinduism have a basically different religious mentality than the religions derived from Judaism. Although Indian Christianity shares some of the tendencies of its religious environment, as we noted in our survey statistics, the push of the Christian Scriptures and teaching is in the semitic direction. Can Christianity really be absorbed into this totally different religio-cultural environment?

Certainly, it cannot be done by the church, but it has already begun among the non-baptised believers as we have seen in our survey and as Kai Baago has described in Subba Rao's theology.[21] I also consider the reason for Sadhu Sundar Singh achieving a truly indigenous theology is the fact that he grew up in a Hindu environment and had only a minimum of theological training.[22] Christianity grew out of Judaism because Christ was incarnated there. However, when He is "grafted into" a totally new tree, we must only expect a new hybrid, a Church of Gentile customs and a theology of Gnostic and mystical ideas. Only then will Christ "of whom and to whom and through whom are all things," be "all in all" among the varying cultures of the world (Rom. 11:20-24, 36).

I disagree therefore, with those who hold the church to blame for lack of progress in developing indigenous church forms. When people hold up the example of how European Christianity absorbed forms from local religions, we must remind them that this took place only when Christianity had become the dominant religion. In our Indian context, however, the church is a very small minority which must struggle against absorption into Hinduism. We are well reminded that only Islam with its strong sense of separate identity has been able to withstand the smothering embrace of Hinduism.

However, some might argue that this is just the danger with the "ishta devata" strategy I am proposing. It will lead not to an indigenous Christianity but to a Christianised Hinduism. Perhaps more accurately we should say a "Christ-ized" Hinduism. I would suggest that really both are the same, and therefore we should not worry about it. We do not want to change the culture or the religious genius of India. We simply want to bring Christ and His Gospel into the centre of it.

We are not interested in proselytization but in evangelisation. Already we have found that Hindus of all education levels welcome Christ to enter Hinduism in this way. One RSS member with whom I discussed this view point agreed wholeheartedly. We should eagerly and confidently accept the invitation, encouraging and supporting our non-baptised believers as they serve in the frontlines of this open battlefield.

As the penetration of Christ into the heart of Hinduism takes place, we will see the demonstration of Jesus' illustrations of yeast, salt, seed, etc. The society will be uplifted and transformed from within. It will gain the new heart for which Gandhi longed. It will gain the transformed caste system for which the *Arya Sama;* is trying. It will gain the spirit of social service which the non-baptised believers are already experiencing.

We look forward to a wonderful cross-fertilisation of prophetic social involvement and personal spiritual maturity; intensity without attachment. However, we must recognize that this high goal can only be reached by entering the society where it wills to be helped. Once Christ is in the mainstream, He will permeate all and work toward a new social, political and economic order.

On our part, it will be essential that we recognize which traditional church practices are proving an embarrassment to the frontline troops. It may be, for example, that we can make a gesture in expression of our affirmation of Hindu religion and culture by ceasing to insist on a change of name at a convert's baptism. We may take a more missiological look at our opposition to certain Hindu cultural practices like the *Tilak* and the intra-caste marriage. However, the real move toward an indigenous Christian faith can never come from the Christian community. It must grow out of the "Churchless Christianity", with the help and encouragement of the church.

INTEGRATED FULFILLMENT OF ALL IN CHRIST:

As part of this move toward a Christ-ized Hinduism, our theologians must do some serious work at integrating the insight of other religions into Christian thought. As we seek to assert the place of Christ in Hinduism and Islam and Buddhist so must we find a place theologically for Krishna, Muhammad and the Buddha. God has done great things through these major figures of religious history. We must not only acknowledge the contributions which these figures have made; we must make them part of our Christian tradition. Only in this way will Christianity truly be the universal religion we claim it to be.

In Christianity every religious seeker must find an integrating fulfillment. We can be sure that as things now stand only a scattered few will embrace the narrow tradition which Christianity represents. The cultural difference is much too great. However, if we present Christ as "the Alpha and Omega" (Rev. 22:13) as He through whom and in whom all things were created so that "in Him all things hold together" (Col. 1:16-17), as the "true light that enlightens every man" (Jn. 1:9), then all spiritual goodness must be understood in some way to proceed from Him and lead to Him (James 1:17).

This will be the theological Christianisation of the "ishta devata" principle. It will be the theological recognition that Christ as Source, Goal and Judge is above every religion, including the Christian religion. It will find the proper place of the historical church in the total Kingdom of God.

Together with knowledgeable and sympathetic converts from these various religions we must work out a kind of "salvation history" within the context of each religio-cultural tradition. Of course, the Incarnation of our Lord into the salvation history of the Jews is a historical fact which makes that history of universal relevance. However, we also know from Scripture that God "has not left himself without witness", even to the extent of saying that the revelation of God in every culture leaves every person "without excuse" (Rom. 1:19-20). Paul could even quote authoritatively from other religious scriptures where he found true insight into our situation before God (Acts 17:28). It is clear in Scripture that God does not despise the searching after Him in other religions (Mal. 1:11, Acts 17:27, 14:16-17). Therefore, we have every theological basis for venturing a fulfilling integration of Christ into the various religio-cultural traditions of our uniting world community.

Our goal is that people of every religion and culture come to see in Christ the necessary affirmation and correction of all they have been striving for. Some scholarly Muslim converts testify that it was the high portrayal of Jesus within their own Koran which led them to investigate more about Him. What Raimundo Panikkar has tried to do in his various books for the Hindu tradition, we must try to do — inspite of the many inevitable mistakes and misunderstandings — for every tradition. The Hindu extends the "ishta devata" principle to assert that all rivers eventually empty into the same ocean. We might assert and demonstrate that this insight is true, if applied to Christ.

"BAPTISM" OF CULTURES IN CHRIST:

Unlike either Hinduism or Islam, Christianity is a culture-free religion. As I have tried to demonstrate in another unpublished paper, the whole ministry of Jesus can be portrayed as a reaction against the ethnicisation of God's covenant with humankind through the children of Abraham (Gen. 12:3). St. Paul correctly caught the essence of this revolt and led the fight against Christianity being tied to any one cultural form.

Jesus gave only the culture-free "new commandment that you love one another" (Jn. 13:34), and Paul insisted that no one judge anyone else as to how that should be carried out. He only insisted that we live so as to show the fruit of the Spirit in our lives through "love, joy, peace, patience..." (Gal. 5:23-24). Thus the Christian ethic is one derived from no culture and yet applicable to all cultures. It judges all cultures and enriches all cultures.

In Africa the ethic of Christian love may be well expressed through polygamy. Among the tribals of Orissa the ethic of Christian love may be well expressed through the annual "mela" in which everyone goes into a drunken brawl but after which all grievances and tensions of the past year are forgotten. In India the ethic of Christian love may be well expressed through caste and family solidarity. In Indonesia we have Christian "adat" and in Africa we have Christian tribal cults. As different as the conservative church at Jerusalem was from the charismatic church at Corinth, so different is the Indonesian Christian "adat" from the African Christian tribal cults. Each expression of devotion to Christ and His Gospel call is as distinctive as the culture in which it sets root.

Only in these diverse and contradictory ways can and should Christianity be the universal religion Christ intended it to be.[3] Even within traditional Christendom the differences between the Quaker, the Pentecostal, the Baptist, the Roman Catholic and the Greek and Russian Orthodox are much more than theological. These are different mentalities, arising out of different cultural histories. Yet, all are one in devotion to Christ. For the ultimate vision is not of one triumphant church but one triumphant Christ. To Him "men/women may bring... the wealth of the nations" (Is. 6:11) with their radically different value systems, organisational structures, styles of living, religious mentalities, cultural expressions, and concepts of human fulfillment.

Our evangelistic goal is not to change any of this "wealth of the nations" but to direct it even now to the Source and Goal who must guide and enrich it to its peculiar fulfillment in Him. The people who receive Christ into their cultural home will decide how He must best feel at home there. If we impose any of our own cultural values upon them in the name of Christ, they must strongly and rightly resist. For it is the "glory of God" and "the lamp" of the lamb which shall provide the light and "by its light shall the nations walk and the kings of the earth shall bring their glory into it" (Rev. 21:23, 24).

"The Kingdom of the world" is to "become the kingdom of our Lord and of His Christ" (Rev. 11:15). Therefore, even now we know that it is God's intention to make the men and women who have been ransomed by the blood of the Lamb "from every tribe and tongue and people and nation" into "a kingdom and priests to our God" to "reign on earth" (Rev. 5:9-10). For even now the ascended Christ is not confined to any heaven but fills "all things" (Eph. 1:23; 4:10); He "is all, and in all" (Col. 3:11).

The Great Commission our Lord gave his disciples was to "disciple all the nations, baptising them" (Mt. 28:19). The total vision we get from Scripture for our task is that of baptismally immersing the nations, the cultures, the "jatis" of the world in the Spirit of Christ so that each peculiar pattern of society on earth may be soaked and permeated with the mind of Christ. Our goal is "baptisma", confrontation with Christ which leads to repentance and renewal for all in whatever way possible. Then each people in their own way and form will glorify God and fulfil God's will of love for them, both now and forever.

Our strategy and implementation of mission must be as comprehensive and long-term as the plan of God "set forth in Christ... before the foundation of the world... to unite all things in him, things in heaven and things on earth" (Eph. 1:10-11). The end looks farther off than ever as Christians decrease to only 16% of the population, and the nations and their cultures are as untouched by Christ as ever (Mt. 23:14).

So often our mission work is motivated by an immature urgency. We win the one in a way which turns away thousands. We thoughtlessly view conversion as merely a religious matter, whereas in fact it is just as much a cultural, economic and social and political matter for the individual, for the church, and for the whole society. God is spirit, but yet not merely spiritual. The "mystery of God's will" is the restoration of the whole good creation which has fallen under the chaos and perversion of sin. His goal, as we know from Scripture, is not a spiritual salvation but a physically "new creation" in which "the perishable puts on the imperishable" (I Cor. 15:54) and a "new Jerusalem" appears in which "the dwelling of God is with men" and women (Rev. 21:2).

Therefore, even now our vision of mission aims toward that final renewal of all things "groaning in travail until now" and awaiting "with eager longing" for the day when, together with the sons of God, "the creation itself will be set free from its bondage to decay and obtain the glorious liberty of the children of God" (Rom. 8:19-23). The overall image of God in Scripture is that of King, the one who inspires and guides every activity of humanity, who is more interested in social justice and righteousness than He is in spiritual songs and solemn assemblies (Amos 5:21-24), who sends His Spirit upon people of Judah *and* people of Tyre to fill them "with ability, with intelligence, with knowledge, and with all craftsmanship" (Ex. 35:31, I Kg. 7:14) to build a house suitable to the glory of the Lord and to the dignity of man/woman created in Gods image. God rejoices in the goodness of His creation like an artist stepping back and looking upon the beauty of his finished piece (Gen. 1:31).

It is no surprise, then, that He continues to lovingly care for all nations, "satisfying them with food and gladness" even while He allowed them "to walk in their own ways" (Acts 14:16-17). He is the one who continued to lovingly give all men and women, life and breath and everything" as He did at first to Adam and Eve in the garden so that He might fellowship with them in love as they gratefully "seek God in the hope that they might feel after him and find him" (Acts 17:25-27), as philosophers and poets of all nations have testified (Acts 17:28). When the love and on-going creativity of God reaches out redemptively to all the cultural life of humanity, can we reach out with any lesser vision?

All the nations, each in its own peculiar way, are to know the Christ "in whom we live and move and have our being" (Acts 17:28), for He "is all and in all" (Col. 3:11). The will of the Creator to restore to Himself all that He has created throughout history is clear, and we are to serve that will:

> On this mountain the Lord of hosts will make for all peoples a feast of fat things, a feast of wine on the lees, of fat things full of marrow, of wine on the lees well refined. And he will destroy on this mountain the covering that is cast over all the peoples, the veil that is spread over all the nations. (Is. 25:6-7; cf: Mt. 8:11, 26:28).

This is the vision with which our Lord inspires and guides us in Holy Scripture. This is the vision to which the "Churchless Christianity" around us serves as a sign and invitation. Our Lord is working now, all around us, to fulfill His redemptive vision. Will we accept the privilege of working with Him?

Footnotes to Chapter Six

N.B.: The footnotes to this chapter were lost during the long delay in publication. I have managed to recover most of the citations, but not the additional commentary.

1. "Baptism, the Church and Koinonia", **Religion and Society** (March, 1972, Vol. 19. no. 1), p. 74.

2. "The Open Church", **The Church: A People's Movement** (NCCI, Nagpur: 1975), pp. 62ff.

3. "On Acknowledging the Lordship of Christ without Shifting Tents", **Religion and Society** (March, 1972, vol. 19, no. 1), p. 67.

4. **The Church in India** (Christian Literature Society, Madras: 1969), p. 77.

5. "Six Door-Opening Actions", **India Church Growth Quarterly** (Oct. - Dec., 1982), p. 245.

6. **Findings** (National Council of Churches, Nagpur: 1983), p. 12. The Bangalore Consultation material is published in **A Call to Discipleship: Baptism and Conversion,** Godwin R. Singh, ed. (ISPCK, Delhi: 1985).

7. **The Church Inside Out** (SCM Press, London: 1964), pp. 183—84.

8. **Christianity among the Religions** (Beacon Press, Boston: 1960), p. 155.

9. **The Church and the Reality of** Christ (Harper & Row, New York: 1962) p. 145.

10. **The Call of the Minaret** (Oxford University Press, New York: 1962), p. 350.

11. **The Church in India,** p. vii. See also Abhishiktananda's article in **The Indian Journal of Theology** issue of July-Sept., 1977 (vol. 16, no. 3), pp. 189—203.

12. **The Book of Concord,** Theodore G. Tappert, ed. (Muhlenberg Press, Phildelaphia: 1959) pp. 416, 418.

16. See, e.g., the life story and reports of Sr. Sesharatnamma in **Pathway to Heaven** (Suvisha Ashram, Bangalore: 1987).

17. "Gurukul Perspective" (July, 1980, no. 19), p. 6.

18. Heiler, The Gospel of Sadhu Sundar Siagh **(Allen & Unwin, London), p. 156.**

19. Kai Baago, **The Movement around Subba Rao** (Christian Literature Society Madras: 1968), pp. 13ff.

20. "Gurukul Perspective" (July, 1980, no. 19), p. 5.

SECTION FOUR

Further Reflections for the Year 2001 Edition

CHAPTER SEVEN

"Follow-Up Reflections on Churchless Christianity"

If you could envision an India won for Christ, what would its religious life be like?

Returning from a recent trip to India, the author of the astounding study Churchless Christianity offers here some summary remarks. They seem wistful—perhaps at first glance, hopelessly ideal or even totally wrongheaded and dangerous.

To read this is like listening in as Paul, in Acts 15, is accorded breathtaking freedom for his Gentile followers—who were not converting to Judaism. Is this really parallel?

Do India's billion need to be Westernized completely to accept Jesus Christ as Lord and the Bible as God's word? Are there really more "non-baptized believers in Christ" in Madras than formal Christians? Are we keeping up with what God is doing? If not, what do we do?

— *Ralph Winter*

Follow-Up Reflections on Churchless Christianity

"DO YOU THINK the vast majority of India will ever join the church?"

"If you could envision an India won for Christ, what would its religious life be like?"

These are the two questions that I've been asking as I have traveled in circles of Christians and non-baptized believers in Christ over the past few months in India.

I have not met anyone who responded affirmatively to the first question. There's an overwhelming recognition that the Western-structured church is basically incompatible with the culture of the nation. I should point out that my question always applies to the institutional (small "c") church. The second question implies my hope and prayer that the Church as the Body of Christ will by God's grace pervade the whole land one day.

Many issues impinge on these two questions. I have found it helpful to divide the matter into two basic topics: spiritual authenticity and cultural forms.

The Issue of Spiritual Authenticity

REACTION TO "FOREIGN" RELIGION

Spiritual authenticity is the critical issue in the Indian mentality. It's the issue that lies behind the guru-principle in Hinduism. It is also one of the dissatisfactions with the Western style of training and appointing spiritual leaders for a congregation.

In all my years in India, I have never heard any disparaging comments regarding my ministry because I am a foreigner, even a representative of past colonial oppression. The people of India look only for one thing in religious leaders: spiritual authenticity. They don't care about the nationality or even the caste (witness, for example, the high-caste following of many mass rally lay preachers) at this point. They will go where they find God's presence.

Another evidence of this principle has been the widespread response to Mrs. Gladys Staines' wonderful witness following the cruel murder of her husband and two sons in northern Orissa. Many Hindu religious leaders and the general public are deeply suspicious and resentful of Christian evangelistic work, especially among the tribals. They feel we go after the "easy prey" among the poor and ignorant and entice them with money and promises. However, all those deep-seated feelings were immediately put aside when they heard this grieving Westerner speak. For example, there was this letter to the editor in the January 28, 1999, issue of the national daily newspaper, *The Hindu*:

> Mrs. Gladys Staines proved to be a true Christian when she said those who were responsible for the death of her husband should be forgiven as it was the will of God. She is an example of divinity in a human being.
>
> We do not come into this world of our own will nor can we postpone death as we wish. Mrs. Staines also proved to be a realized soul when she expressed her satisfaction and gratitude to God for giving that long span of life to her husband to serve the people. All Hindus should take note of divinity in this great Christian woman. —A.V. Hanumantha Rao, Chennai

The issue of baptism is directly related to the issue of spiritual authenticity. Where there is spiritual authenticity, there is no objection to baptism (see the great Hindu philosopher T.M.P. Mahadevan's remarks in *Debate on Mission*).[1] If the majority of Christians were like Mrs. Staines, there is little doubt that most Hindus would wholeheartedly follow that path, even if that path were proposed by Westerners and colonialists.

Example of a social worker

A second evidence of this principle of spiritual authenticity is an encounter I had with a professional social worker. This person is from a devout Christian family and has become quite renowned for his/her (I want to keep the person's identity as concealed as possible) selfless service to the poor.

If anyone asks, the social worker says, "I am a Hindu." She/he has a religiously neutral name. I asked the person what her/his personal faith is, and she/he said, "I am a Christian" without hesitation.

("Hindu" is a term which directly implies identification with the culture and life of India. Therefore, she/he and others readily—and in good conscience—use the term in this way.)

Almost everybody knows everybody else's background in India, especially if they are going to entrust anything to them. I am quite sure many of the Hindu donors to her/his projects know the social worker's background. They have no interest in her/his personal religious denomination. They look at the dedication and the character—and the identification with the national culture.

The unfortunate attitudes toward the Christian church in popular opinion and impression are numerous. For now it is enough to recognize that this person needed to use the term "Hindu" for people to believe and trust her/his intentions. The day may come when she/he can be open about the wellsprings of her/his dedication, and it won't matter anymore.

Advice of a Sannyasi

A third example of this principle is a *Jesu bhakta*, a wandering sannyasi that I met in Chennai. He is a Brahmin believer in Christ, and he has devoted himself to visiting *Jesu bhaktas* (whom I called "non-baptized believers in Christ" in my study) around the country. He has three words of advice which he regularly gives to such people.

His first advice is, "If anyone asks, tell them you are a Hindu." It is acceptable to worship the god of your choice as a Hindu. The statement also indicates that you have identified yourself with the culture, history, traditions, and cause of the nation.

Secondly, he advises *Jesu bhaktas* never to go to a church. He warns that they will usually come after you immediately, embarrassing both you and your family. This will cause unnecessary misunderstanding and opposition with your family.

Thirdly, he advises avoiding going into full-time "church work." Rather, one should stay within one's family and fulfill one's social responsibilities. One's primary call and opportunity is to be a witness there.

I heard many anecdotes from him and others about how such *Jesu bhaktas* are indeed accepted and respected by their families. The authenticity of their faith is recognized and admired. Their faith spreads more easily as these three norms are followed. We must enable the compelling attraction of the Christian faith to shine clearly in the heart of India.

Land of spiritual seekers

Finally, the fact of Hindus yearning for spiritual authenticity provides an ideal opportunity for Christian nurture. The life goal of a sincere Hindu is spiritual growth. One is truly human only to the extent that one has matured spiritually.

The Christian Media Center in Chennai broadcasts radio programs throughout India. Dr. Suviseshamuthu, Director, reports thousands of responses every month, seeking further information and further nurture. Thousands of Hindus—many of them non-baptized believers in Christ—have taken their correspondence Bible study courses. Hindus will go where they receive authentic spiritual help.

Here, then, is the challenge and opportunity for the church. Can we provide the culturally-sensitive, spiritually-authentic nurture materials for which the vast population of India yearns?

In this regard let me add one other observation before moving on to the second issue of cultural forms. I observed above that most *Jesu bhaktas* want to keep aloof from the church. However, that does not mean the church must keep aloof from them. We can—and, I feel, we must—be in relationship with them.

As noted above, they desire nurture materials. In addition, the church can help the individuals and groups (movements?) guard against falling into dangerous heresies. For example, there is an anti-trinitarian trend of Christomonism among *Jesu bhaktas*. By God's grace, God has guided His Church as He promised (Mt. 16:18, Jn. 16:13), and we are responsible to serve as "faithful stewards" (I Cor. 4:1), especially among new believers in Christ.

Of course, we must be extremely aware of distinguishing faith/culture issues in this regard. And that brings us to the second issue: cultural forms.

The Issue of cultural forms

India's cultural forms are deeply rooted and pervasive, having a tradition extending several millennia. India also has a long tradition of defending its cultural integrity against military invaders seeking to impose their cultural and religious forms. Most unfortunately, Christian baptism became involved in those cultural wars (as I discussed in *Churchless Christianity*).[2] However, baptism is a purely spiritual matter which should have no effect on one's cultural practices.

The structured church in India has established its own culture, including its own worship patterns. Christians are comfortable with those forms, for the most part, and nobody is asking them to abandon their preferred culture and religious practices.

Objections to church forms

However, in the reactions to the two questions with which I opened this article, it is evident that the vast majority in India will never conform to Christian cultural forms. As a case in point, the *Jesu bhaktas* prefer to stay away from the church simply because they feel more comfortable in their own cultural forms.

Dayanand Bharati in his book *Living Water and Indian Bowl*[3] outlines in detail and with deep passion these cultural concerns. Recently I participated in a discussion group which came up with the following list of fully twenty "reservations and objections to structured churches" among *Jesu bhaktas*. Many of the objections are minor and some perhaps unacceptable, but all together the list is quite imposing.

a. bad moral reputation of Christians
b. dislike to join socially with Harijans
c. will join in homes and at church during week but not on Sunday
d. discomfort with pattern of Sunday worship
e. feel sitting at worship is disrespectful
f. more comfortable to sit on floor
g. feel inappropriate to wear shoes inside sanctuary
h. dislike Western style of church administration
i. find elections spiritually disruptive

j. cannot understand old Christian language
k. dislike Western-style music—prefering *bhajans*
l. dislike Western-style weddings
m. dislike changes in women's dress
   1) tilak
   2) white sarees
   3) no gold
n. dislike change of name
o. loss of life-cycle rituals (up to 16, classically)
p. loss of frequent festivals
q. loss of cremation ritual by eldest son
r. dislike Christian food (non-vegetarian)
s. reputation of Christians as unpatriotic
t. facing family objections and embarrassment

Once again, the issue is not baptism. Baptism within cultural forms would be quite acceptable. In fact, the group discussed the pros and cons of adapting baptism into a family ritual as most of the Hindu religious customs of initiation are traditionally practiced.

The Issues of faith and culture

Many very difficult issues of faith and culture need to be sorted out. Clearly our *Jesu bhaktas* will probably be the best persons to work on these issues, with the guidance of the Holy Spirit. Hopefully, sensitive Christians also can be helpful in working with them. Some kind of national newsletter or e-mail sharing could be most helpful in stimulating this dialogue.

New forms may require new terms. Old terms—even Biblical terms—may carry too much old (Western) baggage. Instead of "Christian," for example, "*Jesu bhaktas*" is being used, as we have seen. New terms for "church" and "baptism" and "salvation" may evolve as well. I can foresee a less forensic (i.e., "justification") theology of atonement developing, using the concept of God's overwhelming love.

It will be a long and dangerous—but absolutely essential process. The *Jesu bhaktas* will serve as interpreters of the faith to the wider community and as interpreters of the culture to the church. This would enable the vast population of the nation to see beyond cultural mistakes made by missionaries and Christians in the past as well as the present!

The *Jesu bhaktas* will demonstrate to everyone how one can be a *Jesu bhakta* of integrity and a cultural Hindu of integrity at the same time. The Hindu community must realize this, and the Christian church must realize this. In this process, obedience to the command and blessing of baptism will be restored to its proper place in faith and practice.

EVOLVING NEW FORMS

All of the twenty issues listed previously will have to be addressed. In addition, many others will be crucial. India is now a rapidly changing, modern society, so this discussion will be part of a larger national debate on cultural forms.

A Lutheran church in Kodaikanal even now has become a bit of a pilgrimage site. The pastor keeps it open throughout the day. Hindus come and go, by foot and by car. The pastor reports that they come from as far away as Coimbatoro and Chennai. They can pray to Christ privately and secretly in this hill station location. They believe that prayers made in that church are "answered."

Might a more open style of "membership" evolve among *Jesu bhaktas*, more on the temple pattern? In the Roman Catholic churches, for example, they appreciate daily accessibility for private devotion and the anonymous atmosphere of worship and mass rallies.

On the other hand, we also observe in the multiplying Hindu renewal movements that group identification and small group meetings are now common (e.g. Sai Baba and Ayyappa groups). Such group involvement has been central to the Judeo-Christian tradition since the exilic development of the synagogues. It is a pattern we see in Christians throughout the world, also outside the structured church (e.g. the house churches in China, the "no church" groups in Japan, the basic communities in Latin America, the indigenous church movement in Africa). We need to gather for Scriptural study, emotional support, spiritual guidance, prayer, and the Eucharist. Some groups are already forming, whether in a systematic fashion as in the Subba Rao movement or unsystematically as in those visited by our *Jesu bhakta sannyasi.*

All involved need to do some bold—and controversial — envisioning, as suggested in my second opening question: "If you could envision an India won for Christ, what would its religious life be like?"

What might India look like? I see pilgrimage sites and ashrams scattered throughout the land. I see church year festivals and saints days that are now "minor" developing into major social events, and many new Christian family rituals. I see roadside shrines everywhere: "Father" shrines for protection, "Son" shrines for forgiveness, "Holy Spirit" shrines to pray for help and guidance and strength. (We already see such shrines along the roads in Kerala, placed by Roman Catholic churches.) I see pictures of Jesus, incense to Him in puja rooms, Indian Christian art, music, poetry, *bhajans* and a flourishing architecture.

Obviously, the religious life of India would be as different from the religious life of the West as the entire culture is different. Nobody in the East or West—or in the heavens above—would want it any different.

---

1. Mahadevan, T.M.P., "The Christian Image in India." *Debate on Mission.* pp. 299-305, esp. pp. 301-302, Herbert E. Hoefer, ed., Gurukul Lutheran Theological College and Research Institute, Madras. 1979.

2. Hoefer, Herbert E., *Churchless Christianity.* Gurukul Lutheran Theological College and Research Institute, Madras, 1991, pp. 153-168.

3. Bharati, Dayanand., *Living Water and Indian Bowl.* ISPCK

CHAPTER EIGHT

"The Conversion Confusion"

This material was orginally presented at a "Rethinking" conference in Chennai, India, in February, 2000. Dr. Hoefer's assignment was to present an analysis of the deficiencies of the missionary heritage so that new approaches might be considered.

Chapter Outline:

Is Conversion the Issue?

Is Church Membership Essential?

What does Conversion have to do with Church Membership?

Why not promote Faith Communities rather than Churches?

The Conversion Confusion

Is Conversion the Issue?

The issue of conversion has become increasingly controversial in India. In fact, the definition of conversion has been a great historic controversy also within the church up to the present day. Some say it's a gift of God in Baptism also for infants. Others say it's a decision one can make at the "age of reason." Others say it's a moment, a "warm feeling," speaking in tongues, a born-again experience, and on and on. If Christians themselves are not clear about it, it's no wonder devout Hindus and secular politicians are unclear.

A second issue about which everybody is unclear is the relationship of Baptism to conversion. As mentioned above, some say Baptism is the very act of conversion. Others say Baptism is a public testimony of one's conversion decision. Others say "Baptism in the Spirit" is the only baptism that matters. Some say Baptism is water essential for salvation; others say it's necessary but not essential; others say it's not even necessary. In the debate about conversion and Baptism in India, what are we Christians going to say that we can all agree on and others can understand?

Finally, a third controversy is what conversion and Baptism have to do with membership in a church. Can one be converted to Christ and never join a congregation? Once one is baptized, must one join a congregation? Does conversion/Baptism put one into the "invisible Church" so that one's membership in an organizational church really doesn't matter? Can Holy Communion be offered to an unbaptized convert? How about the other services of the church like marriage or burial?

My experience in India is that this third controversy is the critical one. It's membership in a church that is so contrary to Hindu piety, so upsetting to Hindu families, and so threatening to Hindu politicians. If we can clearly state that one can convert to faith in Jesus and one can even be baptized, without ever joining a church, most of our difficulties with the Hindu community and the political parties will be over. It's conversion into a new culture, it's baptism into a new community, that is the problem.

Is Church Membership Essential?

Christianity grew out of Judaism. Judaism is an ethnic religion. It is a tradition of a people. They gather in worship to celebrate their identity. Christianity began with that tradition. The early congregations functioned like Jewish synagogues. The Christians gathered once a week as in their Jewish heritage. They read and interpreted the Scriptures. They enforced spiritual and moral discipline. They married among each other. Even the initial Gentile converts were accustomed to such a spiritual life, as most came from the "God-fearers" who habitually had participated in synagogue life.

This was the early pattern of Christian life. Converts joined a new community. You were baptized into a church. The pattern was set and continued through the centuries.

However, we must question if this pattern is of the essence of the Gospel, if it is commanded by God. We can readily think of many Biblical exceptions to the rule: Naaman, Cornelius, the jailer at Philippi, Bartimaeus, the Ethiopian eunuch, the Samaritan woman at the well, the Samaritan leper, centurion at the cross, the Gadarene demoniac, and on and on. These all seem to have been converts. Some were baptized. We don't know that any joined a congregation, and we know assuredly that many did not.

They all gave a public testimony to Christ. They all seemed to accept Him as their Lord and Savior. None was required to join a congregation. In fact, a few were specifically instructed not to leave their community and not to join the convert community. Conversion need not follow the Jewish community/synagogue model of Christian life.

In regard to the episcopacy, a traditional dictum has been that the episcopal order is of the "bene esse" of the church, but not of the "esse" of the church. Having bishops can be acknowledged as good for an effective church and ministry, but it is not essential for a church and a ministry to be valid. Similarly, on the basis of Mark 16:16, it's been summarized that baptism is necessary, but not absolutely necessary. We seem to have a similar situation with the matter of church membership. It is good but not essential. It is necessary but not absolutely necessary.

What Does Conversion Have to do with Church Membership?

Every pastor knows from personal experience that church membership is no guarantee of conversion. How many times have we conducted a Christian rite (a Baptism, a wedding, a Confirmation, a Lord's Supper, a funeral) having plenty of doubt in our minds about the Christian convictions of the participants. We know all too well that many church members see their membership rather than their conversion as their assurance of salvation.

We know how personally disconcerting it is to find people outside of the congregation whose faith outshines many for whom we conduct all the rites (cf. Lk. 7:9). The pastors who minister to non-baptized believers in India certainly express this godly amazement (see chapter 1). We all know from firsthand experience that there is a difference between conversion and church membership.

At a conference in January 2000, an evangelist shared the following incident. The local tahsildar (government official) came to know of his evangelistic work and approached him. He asked, "Are you converting anyone?" "Well, what do you mean by conversion? Is it alright if people pray to Jesus, learn about Him, guide their life after Him, and accept Him in their hearts?" "That's all alright, but no conversions!"

The official's concern was not spiritual but political, not moral but cultural, not individual but communal. The evangelist said he left church membership up to the converts. They could join the nearby city congregation if they wished. It was good but not essential. It was their decision how they wanted to grow and live in the faith.

Why Not Promote Faith Communities rather than Churches?

We also must distinguish between church communities and faith communities. The church is a faith community, but not all faith communities are churches. One can be a part of a Bible Study group or a prayer group quite separate from one's congregation. A faith community may be a group with whom one relates face-to-face, or one may participate at a distance. No doubt, Naaman and the Ethiopian eunuch and the Gadarene demoniac and the others felt they were part of the faith community, though they never had face-to-face contact. The faith community is the classical "invisible Church," with a capital "C." One can be part of the Church and never part of the visible church.

The objections to conversion in India center around the cultural and political issues of church membership. Politicians realize that church membership means new community affiliation and new political influence. It means obedience to a new organization's rules and a clergy person and a community discipline. Families and cultural leaders fear a self-removal from traditions and responsibilities. Conversion isn't the issue. Baptism isn't the issue. Church membership is the issue.

If one remains within the family and the culture and the political party, there is no problem. Can one be a loyal member of the BJP as a Christian? If so, no problem.

Finally, there are styles of faith community evolving in India, which are not the hierarchical, Western-style organizations. The Sri Narayana and the Sai Baba groups, for example, are much more informal. They don't have membership rolls or required attendance or ordained clergy or formal discipline. Yet, they are powerful forces in people's lives. They follow the cultural tradition of providing religious opportunities rather than religious laws. They are faith communities, not "churches."

Any religion must have standards. It must stand for something. It must hold up lofty goals and expectations. It must identify for its followers what is good and necessary and helpful. There is no objection to such religious teaching, also among the most strident Hindu fundamentalists. The objection comes when demands are made, when separation is expected, when affiliations are changed. Can conversion be to the standard and not to the church?

Membership in the Church (capital "C) is not a matter of joining an organization or conformance to institutional patterns or obedience to appointed individuals. It is a matter of faith, of relationship to God in Christ. It's the same issue St. Paul dealt with time and again in his day, and which we institutionalized Christians need to hear again and again:

"Do not let what you eat (we might add: or any other non-spiritual requirement) cause the ruin of one for whom Christ died.... for the Kingdom of God does not mean food and drink but righteousness and peace and joy in the Holy Spirit; he who thus serves Christ is acceptable to God and approved by all" (Rom 14:15-18).

CHAPTER NINE

What Does It Mean to be in a Caste?

Chapter Outline:

What Does It Mean to be in a Caste?

People in the West wonder why it is so difficult for many people in India to accept baptism. The usual answer is that it affects their caste status. Western Christians' response typically is silence. So often, however, beneath that silence is the question, "So what?"

Even deeper is the thought that the command of Baptism is simply to be obeyed. Jesus called His followers to "take up their cross," to "not love father or mother more than Me," to "store up treasure in heaven," etc. What earthly tie can be so great that one would disobey the divine command and perhaps forfeit the heavenly call?

On the one hand, Western Christians do not want to be judgmental. On the other hand, they simply do not understand. This chapter is an attempt to help Western Christians understand.

I do not plan to detail the many theories about the history and origin of the caste system in India. These are readily available in sociology and anthropology books. For our purposes here I will simply outline the most common theories.

Theories of Origin

One is the claim that caste originated in trades. Therefore, the four major castes originally simply were family traditions of priesthood or *Brahmins*, warrior or *Kshatriyas*, business or *Vaishyas*, and farming or *Sudras*. Note that different theorists assign different historic roles to these divisions, but the fact of these basic divisions is the same. It was orginally a simple apprenticeship system. Over time the prestige of the societal role developed into a hierarchical system.

Related to this theory is the claim that originally these groups were not passed down along family lines but were informal gatherings of people with those particular gifts. Those philosophically and spiritually inclined became priests. Those with an ethical commitment to defend people against evil became warriors. Those attracted to the adventure of business gathered with like-minded people. Those of a simpler nature were content to work the land.

A third theory is a political analysis. The claim is that there was no caste system in India before the Aryan invasions around 2000 B.C. When the Aryans became victorious over the simple, peace-loving Indians, they invented the caste system and the related philosophies of reincarnation in order to ensure their ascendant position in the society.

This theory is most common among the lowest castes, and especially among the outcastes, who claim to be the original Indians.

Finally, there is the religious claim for the system. This claim is that caste originates from the eternal Brahma (Soul). It originates in the eternal "dharma" (moral order) of the universe. The mythology is that at creation the Brahmin caste appeared out of Brahma's head, the Kshatriyas from his shoulders, the Vaisyas from his torso, and the Sudras from his legs.

Caste as Identity

We must be clear that one does not change castes in India. You are the caste of your parents. If it is an inter-caste marriage—which is highly rare and strongly opposed to this day—you are the lower caste. A person can attain great political power and economic status, but you are always your caste. With some exception in urban situations, your intimate social contacts (friendships, marriage, celebrations, etc.) are with your caste members. Therefore, one can be quite poor and still be a high caste person, and one can be a high government official but people are still quite aware what your social ranking is. Everybody is aware of it all the time.

As in any traditional society, you do not *find* your identity in life. You are *given* it. You are the member of this group or that. That is who you are. That is who you will always be. That is with whom your future and the future of your children and grandchildren are bound.

One's caste is one's identity. The closest we come to this sense of personal identity in the West is our gender. Every gene of your body is either male or female. You are totally a male or a female (excluding the peculiar situation of, say, homosexuals).

To put the practical question directly, we might ask ourselves if we would hesitate to convert to Christianity if it meant that we would have to enter the world of the opposite sex to do it. We would have to live like them, dress like them, eat like them, feel like them, be like them. We would have to live as a man in a woman's world or as a woman in a man's world. Would we hesitate? Would we try to find some alternate way to answer God's call?

Joining the"Dalits"

About 85% of Christians in India are *dalits*. This is the term that political and cultural leaders of the untouchables have adopted for themselves. Fifty years ago Mahatma Gandhi tried to give them a new name: *Harijans* or children of God. However, the term never caught on, probably because it was once again given from outside rather than generated from within. As an assertion of their human dignity, the untouchables assert their right to name themselves. In this process, they have also included the others in India who are excluded from the four castes: the *tribals*.

Harijans are approximately 12% of the Indian population and tribals 6%. Again, I won't go into the long, sordid history of social and economic oppression of these groups in India. However, the anger over past and present mistreatment seethes among these people just as it does in parts of the African-American community in the United States. The movement to Christianity in the past and also today among these peoples of India is a profound movement of new personal dignity and social liberation.

How would you feel as a caste person who is invited (commanded?) to join the church? In the USA, most of our congregations are divided along socio-economic lines. However, these lines do not come near the intensity of the Indian caste system. Our groupings are usually matters of comfort, not of identity. To pursue my earlier illustration, would we be willing to dress and act and talk and move like the opposite sex in order to be part of a congregation? To push the illustration further, would we be willing as a male to live with a group of angry feminists or as a woman with a group of redneck woman-haters? That is how a caste convert feels.

Added to this, is the fact that the church is the one organization dalits have for themselves. In the church, they can develop their abilities and express their dignity and assert their leadership. In rural situations especially, caste people hold all the levers of social, political, and economic power. If one of them joined the church, s/he would inevitably become the de facto agent of power. The dalits would be under the same thumb within the church as they are outside the church. Even if the caste convert and the congregation are most accomodating, everyone is very uncomfortable.

Feelings about the System

Caste people are generally very comfortable with the caste system. It is a social network that is amazingly reliable and effective. This is the group that will always be there for you. In a country like India where there is very little financial security, the one place you can turn in desperate straits is your caste. In a recent survey, Indian people had the second highest "very happy" percentage of any people in the world (37% compared to the USA at 42%). In spite of all the economic pressures in the country, the amount of happiness is remarkable. I would attribute it largely to the security and identity of the caste system.

However, the situation and feelings of the Christian dalits are very different. In 1999 there was a story on the television series "ER" in which two young men were rushed into the emergency room, both shot. One was white and the other Black. The lead doctor worked on both of them, but there was a background that the Black young man probably had been shot in a drug war and the white youth was an innocent victim. At the end, it turned out to be just the opposite, and the white man lived and the Black man died. In the concluding scene, the doctor asks a Black nurse if she thought his handling of the situation had anything to do with race. Her response was: "With us Blacks, everything has to do with race."

The world looks very different when you're at the bottom looking up. When you're at the bottom, you are very sensitive and cautious and vulnerable. You become defensive and aggressive. You interpret everything in terms of your historically oppressed position. Perhaps you overreact. Perhaps you just see the deep truth that others deny or are blind to.

It's certainly true that Blacks are much more race conscious in the United States that Whites are. It's understandable. Similarly, dalits in India are much more aware of caste discrimination that high caste people are. They may not intend to be offensive and may profess a lack of caste-consciousness. However, dalits do not perceive or experience it that way - just as Blacks in the USA do not.

Feelings within the System

Likewise, there are strong hierarchical caste feelings within the dalits themselves. They resist a marriage below them within the dalit ranks as vehemently as a high caste family will resist within their ranks. There was a story of a community that praised and defended a young dalit man who married a Brahmin girl. However, they just as vehemently opposed when another man from their community wanted to marry a street cleaner's daughter.

Two Christians were studying together in the States and returning home. One was of a higher dalit ranking than the other. Because of their commonality in the States, they became fast friends. As they prepared for the return trip, the lower dalit asked the other if he would take some of his hand luggage, as he had too much to carry. The friend objected, saying that he shouldn't take so much. The former became totally offended at the refusal. It was not a practical matter. It was a personal matter: Do you think you're too good to carry my things? It may not have been intended that way at all. On the other hand, the deeper feelings of the other person may have been correctly perceived. The sensitivity and intensity are clear.

A new group of students is meeting their teacher in India. As the teacher introduces himself, he mentions the town he is from. The dalit students immediately recognize the town is preponderantly people of a higher caste. They perceive that teacher is subtly but clearly indicating his rank over against them. They resent it.

When we first arrived in India, we became friends with a college student named Sathi. It turns out that he was a Brahmin. Brahmins are the one caste that is generally physically identifiable. They are lighter-skinned. They have a particular nose. Because they do not intermarry with other castes, these traits are quite universal. Other caste people are not so readily identifiable by looks, so this is one of the arguments in favor of the political origin of the caste system mentioned above.

Brahmins also have a special "air" about them. They have a sense of refinement and dignity that is admirable. They know who they are. They don't have to flout it. Usually they are quite humble and unassuming. However, they are also quite strict about the lines that are drawn: what they will eat, with whom they will eat, how they will dress, etc. Brahmins typically are not wealthy or ostentatious. They are devout Hindus who are vegetarians, highly moral, and philosophically educated and refined. They typically live simply, but they are the nobility of India. Many of them are bureaucrats. (The British quite astutely recruited them in that role, between them and the masses!) Many are politicians. They command respect simply by their being.

To get back to Sathi, he dropped out of college. To our astonishment, even without a college degree he quickly got a good job as a traveling salesperson. He excelled at the work. Then, to our astonishment once again, he resigned and immediately got another highly coveted position as a salesperson. Once again, he excelled. I asked him how it was that he could sell so easily. He just smiled and said, "I simply go into a store. They immediately recognize who I am. They give me a seat. I tell them they need to restock on this and that, and they readily give me their orders." There is no worse karma than opposing or disrespecting a Brahmin, even when he's an uninvited salesperson in your shop.

Upper caste persons are very comfortable with themselves. They often have dignity and "class." They are born into it and live it out. The people below feel it and often resent it. But they are socialized to live with it. Some at the very bottom have become so angry that they have tried to leave the caste system for Christianity.

Perspectives on Conversion

One pastor tells the story of his father. His caste is low but highly numerous in his state of Kerala. His father went with a friend of that same caste to meet a Buddhist priest some 70 years ago. It was the time when the great dalit leader Ambedkar had finally decided to lead all his followers (primarily in the state of Maharashtra) to Buddhism. He had considered the other non-caste religion of Christianity, but decided to opt for a religion that had its historic beginnings on Indian soil. When the two young men got to the agreed upon location, the priest did not show up. They had decided to commit their life to oppose the caste system. Now they returned disappointed. The friend became an important political leader in the Communist Party, working against caste discrimination. The pastor's father stopped on the way back to discuss with one of our Lutheran missionaries and became a Christian and one of the first pastors of our India Evangelical Lutheran Church. The people at the bottom are not appreciative of the caste system. It is the system that has kept them in social disgrace, economic dependency, and political powerlessness for millennia.

One can appreciate why dalits would want to convert. One also appreciates why high caste coverts would hesitate to join the church through baptism. A high caste convert typically has no community. The dalits don't know what to do with him/her. They don't want to give their sons or daughters in marriage. It won't work well across caste lines. The way of life is too different.

If a caste Hindu coverts, typically he will also lose his old community. They consider him to have disgraced himself and his family and his caste, by joining the outcastes. Here is a small portion of a letter one new convert recently received from his mother:

> *Once you decide to convert yourself to one thing to another thing, you can convert yourself to anything. You can find a mother of your own choice, father of your own choice, sisters and brothers of your own choice. You can convert your nationality, race....It could have been very, very easier for me to console myself if you were dead than hearing this nonsense. You are a murderer, liar, criminal, actor, cheater, and bluffer, most of all a heartless and selfish person.*

The letter goes on and on. The family feels betrayed and disowned. When you know you will hurt your loved ones so deeply, would you get baptized? From their perspective, you have rejected who you are, who they are. You have willfully decided against all that your family is and hoped you to be. You have taken up a new, hostile identity: "You are no longer one of us. You are one of them."

Would you remain as a non-baptized believer in Christ, within your family, within your caste? Would you resolve, with God's help, to be a light and a leaven and an ambassador of Christ as a member of your own community and forego the blessing of Baptism?

CHAPTER TEN

"The Burden of the Past"

This material was orginally presented at a "Rethinking" conference in Chennai, India, in February, 2000.Dr. Hoefer's assignment was to present an analysis of the deficiencies of the missionary heritage so that new approaches might be considered.

Chapter Outline:

A. **Effects of the Missionary Heritage**
   1. In worship
   2. In culture
   3. In community

B. **Limits of the Missionary Heritage**
   1. Lack of a Theology of Creation
   2. Lack of a Theology of the Kingdom
   3. Lack of a Theology of Experience
   4. Lack of a Spontaneous Spirituality
   5. Lack of a Theology of Witness
   6. Lack of a Theology of History
   7. Lack of Church Structures for Mission
   8. Lack of an "Evocative" Theology
   9. Role of the Church in the Kingdom

"The Burden of the Past"

A conversation was reported between the late Prime Minister Indira Gandhi and a church leader from India. The Prime Minister challenged the church leader as to why there were less than 3% Christians in India after the West had expended so much money and so much missionary effort over so many years. This chapter will attempt to suggest several reasons for why this is true.

Effects of the Missionary Heritage

In Worship

My first exposure to Christianity in India came on my first Sunday in the country, in July 1968. My wife and I had enrolled in the Tamil language school at the United Theological Seminary. We went to the Sunday worship at the Lutheran congregation nearby. We had been looking forward to this opportunity to experience Indian Christianity first hand.

Actually, I was also looking forward to getting away from the drab, boring liturgy on which I had been raised in the States. But, as you might guess, I found exactly what I had left, only it was sung yet more slowly and yet more unenthusiastically. In sum, it was the same liturgy, but worse!

I thought, "Well, this is an urban congregation. Things will be different in the village." What I found when we finally got to visit remote villages and join in their worship, was the same liturgy, yet worse. Except that there was one moment of real enthusiasm and strong singing, when—as you might guess—the Tamil lyric was sung toward the end of the worship.

Historically, the Western missionaries had passed on what they knew, both in the Gospel *and* in the cultural forms. They did not do this with an agenda of destroying or even displacing Indian culture. They wanted to share the classic, proven heritage of the church through the ages. Our Missouri Synod missionaries honestly felt the Western liturgy was a treasure to be shared.

To my even greater surprise, this had happened not only in my Missouri Synod's mission history but almost across the board. I know of one exception in the area of worship forms which is the Andhra Evangelical Lutheran Church. They received the blessing of a talented musician among their early converts and far-sighted missionaries who had him cast the traditional Lutheran liturgy into indigenous forms. I've not had the privilege of participating in their worship, but I've heard it is an inspiring experience.

But something even more surprising about those early experiences hit me. In spite of all the drabness and slowness in the liturgy, both young and old use it for meaningful worship—they come to worship! What a testimony to the power of the Holy Spirit among these people, I thought – and still think. Where pastors in the West experiment with ever-new forms to try to attract people to worship, in India they come in flocks even when it's the same, boring form Sunday after Sunday. One stands in awe of the Indian church. Certainly there are significant forms which the Indian church itself has created such as processions and funeral forms and bhajans (these are traditional antiphonal chants between a guru and his disciples). However, these have not displaced the decidedly Western form which was established initially by early missionaries.

In Culture

This early experience of worship forms was, of course, just a foretaste of things to come. Let's take the matter of food. Christians are renowned in India as meat eaters. In fact, it is a standard expression at pastoral conferences that "We haven't really eaten unless we've had meat." Where did this habit come from? Certainly there was meat eating in India before the missionaries came on the scene. The poor of the land would eat anything just to survive, and most of the converts came from the poor. However, there was the general cultural standard that vegetarianism is the ideal. Christians by and large have rejected that cultural standard, seemingly following the lead of the Western missionaries once again.

What this represents is *not* Western cultural imperialism. On the one hand, we have Westerners who were simply following their own preferred eating habits. On the other hand, we have people convinced of the freedom of the Gospel. There is no reason that people cannot eat meat. God had specifically allowed it in the new covenant with Noah (Gen. 9:3). He had specifically confronted

Peter with it in the vision at Joppa (Acts 10:15). The Christian faith is a spiritual celebration of freedom, not a religious obedience to laws and superstitions.

Within the church in India, meat eating also came to be linked with baptism. A Hindu convert might be expected to eat beef before he would be baptized. Why? To demonstrate that he was free from old superstitions connected with anti-Christian beliefs like reincarnation. Similarly, Muslim converts might have to demonstrate their rejection of their previous faith by eating pork. If a convert wanted to have meal fellowship with other Christians, the assumption would be that s/he would eat meat.

Such cultural insensitivity was true not just a century ago among the early, "unreflective" missionaries. I blush to relate another incident I experienced just 25 years ago. Our Missouri Synod had a long tradition of Muslim missions. In fact, there was criticism in the home church that the Mission Board was skimming off the cream of the crop every year, training them thoroughly in Islamics and in Arabic, and sending them off to India.

I was sitting on the verandah with one of these long term Muslim missionaries. We happened to be eating pork. One of the rare Muslim converts happened to come by. This senior missionary beckoned the young man to join us and urged him to eat some of the pork. He mocked him for his hesitation. I vividly recall the confusion in the young man's face.

Here was the revered father in the faith who had brought him to the Lord. His spiritual mentor was insisting that he do something that clearly made him sick to his stomach.

Was this a test of faith? Was this the next, necessary step in true submission? To my joy, the young man steadfastly yet politely refused and soon went on his way. However, I had experienced in person what I had long read about in theory: the destruction of culture in the name of Christianity.

In Community

Let me pursue this sad story to illustrate another aspect of the great problem we missionaries have created for the Christian community. Also after his baptism, *both* the Christians and the Muslims continued to see him as a "Muslim." For the general Muslim community, he was an embarrassment and an insult. He was an infidel who had degraded the holy faith before the world. He deserved far worse according to the Koran, but at least he deserved social exclusion. His experience of social exclusion would *not* be limited to his past religious community. His new religious community as well had no place for him either. Assuredly, the missionaries gave him employment as an evangelist but he had no real friends. He was a Muslim among Hindu converts. Only the missionaries would receive him, though with increasing impatience. Finally, scandal arose: No Christian family could be found to give him a bride, so he had gone out and arranged a Muslim bride for himself. How could he continue in the employ of the church? How could he be an evangelist? Shouldn't some sincere, true witness to the Gospel be put in his place?

In a publication from Hawaii called *Hinduism Today* there was a challenging article by Swami Dayanandan entitled "Conversion as an Act of Violence" (*Hinduism Today*, November 1999, page 52). Here is his comment on baptism, quite apropos to this young man's situation:

> *"Religious conversion.... Is an act of violence because it hurts deeply, not only the other members of the family of the converted, but the entire community.... When the hurt of the religious becomes acute, it explodes into violence."*

The more religiously sensitive one is the more a conversion hurts, and the more one is provoked to a violent response.

Once again, however, we have the biblical mandate. Our Lord Himself has told us that He did "not come to bring peace but a sword... and to turn a man against his father, a daughter against her mother.... Anyone who loves his father or mother more than Me is not worthy of me.... And anyone who does not take up his cross and follow Me is not worthy of Me" (Mt. 10:34-37). It would be unfair to call the violence of conversion a form of cultural imperialism. It is the inevitable result of the Gospel call, but to what degree?

On the other hand, marriage and family are orders of God's creation. Every society strives to keep these foundations intact. Any time we undermine an order of God's creation we violate His good intent for that society. Therefore, Paul teaches the Corinthian congregation, "If any brother has a wife who is not a believer and she is willing to live with him, he must not divorce her." He goes on to assert, rather mysteriously, that such respect for God's order of creation has saving implications: "For the unbelieving wife has been sanctified through her believing husband. Otherwise, your children would be unclean, but as it is, they are holy" (I Cor. 7:12-14).

Culture is another of these orders of creation which we are called to keep intact. In the Old Testament, certainly the sinful aspects of Canaanite religion were to be rejected, such as idol worship and temple prostitution. However, we find archaeologically that the Israelites learned from the Canaanites' temple architecture and replicated it in their own temple, for example. Strikingly, the apostle Thomas seems to have done the same thing with Hindu temple architecture when he came, judging by the famous St. Mary's Church outside Nagercoil.

Similarly, the Jerusalem Council in Acts 15 affirmed that Gentile converts did not have to become cultural Jews. Their culture was to be affirmed in anything that did not contradict the Gospel. (I have written further on the application of this Reformation principle to issues of faith and culture in "Church-State-Society," pp. 74-77, CLS, 1982.)

Are we carrying on our evangelistic work ethically if we do not provide for people's innate social/fellowship needs? As I documented in the interviews in the first chapter of this book, the Christian congregations in rural Tamil Nadu did not want the converts from castes in their fellowship. It would upset their entire social and administrative structure. One evangelist has poignantly asked, "If we are not ready to provide a community for our converts, how can we ethically go out and evangelize?" Is the only alternative to create "compound Christians" as was typically done in North India? There has to be a better way.

Limits of the Missionary Heritage

Lack of a Theology of Creation

Here is where Roman Catholic theology and missiology have proven far superior to our Protestant attempts, in my opinion. From Pope Gregory the Great's famous edict in the sixth century until today, Roman Catholic missionaries have affirmed local customs, even religious practices as "outward joys" leading "by way of exchange" to "the true inner joy," going "upward step by step and pace by pace." (See *From Jerusalem to Irian Jaya* by Ruth Tucker, Zondervan, 1983, page 44.)

Why have they been able to take such a broader, more progressive approach? I think it is because of their philosophical training. Roman Catholic theology is developed within the broad framework of all human thought. Protestant theology tends to be much more narrowly biblical in focus. St. Thomas Aquinas could draw freely on the insights of Aristotle in working out the implications of the faith. Luther, in contrast, called philosophy a whore. An implication of this suspicion and rejection of general human knowledge among Protestant missionaries has been a suspicion and rejection of general non-Christian culture.

We need to challenge this Protestant viewpoint. Was God in India before the Christian missionaries arrived? Was God at work for good among these people that He loved and valued and for Whom Christ died? Of course.

- He had "shepherds" and "anointed" ones and "servants" here just as He did among the heathen Persians and Babylonians (cf. Is. 44:28-45:1, Jer. 25:8).
- He had inspired profound religious truths here as He had among the Greeks, "as some of your own poets have said" (cf. Acts 17:28).
- God had given great wisdom to the Egyptians, and Solomon was inspired to include the "Sayings of the Wise" in his Book of Proverbs (cf. Prov. 22:17-23:14).
- Amos tells us that God had brought up the "Philistines from Caphtor and the Arameans from Kir" just as much as the Israelites from Egypt (Amos 9:7).
- "Where can I go from your Spirit?... If I go up to the heavens, you are there." (Ps. 139:7-8) If I go to India, you are there.

As Henry Blackaby's workbook, *Experiencing God* clearly presents, God is always working.

Lack of a Theology of the Kingdom

The Kingdom of God is more than the Church—local or global. The work of God is bigger than the work of the Church. We Protestants lack a theology of creation as the broader context for our theology of salvation. We need the help of our brothers and sisters in the ancient churches of the Roman Catholic and Orthodox traditions who are more advanced in this area of thinking and action. Perhaps our missiology has been simplistic because our theology has been simplistic.

Why couldn't we have used bhajans instead of liturgy? Why couldn't we have built temples and mandapams—a covered rest areas in front of a temple? Why couldn't we cite great Hindu poets? Why not acknowledge the great wisdom of the Hindu sages? To do so would merely be to acknowledge the greatness of God.

Why can't Christian men wear the veshti (skirt-like cloth) and Christian women the tilak (decorative dot on the forehead)? Why can't we be vegetarian, as God had ordained in the original creation (cf. Gen. 1:29)? Why do we have to have pastors and bishops and divisive elections and committees for everything under the sun? The fact is there is no reason the Indian church cannot be Indian, or "Hindu" in the cultural sense.

But the fact is that we are a culturally Westernized community, from the way we dress to the way we worship to the way we organize ourselves. It is the burden of *our* past. We cannot escape it. But we do not have to drag others into it. We can rejoice that followers of Christ might yet be freed from the cultural entrapments of the missionary era. We certainly don't want to replicate the church in India. We know that the vast population of India will never join this organization. It just doesn't fit the culture.

Instead, we want to do all we can to release a discipleship of Jesus that flows smoothly along the highways and byways of this great land. Instead of hymns which are heavy with doctrinal theology, we'll have lyrics which bounce with simple praise. Instead of congregational activities, we'll emphasize private family and individual devotional practices.

Lack of a Theology of Experience

Of all Protestant church bodies, the one—in my opinion—that comes the closest to the heart of India is the Pentecostal. I realize they are often the most offensive in their evangelistic methods and cultural restrictions. However, they have a central emphasis in their theology and practice which reaches right to the heart of Indian religiosity.

Traditional Hindu religiosity emphasizes three sources of authority in discovering religious truth:

- *srti* or ancient writings;
- *yukti* or rational thought; and the most important
- *anubhava* or experience.

The purpose of using srti and yukti is only to get to one's own anubhav. Only when I personally experience the truth witnessed in the writings and explained by the philosophers, will I know it is true.

Of course, this emphasis on anubhava is central to Pentecostal theology and practice as well. An Indian seeker will want confirmation through visions and miracles and answered prayers and healings. Most other denominations—and here I can include the Roman Catholics and the Orthodox as well—are uncomfortable with all this subjectivity. They prefer to remain at srti—in this case the Bible—and yukti—the dogma, but the Indian drive is for anubhava. The Pentecostals will gladly and skillfully lead them there, by the Holy Spirit.

Lack of a Spontaneous Spirituality

Another area where I feel our Pentecostal brethren are closer to the general religious culture of India is in their selection of clergy. We have formalized, structured, and centralized the appointment of spiritual leaders. In contrast, among the Pentecostals one must gather a new congregation of believers and thereby become recognized and ordained as a pastor. People come because of the attractive spirituality of the leader, similar to the "guru" tradition of Hinduism.

In contrast, we non-pentecostals train our future pastors in seminaries and assign them to congregations. These individuals may or may not be spiritual leaders. They may only be church leaders. They may be more like *pujaris*, simply performing religious rituals for the people. They are leaders by training and assignment, not be popular acclamation as with a guru.

Likewise, our congregational life is a structured spirituality, quite unlike the traditional pattern of Hindu spirituality around us. We have membership rolls and times and days of worship. At other times, our worship centers are locked shut, quite in contrast to the spontaneous pattern of worship typical around India.

In this respect, Roman Catholic churches have structured themselves more closely to the cultural pattern than the Protestant churches. Worshippers can come and go, even on a Sunday morning, and no one particularly notices. Roman Catholic church buildings also are often kept open, at least during the day, and many have a roadside shrine as well for those who feel moved to worship more spontaneously during the week.

Lack of a Theology of Witness

There is a big difference between the call to be a witness to the faith and the expectation to be a demonstrator of the faith. All Christians are called to be witnesses (Acts 1:8, I Pet. 3:15) and leaven (Lk. 13:21) and salt (Mt. 5:13) and light (Mt. 5:14). Not all Christians have the spiritual gifts of evangelism or the call to martyrdom. We are all called to be disciples, but not necessarily heroes, of the faith.

The Protestant missionary movement was motivated by a theology of heroic demonstrations of the faith. The true Christian will be a missionary, a hero, a martyr. This is how the missionaries viewed their own life, and this is what they expected of their converts.

Once again, this was not cultural imperialism. This is how the missionaries sincerely understood the biblical call for everyone:

> The true disciple is to "hate his father and mother... and carry his cross." Lk. 14:26-27

> "What does a believer have in common with an unbeliever?...Therefore, come out and be separate, says the Lord." II Cor. 6:15, 17

The missionaries were not demanding of their converts anything more than they demanded of themselves, anything more than God expected. God expects us to demonstrate our faith heroically. Jesus' first disciples "left everything and followed Him" (Lk 5:112), and so must we.

However, while there were heroes of the faith in both the Old Testament and the New Testament, we never see this as the norm. There are situations where we are to "come out and be separate" and to accept martyrdom, but this is never presented as the normal call, for example:

- We do not express our faith by separating ourselves but by involving ourselves (Jn. 17:15-18).
- The demonstration of our faith is not by ostentatiously changing our name or our dress but by changing our life (Dt. 4:5-8, Mt. 5:16, I Pet. 3:3-4).
- Under normal circumstances, the mark of the covenant to which we are committed is quite invisible: circumcision and baptism.
- The Jerusalem Council in Acts 15 decided that Gentile converts did not have to demonstrate the genuineness of their faith by heroic breaks with the culture.

Over and over again, Paul insists the call of God is not to abrasive demonstrations. "For the kingdom of God is not a matter of eating and drinking, but of righteousness, peace, and joy in the Holy Spirit" (Rom. 8:17, I Cor. 8). Furthermore, when heroic demonstrations are insisted upon—Paul cautions—we will only cause those who are weak in the faith "to stumble" on their path to the Lord (I Cor. 8:9). And we certainly have seen that prove true as a result of this faulty missionary theology. How many people have we scared away by what we have expected of converts? Humanly speaking:

By the way we have won the one,
we have lost the thousands.

We have unnecessarily alienated the vast majority of the country. We have presented a faith which destroys families and cultures and accepted morals. Of course, any sensitive, sensible citizen of India must reject and oppose this kind of Christianity. In order to inhibit backsliding, we have removed them from their God-given communities of support and from their natural opportunities to witness.

In contrast, let me share a couple more experiences. When I was visiting a small town in Tamil Nadu last year, a lay evangelist took me to a slum area where God was bringing together a congregation. When they had the dedication of their little mud-walled, thatch-roofed building, he said, Muslim and Hindu leaders from the community were invited to speak. They praised the work of the evangelist among them. They said the converts were not carousing as before. The community was much quieter and more peaceful. In biblical terms, they were the light, the leaven, the salt permeating the society with "righteousness, peace, and joy in the Holy Spirit." The Kingdom of God was welcomed. The thousands were being won.

Another time. I was sitting in the train with all the other people in my second class sleeper. Nobody opened up any conversations with each other. However, a husband and wife were having a conversation about the role of priests in their church. Another man quietly read from his Bible the last thing at night and the first thing in the morning. I'm sure they would have been ready as St. Peter urged "to give the reason for the hope" that they have "with gentleness and respect" (I Pet. 3:15).

This is the theology of witness to which we are called and which God can bless to win the thousands. We don't have to rub our differences in people's faces. Our witness will be much more effective when it is done "with gentleness and respect."

Lack of a Theology of History

Closely related to the above problem of proper witnessing is the issue of a proper theology of history in our mission thinking. The Protestant traditions which produced the great mission outreach of the last two centuries had two serious weaknesses in this regard: repristinization and perfectionism.

Repristinization is the view of history which looks back to a glorious period which needs to be restored. These Protestant traditions viewed the first three centuries of Christian history as the time when the church was pure and obedient. Then the church fell into serious decay and disobedience for over a millenium. In the 16th century Reformation movements they see God's work to restore the original, true church he had founded.

Related to this view of world history is a similar view of personal history. Just as the church is called to perfection, so are we: "Be perfect as your Father is perfect" (Mt. 5:47). The call to heroism we discussed before is a dimension of this perfectionist theology. We are "to restore the church of heroes of the faith." Although the churches in Europe were and are faltering, we, as missionaries, must seek to achieve it on this new soil—we are led to believe.

But, there are many ways in which this theology in taken too far. First, one simply needs to point to the reality of the New Testament church evident in I Corinthians and to the on-going struggle with sin evident in Romans chapter 7. Rather than list other arguments here, it is important to see how this improper theology seriously hurt the mission work in India. Perhaps two additional stories will help.

In my early mission work in the early 70s, a conflict arose between our church and a Roman Catholic priest who was starting work where we had congregations. Part of his approach was presenting new converts with cows and promising parents that their children would be given places in boarding schools. I confronted him on this, and he replied simply, "I know these converts are not genuine. We are interested in their children."

On another occasion, when I had first come as a missionary in India, one of our senior missionaries was taking me around his town, and he commented, "You know, after a while you can tell on the street who are the Christians." I looked around incredulously, as all the people walking around looked pretty much the same to me. However, I came to see the truth of his comment. There is a certain bounce in the step and look in the eyes and sense of presence among the Christians. These people are changed!

The contrast is especially strong among dalit converts. You can see the self-dignity and spiritual growth in any congregational worship in contrast to where those dalits were before and where many still are. They have grown in their awareness of being a child of God. They are not perfect in sanctification and they never will be, but they are living out their "new creation" (II Cor. 5:17).

We are unfair to converts when we demand that they be perfect. We are unfair to the church when we expect it to rise above all the problems of its society. We should reject such expectations. Part of the burden of our missionary past is these unfair expectations. Western missionaries failed to recognize the beam of cultural sins in their own eyes, while demanding partner churches take out the speck in their eyes (Mt. 7:3-5). The true Gospel of forgiveness and hope and renewal has been rejected in the process.

Jesus told us the spread of the kingdom is gradual but sure, like a seed and like yeast (Mt. 13:31-33). There will be "hard ground" (Mt. 13:4) and "weeds" (Mt. 13:25) and "bad fish" (Mt. 13:48), but God's Word "will not return empty" (Is. 55:11). This is the biblical perspective of mission with a proper theology of history. It takes time, and it is never perfect on earth.

Lack of Church Structures for Mission

Perhaps one of the most burdensome heritages from the missionary past is the lack of organizational church structures for mission. The missionaries provided institutional structures which were used—and still can be used effectively for mission. Particularly medical institutions and institutions for the handicapped. Many criticize these institutions as financial and organizational burdens on the church. In terms of mission potential, however, I consider them very valuable resources.

I also do not consider the pastor/congregation structure a burden from the missionary past. Certainly this structure has biblical precedents and historic continuity. As a method of teaching and growing in the faith, the pastor/congregation structure is highly useful. We have some missionary patterns of ordination, seminary training, administrative patterns, financial support, etc. which are problematic

Our burden from the missionary past is that we have no church structures for mission outreach. We have focussed our parish life on shepherding a flock, with an occasional nod in the direction of mission outreach beyond the flock (cf. Jn. 10:16). The mentality of the parish and the training of the pastors are overwhelmingly inward-looking. This is true not only in India but around the world. It's simply the nature of the structure.

Our missionary heritage, therefore, has not provided us with church structures for mission. We can see such structures in the Old Testament in the "attraction" role of Israel's righteous laws (Dt. 4:5-8) and of the grand Jerusalem temple (II Chron. 6:32-33). The Roman Catholic evangelistic approach is largely drawn from this model. They do not go around asking people to consider the Christian faith. They carry out service. They build a huge cathedral. People are attracted. They come and inquire and join. God has obviously blessed this historic structure, for half of those who call themselves Christians in the world are in the Roman Catholic fold, which continues to grow.

Another highly successful church structure for mission has been the monastic orders. Historically, the great missionary outreach efforts of the Roman Catholic Church have not come through their parish structures but through their monastic orders. What a powerful, flexible church mission structure the monastic order is.

Trained, dedicated, unmarried women and men are ready to go anywhere needed.

We see another possible structure model in Jesus travelling from village to village with His disciples, in Jesus sending them out two-by-two, in the church of Antioch commissioning Barnabas and Saul, and in the pattern of travelling evangelists. The Church of Jesus Christ, Latter Day Saints (Mormons) have adopted this structure, and it has proved highly successful.

Evangelistically committed Protestant Christians in India have had to go outside of church structures in order to organize themselves effectively for mission. They have formed para-church organizations and mission societies. However, these efforts have often been in tension with the church structures, rather than integral with and encouraged by them.

Lack of an "Evocative" Theology

Western theology is based upon Western philosophy, particularly Western logic. It is deductive and systematic. Its goal is logically arranged syllogisms and dogmas. Theology is reduced to rationalism.

Indian religious philosophy is much more profound and varied. There is recognition that religious thought must be integral with all other thought, for truth can be only one. There are logical systems which are drawn from the paradoxical character of ultimate realities, so what are logical contradictions in Western philosophy are profound truths in Indian logic. There is the recognition that religious and ultimate truth must not be reduced to simple dogmatic statements. Religious truth is not merely rational. It also is never irrational. It is super-rational.

In order to convey these insights which are beyond rationality, Indian religious philosophers used evocative theology. What I mean by this term is the goal of evoking spiritual insight, not through hard logic but through creative insight. The religious philosopher will used stories, parables, allegories, and "koans" to stimulate insight. Typically, it is an "Aha!" experience.

Indeed, this non-rational approach to religious teaching is much closer to the writings of the Bible. Prophets used allegories and symbolic acts to convey their message. The Wisdom literature abounds in allegories and imaginative, evocative imagery. Jesus used parables and hyperbole. Paul used mystical language (e.g., being "in Christ," "dying and rising" with Christ, Christ living "in me," etc.).

Actually all theology begins and ends in mysticism. Rational argument only guards against error. It does not embody the truth. It must lead to faith and commitment and inspiration. Any theology which does not evoke such a spiritual response is lifeless and purposeless.

In my opinion, the one theologian of India who expressed the biblical message in truly Indian forms was Sadhu Sunder Singh. He had only a minimal exposure to Western theological training. He quickly freed himself from that misorientation and deculturalization. His message was continually conveyed in provocative and evocative parables, stories, and allegories. Similarly, the most powerful village preaching I have heard is in simple telling of Bible stories. This approach reaches the heart, beyond the mind. This is where the Holy Spirit can work faith and repentance and renewal of life.

Role of the Church in the Kingdom

The goal is not to replace the church. As an organization, it is here to stay. It is its own cultural group, among the wide array of sub-cultures in this land. They should be allowed to worship and to organize as they wish. In my interviews for the initial research for this book, I found that the Christians really didn't want these high caste non-baptized believers in Christ in their churches. That would change all the social dynamics. They would lose all their positions of status and power in the organization the moment a traditional village leader joined.

We should let the church be primarily a forum for the dalits. They need this base. They deserve this opportunity to develop and exercise their potentialities. The mass conversions to Christianity, especially in the South and among the tribes, was, in large part, a movement of social liberation. They were rejecting the despised role they had endured for so long within Hinduism. Christianity was a marvelous way out, and it still is for many.

However, we must never let the theology of the church become the theology of the kingdom. Dalit theology must speak out against the caste system and all it has done to oppress and suppress the poorest and weakest. But kingdom theology calls us to reflect further. Is the caste system itself sinful? Is it any more sinful than any other system of social organization? Its abuses must be opposed, but its benefits also must be affirmed in a theology that affirms culture as part of God's Kingdom work.

A century ago the conversion to Christianity brought social prestige and financial benefit. I remember asking one of the first converts in a village congregation why he originally decided to become a Christian. He said, "I saw the missionary wearing shoes, and I thought I'd like to wear shoes too." There were incentives and expectations at that time but the movement was far deeper than that. It was a movement of the soul, and it still is.

We know it is no longer the case that there are economic advantages for a dalit to convert in fact, just the opposite. Yet, the conversions among the dalits continue. Why? Because downtrodden people need the opportunity to assert their self-dignity. It may cost their stomach, but they will save their soul.

The church will assert its dignity as a child of God in terms of the issues it faces. The culture of India was not the culture of the dalits. They were excluded from it, so, of course, they want to replace it. They should have a theology of righteous anger.

The cultural experience of most in India has been different. These will be moved by the same Spirit to assert their identity as children of God in terms that fit their cultural situation. Each must hear and affirm and trust the other. In a country as culturally diverse as India, there must be theologies and approaches to truth as "different" as James and Paul, as Jesus and the author of Hebrews, as John and Jeremiah. Yet they are part of the one, faithful witness.

We must affirm the role of the church, the Westernized church, in the mission of God. The Indian church can reach the 20% dalit population. However, God is not limited to the existing church. There is so much more to do that this church with its burden of the missionary past cannot carry forward. God's Kingdom work is far greater than the Church's work. Will the Church serve the Kingdom beyond its borders? Will we?

As the early chapters of this book attest, the fact is that God is moving beyond. He has moved beyond. The Spirit blows where He pleases (Jn. 3:8). The only question is if we will be keeping up with Him.

CHAPTER ELEVEN

"Christ-Followers in India Flourishing—But Outside the Church"

A Review of Churchless Christianity, *Herbert E. Hoefer*
—H. L. Richard

Here a younger man brings to light a truly epochal study not yet taken seriously. Is it too radical for us? Is this like Peter at first protesting against God's welcome to the Gentile household of Cornelius?

A Missouri Synod Lutheran missionary, Herbert Hoefer, made a careful study some years ago, describing it in a small book entitled Churchless Christianty. *But it was not hailed at that time as a landmark study which it truly is. H.L. Richard then wrote up a fifteen page review of it, these words here are a condensed version of that review (a review of a review).*

—Ralph Winter

Christ-Followers in India Flourishing— But Outside the Church

IN STRIKING RESEARCH undertaken in the mid-eighties and published in 1991, Herbert E. Hoefer found that the people of Madras City are far closer to historic Christianity than the populace of any cities in the western Christian world could ever claim to be. Yet these are not Christians, but rather Hindus and Muslims. In their midst is a significant number of true believers in Christ who openly confess to faith in fundamental Biblical doctrines, yet remain outside the institutional church. It was the locating and understanding of these that especially motivated Hoefer's research.

Fundamental questions on the nature of Christianity and the Church are raised by this study. The colonial legacy of Christianity as a foreign religion is taken seriously, and steps toward transcending the constrictions of this heritage are suggested. Dr. Herber Hoefer, author of *Churchless Christianity*, knows he is treading new ground, and so is careful to document his facts and conclusions while allowing that his views are far from definitive, but rather only exploratory.

A Brief Background

In October of 1980 Hoefer surveyed pastors in three Lutheran as well as five Church of South India dioceses regarding their knowledge of unbaptized believers in Christ. That study identified 246 believers, more than 80 of whom Hoefer proceeded to personally contact. Though these people were traditionally thought of as "secret believers," Hoefer notes that just 6 percent of the pastors queried indicated that they felt the people were denying Christ by not taking baptism. "In most cases the pastors also reported that the non-baptized believer welcomes him and other church workers to his/her home. Their faith in Christ is public, and their relation to the church is as close as possible" (xii).

It is important to note that throughout his study Hoefer is careful to maintain a high definition of what constitutes a believer in Christ. He describes a meeting with some Hindu families who had a high view of Christ (as an *avatara*, but not sinless), and pride in their stand for religious harmony and learning from the best in all religions. He comments:

> *Such people—who are, of course, very numerous—I do not classify as non-baptized believers in Christ. They have neither orthodox belief nor devoted practice which is expected of a follower of Christ. Jesus has no special place in their spiritual life, and they have made no break with their Hindu pattern of worship. (11)*

It is demonstrated that low-caste unbaptized believers are often outside the church due to political and economic pressure. The church is composed, largely, of lower-caste people, and cultural change in joining the church is, for them, minimized. The largest problem in embracing Christianity and the Church for these low-caste people is the loss of government benefits involved in any legal change from Hindu to Christian religion. For the high-caste non-baptized believer in Christ (NBBC), however, the issue is social. His family and social group are far removed culturally from "Christian" society, and cannot understand conversion in anything but sociological terms. Hoefer summarizes the impossible predicament of the high- caste NBBC by pointing out:

> *We cannot ignore the close association in Indian tradition between religion and culture. The NBBC is caught in a predicament where he wants to distinguish between these two in his life, whereas neither most of his Hindu kinsmen nor most of his Christian co-believers are able to. The common Protestant reaction to the close association of Indian culture with Hindu religion has been to develop a separate culture for the new religion: differences in devotions, festivals, names, appearance, lifestyle, worship, gestures, etc. If you are to join this religion, you must get accustomed to its culture. This is the basis for all the accusations about a 'forsaking' of the family heritage.*
>
> *The NBBC is trying to change religion without changing culture, even to the extent of asserting that he's not really changing religion at all. Unfortunately, he suffers*

> *from suspicion and rejection on the part of both Hindu kinsmen and Christian co-believers. Even if one is baptized, but does not participate in the mores of the Christian "culture," he will not be accepted. Sometimes the only way he can assert his cultural identity is by keeping aloof from the Christian community—which doesn't really know what to do with him anyway. The tragic consequence of this strategic aloofness is that the Christian community can then self-righteously judge the genuineness of his faith, and the NBBC ends up even more isolated and deprived spiritually. (51-52)*

Hoefer is rightly sympathetic to people in this situation, and demonstrates that their religious activity, while centered on Christ, often follows a Hindu rather than traditionally Christian pattern. That is, the church building is used like a temple for occasional visits when the need is felt; a picture of Christ is central to their devotion; they attend large Christian conventions rather on the pattern of taking a pilgrimage; and they follow an *ishta devata* theology of Jesus as a personal, chosen deity among many gods, if not in abstract theology, at least in practice in their highly pressurized situations. Interestingly, Hoefer comments that "these spiritual seekers are on the Indian quest for *shanti*, and they have found it in Christ. They are still Indians, they haven't yet become Protestants" (61). His highly appreciative closing summary must be quoted in full:

> *The general portrait of the non-baptized believer in Christ in rural Tamil Nadu, no matter from what background he may come, is an encouraging one. He is a thoughtful and sincere person who takes his spiritual life seriously. He responds with gratitude and faithfulness when he has reached conviction about the love and power of Christ. Most often this conviction comes in some experience of healing, but it also often derives from the experience in a Christian school. The strength of his relationship with the church depends on whether the local congregation is of his own caste background or not. He clearly needs this relationship because of the financial, social, and spiritual problems he faces. In spite of all these problems, however, he/she presents us with a clear Indian experience of Christ as the fulfilment of the traditional spiritual quest*

for peace of mind and a clean heart. The non-baptized believer of rural Tamil Nadu is an admirable person. Thanks be to God. (63)

Having become convinced of the quality of faith of the NBBCs, Hoefer sought a way to gauge their quantity. A survey of Madras City was the simplest way to get solid data on this, and had the advantage of providing an urban counterpart to the less scientific rural study. As the Department of Statistics at Madras Christian College had previously done political surveys, it was equipped for a broad-based analysis. Hoefer explains:

We decided to broaden the Madras City study in order to give us an idea of the place of Jesus Christ in the faith and practice of the whole population, not only the NBBCs. For our theological understanding and practical planning it is important to know the general background of which the non-baptized believer is a particular phenomenon. The questionnaire was designed in order to give us a clear idea of how Hindus and Muslims are already related to Christ and how we might best reach them. (69)

No unbaptized believers were identified among the Muslim sample population. But "our primary problem seems to be lack of effort rather than lack of results. Once again, the sociological differences between the Christian and the Muslim community are the major barrier" (97). Among the Hindu population the results were striking indeed. "In Madras City our regular church ministries are reaching primarily 12 percent of the population, the Harijan community," he notes (93).[1] Yet Hoefer found the number of high-caste Hindus who worship Christ equal to the entire Protestant population of Madras! It must be noted again that Hoefer employed a high definition for an NBBC. He points out that "even if we take the 'hard-core' figures of those who worship only Jesus, in terms of numbers the Hindu Harijan worshippers are only one-half of the total [NBBCs]. There are as many Protestants wholly devoted to the worship of Christ as there are people of all castes outside the church. The 'churchless Christianity' is a diverse group but certainly united in firm devotion to Christ under most difficult circumstances" (96).

Sorting It Out

"What does all this mean?" asks Hoefer as he begins his final section evaluating all the data. He again carefully warns against taking his suggestions as anything more than tentative. God has done an unexpected work and we must continue to observe and learn from it. The primary point, without which all discussion of the subject will be misdirected, is to see that the "problem" of these believers staying outside the church has nothing to do with theology but rather with sociology. As Hoefer says:

> *The issue is the sociological distortion of theology in practice. If baptism and the church were carried out in practice as our theology conceives them, there would be no problem and there would be no non-baptized believers. It is clear, furthermore, that the communalized nature of the church exists quite apart from baptism. Even among the non-sacramental churches where baptism is considered unnecessary (e.g. the Salvation Army) or merely symbolic (e.g. the Baptists), the church is just as exclusively communal as among those churches who emphasize the necessity of baptism. The character of the church is formed by the structure of the society irrespective of the theology or practice of baptism.*[2] *Therefore, the primary questions raised for us by the phenomenon of non-baptized believers in Christ around us are not about their authenticity but about ours; about our recognition of sociological realities in ecclesiastical structures and mission planning and about developing a style of church fellowship which makes the call of Christ and gift of His Spirit available to all in the fullest possible freedom and power. (146)*

In the final chapter Hoefer considers implications for the future. New structures are needed as well as new missiological insight. This is especially imperative in light of the irrelevance of present Christian activity:

> It is important for the church to share its inner experience *and "mysteries" in a manner which is acceptable to those it seeks to reach. Most of the 80 percent of India around us feel no need for what we have to offer. They are quite proud of their own spiritual heritage, even if they have never drawn upon it seriously themselves. (191)*

> *At issue is really a matter of fundamental mentality, not merely a change of candles to oil lamps. Can Christianity really be absorbed into this totally different religio-cultural environment? Certainly, it cannot be done by the church, but it has already begun among the non-baptized believers as we have seen in our survey. Christianity grew out of Judaism because Christ was incarnated there. However, when He was "grafted into" a totally new tree, we must only expect a new hybrid, a Church of Gentile customs and a theology of Gnostic and mystical ideas. Only then will Christ "of whom and to whom and through whom are all things" be "all in all" among the varying cultures of the world.*
>
> *However, some might argue that this [the "smothering embrace of Hinduism"] is the danger with the ishta devata strategy I am proposing. It will lead not to an indigenous Christianity but to a Christianized Hinduism. Perhaps more accurately we should say a Christ-ized Hinduism. I would suggest that really both are the same, and therefore we should not worry about it. We do not want to change the culture or the religious genius of India. We simply want to bring Christ and His Gospel into the center of it.*
>
> *The real move toward an indigenous Christian faith can never come from the Christian community. It must grow out of the 'Churchless Christianity', with the help and encouragement of the church. (200-201)*

One leaves Hoefer rather gasping for breath as his vision stretches so far beyond our normal parameters of thought. Our emotional ties to historic Christianity and its cultural forms inevitably give birth to feelings of uneasiness as we think of "Christ-ized Hinduism."[3] But Hoefer has wrestled with the complex and disturbing rise of what Robin Boyd called the "Latin captivity of the Indian church."[4] He confesses to having learned a great deal from Hindus and high- caste NBBCs regarding the fact that Christ is "captivated" within the Indian church. He says he writes on behalf of numerous Christian workers, of whom "many are bending and ignoring missiologically frustrating church practices in order that the call and nurture of the Gospel can readily go beyond the church walls. Their greatest frustration and anger is directed not against the non-baptized believers but against the rigid church rules and rigid congregational attitude which hinder the free flow of the Gospel into the community. They want to be servants of the Kingdom, rather than servants of the church" (xii-xiii).

Nonetheless, one must question whether Hoefer in the end is either too traditionally attached to the church or just not careful enough to define what he means in saying that this churchless Christianity needs the church. Did Gentile Christianity need the Jerusalem church? Arguably, it needed to be protected from that church. It needed sensitive apostles from that church, and this seems the parallel to today. India's NBBCs need to be guarded against a great deal of trouble that Christians will cause them (clearly enough demonstrated in Hoefer's study), but they certainly need help. May all potential helpers be as careful and quick as the apostle Paul to renounce oversight and insist on immediate leadership from within the local context! Herbert Hoefer's study documenting the existence and vitality of faith in Christ outside the institutional church may well be the most significant missiological publication related to India to have appeared in the second half of the twentieth century. On the basis of experiential findings, followed up with careful research, Hoefer challenges the assumptions and practices of established church and mission structures. He calls for a paradigm shift in thinking about service for Christ in India, and for radical adjustment of ministry models to deal with a significant but ignored work of the Holy Spirit in our midst. In eight years since the publication of *Churchless Christianity*, little notice seems to have been taken, debate has not been stirred and, most tragically, ministry strategies that affirm and empower the NBBC have not been born.

Yet this is a book that demands debate and response. But where and by whom might this begin? Hoefer's is yet one more voice against the "captivated" Christ of the Indian church. What hope lies in his plea that "what we desperately need is that these mumblings of frustration become a rising chorus of objection which we can no longer ignore" (xiv)? After a century of refining its ability to ignore just such "mumblings of frustration" and "anger against church rules and rigid congregational attitudes," one wonders if even a "rising chorus of objection" would be greeted by institutional leaders with anything other than rebuke for lack of humility and ungodly impatience. Rather than vainly objecting to the church, the need is for pioneer ministries within Hindu contexts to be born—movements to empower NBBCs and help them forward in Biblical and contextual discipleship. As a new reality in discipleship to Christ emerges, the existing churches will adapt or die. Thus it happened in the first century as the Gentile churches overtook the Jewish; herein lies the hope of India in the 21st century. Herbert Hoefer has given a foundation for hope and a direction for planning; who now will take action?

---

1. Terminology related to caste is almost as controversial as caste itself. Hoefer at one point is careful to point out that by speaking of "high" caste he is merely using traditional terminology and does not at all accept that there are higher and lower people. His chosen term for what are traditionally called "outcastes" (or Pariahs or panchamas or Scheduled Castes) is the Gandhi-coined term "Harijan," meaning people of God. This is now for many as unacceptable a term as those previously mentioned as it is considered condescending. The politically correct term of the hour is Dalit, which means "the oppressed."

2. It seems strange that in his long and helpful discussion of baptism Hoefer never refers to the complex legal issues involved therein, which most strikingly demonstrate that the baptism of non-Christians in India involves decidedly extra-Biblical (if not anti-Biblical) elements. (On this see Saldanha, J., Conversion and Indian Civil Law, Theological Publications in India, Bangalore, 1981.) Further, he makes no concrete suggestions on the line of re-conceptualizing baptism in terms of the initiatory rites (often involving water) of numerous schools and sects of Hinduism. Omitting these rather obvious points is the only major flaw in his study.

3. Hoefer does not seem to be careful enough in defining this striking terminology. At this point he is clearly viewing Hinduism as primarily cultural phenomena. On this point see the striking analysis of Hans Staffner in *Jesus Christ and the Hindu Community* (Gujarat Sahitya Prakash, Anand, 1988). Staffner argues that "Hinduism is a culture that has room for many religions" and "Christianity is a religion which can become incarnate in any culture."

4. Boyd, Robin H., *India and the Latin Captivity of the Church*, Cambridge University Press, London, 1974.

Bibliography

ABHISHIKTANANDA

1969 **The Church in India,** Madras: CLS.

ALLEN E.L.

1960 **Christianity among the Religions.** Boston:Beacon Press.

ALLAN, ROLAND

1930 **Missionary Methods - St.Paul's or Ours?** London: World Dominion Press.

ALTHAUS, PAUL

1966 **The Theology of Martin Luther.** Philadelphia: Fortress Press.

BAAGO, KAJ (Ed.)

1969 **Pioneers of Indigenous Christianity.** Madras: CLS/CISRS.

1968 **The Movement Around Subba Rao:** A study of the Hindu Christian Movement around K. SubbaRao in Andhra Pradesh, Madras: CLS.

CRAGG, KENNETH

1964 **The Call of the Minaret.** New York: Oxford UniversityPress.

FORRESTER, DUNCAN

1979 **Caste and Christianity:** (Attitudes and policies on Caste of Anglo-Saxon Protestant Missions in India). London: Curzon Press Ltd.

HAYWARD, VICTOR E.W.

1966 **The Church as Christian Community.** London: Lutherworth Press.

HEILER, FRIEDRICH

1927 **The Gospel of Sadhu Sundar Singh.** New York: Oxford University Press.

HOEFER, HERBERT E. (Ed.)

1981 **Christian Art in India.** Madras Gurukul Pub.

1982 **Church-State-Society.** Madras: CLS,

1979 **Debate on Mission: Issues from the Indian Context.** Madras: Gurukul Pub.

HOEKENDIJK, J.C.

1966 **The Church Inside Out.** London: SCM Press.

KNOX, JOHN

1962 **The Church and the Reality of Christ.** New York: Harper & Row.

McGAVRAN, DONALD M.

1957 **How Churches Grow?** London: World Dominion Press.

1970 **Understanding Church Growth.** Grand Rapids, Michigan: William B. Eardmans Pub. Co.

1979 **Understanding Church Growth in India.** Bombay: Gospel Literature Service.

NEILL, STEPHEN

1964 **Christian Missions,** Great Britain: Penguin Press

PANIKKAR, K.M.

1960 **Hindu Society at Cross Roads.** Bombay: Asia Pub. House.

ROBERT, K.J.

1977 **Caste and Christianity.** Madras: Nadar Christian Welfare Association.

SESHARATNAMMA

1987 **Pathway to Heaven.** Suvisesha Ashram, Bangalore.

SINGH, GODWIN R.

1985 **A Call to Dicsipleship: Baptism and Conversion.** Delhi: ISPCK.

SINGH, SADHU SUNDAR

1969 **With or Without Christ.** Madras: CLS.

25. TAPPERT, THEODORE G. (Ed.)

1959 **The Book of Concord.** Philadelphia: Muhlenberg Press.

THOMAS, M.M.

1976 **The Acknowledged Christ of the Indian Renaissance.** Indian Theological Library, Series No. 4, Madras.

1977 **Same Theological Dialogues.** Indian Christian Thought Series, No. 14, Madras: CLS.

WARD, MARCUS

1946 **Our Theological Task.** India: CLS.

DAVID LYON AND ALBERT MANUEL (Ed.)

1967 **FINDINGS** of the National Consultation of the Missions of the Church in Contemporary India held at Nasrapur, 1966 in **Renewal of Mission,** Madras: CLS.

APPENDICES

Appendices Outline:

APPENDIX I

QUESTIONNAIRE

'A STUDY ON THE RELIGIOUS FAITH OF THE PEOPLE OF MADRAS CITY WITH SPECIAL REFERENCE TO THE PLACE OF JESUS CHRIST'

A Survey conducted by
Gurukul Lutheran Theological College and Research Institute,
Madras 600 010.
with the help of the Department of Statistics,
Madras Christian College

4. Age : 15–20 ( ) 21–25 ( ) 26–30 ( ) 31–40 ( ) 41–50 ( ) 51–60 ( ) 60 + ( )

5. Sex : Male ( ) Female ( )

6. Occupation
   Teacher ( ) Housewife ( ) Business ( ) Non Govt. officer ( )
   Executive ( ) Professional ( ) Other ( )......

7. Caste: ....

8. Religion
   Hindu ( ) Muslim ( ) Orthodox ( ) Protestant ( )
   Roman Catholic ( ) Other ....

9. Education
   None ( ) Std. 1–8 ( ) Std. 9–11 ( ) SSLC/PUC ( )
   Graduate ( ) Post-Graduate ( )

10. Income Group
    Lower Income ( ) Middle Income ( ) Higher Income ( )

11. Native Place
Kerala ( ) Southern Tamilnadu ( ) Madras ( )
Elsewhere ( )

I. Opportunities to learn about Jesus

Key: Yes, I learned much
Yes, I learned a little bit
Yes, but I did not like what I saw
Yes, but I learned nothing
No, I did not have the opportunity

A. OPPORTUNITIES TO LEARN ABOUT JESUS THROUGH INSTITUTIONS

12. In a Sunday School
Much ( ) a little ( ) not like ( ) nothing ( ) No ( )

13. In a Christian School
Much ( ) a little ( ) not like ( ) nothing ( ) No ( )

14. In a Christian Hospital
Much ( ) a little ( ) not like ( ) nothing ( ) No ( )

15. Through seeing Christian Social Service
Much ( ) a little ( ) not like ( ) nothing ( ) No ( )

16. Through visiting Velankanni
Much ( ) a little ( ) not like ( ) nothing ( ) No ( )

B. OPPORTUNITIES TO LEARN ABOUT JESUS THROUGH MASS MEDIA:

17. Through Radio programmes
Much ( ) a little ( ) not like ( ) nothing ( ) No ( )

18. Through TV Programmes
Much ( ) a little ( ) not like ( ) nothing ( ) No ( )

19. Through Movie Programmes
Much ( ) a little ( ) not like ( ) nothing ( ) No ( )

20. Through reading the Bible
Much ( ) a little ( ) not like ( ) nothing ( ) No ( )

21. Through Christian Tracts
Much ( ) a little ( ) not like ( ) nothing ( ) No ( )

22. Through Christian literature
Much ( ) a little ( ) not like ( ) nothing ( ) No ( )

23. Through big Christian meetings
Much ( ) a little ( ) not like ( ) nothing ( ) No ( )

24. Through Christian Street preaching
Much ( ) a little ( ) not like ( ) nothing ( ) No ( )

C. OPPORTUNITIES TO LEARN ABOUT JESUS THROUGH PERSONAL CONTACTS:

25. Through a Christian family
Much ( ) a little ( ) not like ( ) nothing ( ) No ( )

26. Through marriage to a Christian
Much ( ) a little ( ) not like ( ) nothing ( ) No ( )

27. Through contacts with individual Christians
Much ( ) a little ( ) not like ( ) nothing ( ) No ( )

28. Through discussions with Christian Evangelists
Much ( ) a little ( ) not like ( ) nothing ( ) No ( )

29. Through Children studying in Christian School
Much ( ) a little ( ) not like ( ) nothing ( ) No ( )

30. Through attending Christian funeral
Much ( ) a little ( ) not like ( ) nothing ( ) No ( )

31. Through attending Christian Wedding
Much ( ) a little ( ) not like ( ) nothing ( ) No ( )

32. Through joining in Christian Church Worship
Much ( ) a little ( ) not like ( ) nothing ( ) No ( )
Others ....

II. Attitude toward Bible and Pictures

33. It is good to have a copy of the Bible in every home
    - a. ( ) Whole heartedly agree with the statement
    - b. ( ) Agree
    - c. ( ) No comments
    - d. ( ) Disagree
    - e. ( ) Strongly disagree

34. It is good to have a picture of Jesus in every home.
    - a. ( ) Whole heartedly agree with the statement
    - b. ( ) Agree
    - c. ( ) No comments
    - d. ( ) Disagree
    - e. ( ) Strongly disagree

III. Understanding concerning Jesus

A. Understanding of nature of Jesus:

35. Which one of these statements do you consider MOST correct
    - a. ( ) Jesus is another god like *Muruga* or *Ganesa*
    - b. ( ) Jesus was a great religious reformer
    - c. ( ) Jesus is like one of the *avatars of Vishnu*
    - d. ( ) Jesus is one of the prophets of God
    - e. ( ) Jesus is one and only true Incarnation of God
    - f. ( ) Jesus is the greatest religious leader of all times
    - g. ( ) Jesus was a misguided person
    - h. Any other ....

B. What one has learned from Jesus:

36. I have not learned anything from Jesus: Yes ( ) No ( )

37. I have learned from Jesus how to pray sincerely
    Much ( ) a little ( ) No

38. I have learned from Jesus how to love others
Much ( ) a little ( ) No ( )

39. I have learned from Jesus how to help the poor and needy
Much ( ) a little ( ) No ( )

40. I have learned from Jesus how to sacrifice for the good of Society
Much ( ) a little ( ) No ( )

41. I have learned from Jesus how to know what God wants of me
Much ( ) a little ( ) No ( )

42. I have learned from Jesus how to have peace and joy in life
Much ( ) a little ( ) No ( )

43. I have learned from Jesus how to receive forgiveness of sins
Much ( ) a little ( ) No ( )

44. I have learned from Jesus how to attain heaven after death
Much ( ) a little ( ) No ( )
Others ....

C. Knowledge about Jesus:

45. Jesus was a living historical person
I agree ( ) I disagree ( ) I don't know ( )

46. Jesus rose from the dead
I agree ( ) I disagree ( ) I don't know ( )

47. Jesus is alive today in heaven
I agree ( ) I disagree ( ) I don't know ( )

48. Jesus raised people from the dead
I agree ( ) I disagree ( ) I dont't know ( )

49. Jesus healed many sick people
I agree ( ) I disagree ( ) I don't know ( )

50. Jesus drove out demons from people
I agree ( ) I disagree ( ) I don't know ( )

51. Jesus has power today to help those who worship Him
I agree ( ) I disagree ( ) I don't know ( )

IV. Personal religious experience concerning Jesus

A. PRAYER TO JESUS IN NEED:

52. I have never prayed to Jesus
Yes ( ) No ( )

53. I have prayed to Jesus but was not helped
Yes ( ) No ( )

54. I prayed to Jesus and I was helped
Yes ( ) No ( )

55. I prayed to Jesus frequently when I am in need
Yes ( ) No ( )

56. I pray to Jesus regularly in my home
Yes ( ) No ( )

57. I prayed before but not now
Yes ( ) No ( )
Others ....

B. EXPERIENCE IN PRAYER TO JESUS:

58. When I prayed to Jesus, I experienced freedom from bad habits
Much ( ) a little ( ) No ( )

59. When I prayed to Jesus, I experienced blessings in my life
Much ( ) a little ( ) No ( )

60. When I prayed to Jesus, I experienced healing of my body
Much ( ) a little ( ) No ( )

61. When I prayed to Jesus, I experienced forgiveness of my sins
Much ( ) a little ( ) No ( )

62. When I prayed to Jesus, I experienced peace of mind in my troubles
Much ( ) a little ( ) No ( )

63. I prayed for someone else
Much ( ) a little ( ) No ( )
Others ....

C. Practices of Worship toward Jesus:

64. I worship Jesus at home privately
Yes ( ) No ( )

65. I worship Jesus together with family members
Yes ( ) No ( )

66. I worship Jesus at Church
Yes ( ) No ( )

67. I worship Jesus along with my other gods
Yes ( ) No ( )

68. I worship only Jesus
Yes ( ) No ( )
Others ....

D. Preferred ways to learn more about Jesus:

69. I would like to learn more about Jesus by worshipping at a Christian Church:
Much interested ( ) a little interested ( ) not interested ( )

70. I would like to learn more about Jesus by reading the Bible at home:
Much interested ( ) a little interested ( ) not interested ( )

71. I would like to learn more about Jesus by discussing with a Christian Evangelist:
Much interested ( ) a little interested ( ) not interested ( )

72. I would like to learn more about Jesus as part of an open discussion group:

Much interested ( ) a little interested ( ) not interested ( )

73. I would like to learn more about Jesus by listening to the Radio:

Much interested ( ) a little interested ( ) not interested ( )

74. I would like to learn more about Jesus by attending big Christian meetings:

Much interested ( ) a little interested ( ) not interested ( )

75. I would like to learn more about Jesus through reading Christian literature:

Much interested ( ) a little interested ( ) not interested ( )
Other ....

V. Other attitudes and experiences

76. Can one Worship only Jesus without changing his/her religion?

a. ( ) Yes
b. ( ) No
c. ( ) Can't say

77. The only true way to worship God is to worship Jesus Christ

a. ( ) Whole heartedly agree with the statement
b. ( ) Agree
c. ( ) No comments
d. ( ) Disagree
e. ( ) Strongly disagree

78. Do you have relatives who are Christians?

Yes ( ) No ( )

79. Do you have relatives or friends who worship only Jesus but are not Christians?

Yes ( ) No ( ) No idea ( )

APPENDIX II

GENERAL DATA ON HINDUS, MUSLIMS AND OTHERS

TABLE ONE: BIO DATA

Age

	15–20	21–25	26–30	31–40	41–50	51–60	61 & Above	Blank
*	128	128	132	153	93	64	28	0
**	17.63	17.63	18.18	21.07	12.81	8.82	3.86	0.0

Sex

Male	Female	Blank
365	357	4
50.28	49.17	0.55

Occupation

Teacher	H. Wife	Business	NGO's	Executive	Professional	Others	Blank
11	235	84	32	16	35	312	1
1.52	32.37	11.57	4.41	2.20	4.82	42.98	0.14

* Data in the first row are actual numbers of respondents

** Data in the second row are Percentages of each category

Caste

High Caste	Scheduled Caste	Others	Blank
382	77	266	1
52.62	10.61	36.64	0.14

Religion

Hindu	Muslim	Orthodox	Protestant Christian	Roman Catholic	Others	Blank
645	75	0	0	0	6	0
88.84	10.33	0.0	0.0	0.0	0.83	0.0

Education

None	Std. 1–8	Std. 9–11	SSLC/ PUC	Graduate	Post-Grad.	Blank
57	251	78	228	90	21.	1
7.85	34.57	10.74	31.40	12.40	2.89	0.14

Income group

Low Income Group	High Income Group	Middle Income Group
232	343	151
31.96	47.25	20.80

Native Place

Kerala	South Tamil Nadu	Madras	Others	Blank
37.	135.	419.	135.	0.
5.10	18.60	57.71	18.60	0.0

TABLE TWO

OPPORTUNITIES TO LEARN ABOUT JESUS

A. Through Institutions

In a Sunday School

Much	Little	Not Like	Nothing	No	Blank
21	13	0	1	691	0
2.89	1.79	0.0	0.14	95.18	0.0

In a Christian School

Much	Little	Not Like	Nothing	No	Blank
106	97	0	6	517	0
14.60	13.36	0.0	0.83	71.21	0.0

In a Christian Hospital

Much	Little	Not Like	Nothing	No	Blank
22	34	1	8	661	0
3.03	4.68	0.14	1.10	91.05	0.0

Seeing Christian Social Work

Much	Little	Not Like	Nothing	No	Blank
25	85	0	3	613	0
3.44	11.71	0.0	0.41	84.44	0.0

Visiting Velankanni

Much	Little	Not Like	Nothing	No	Blank
35	114	0	47	530	0
4.82	15.70	0.0	6.47	73.00	0.0

B. THROUGH MASS MEDIA

Radio Programme

Much	Little	Not Like	Nothing	No	Blank
132	255	2	11	326	0
18.18	35.12	0.28	1.52	44.90	0.0

T.V. Programme

Much	Little	Not Like	Nothing	No	Blank
72	206	3	6	439	0
9.92	28.37	0.41	0.83	60.47	0.0

Movie Programme

Much	Little	Not Like	Nothing	No	Blank
141	330	2	10	243	0
19.42	45.45	0.28	1.38	33.47	0.0

Reading the Bible

Much	Little	Not Like	Nothing	No	Blank
37	142	4	4	539	0
5.10	19.56	0.55	0.55	74.24	0.0

Christian Tracts

Much	Little	Not Like	Nothing	No	Blank
64	303	4	10	345	0
8.82	41.74	0.55	1.38	47.52	0.0

Christian Literature

Much	Little	Not Like	Nothing	No	Blank
29	171	4	3	519	0
3.99	23.55	0.55	0.41	71.49	0.0

Big Meetings

Much	Little	Not Like	Nothing	No	Blank
26	70	5	4	621	0
3.58	9.64	0.69	0.55	85.54	0.0

Street Preaching

Much	Little	Not Like	Nothing	No	Blank
56	270	9	37	354	0
7.71	37.19	1.24	5.10	48.76	0.0

C. Through Personal Contacts

Christian Family

Much	Little	Not Like	Nothing	No	Blank
191	133	2	75	325	0
26.31	18.32	0.28	10.33	44.77	0.0

Through Marriage

Much	Little	Not Like	Nothing	No	Blank
4	4	0	1	717	0
0.55	0.55	0.0	0.14	98.76	0.0

Individual Christian

Much	Little	Not Like	Nothing	No	Blank
209	140	3	89	285	0
28.79	19.28	0.41	12.26	39.26	0.0

Discussion with Evangelist

Much	Little	Not Like	Nothing	No	Blank
14	22	2	3	685	0
1.93	3.03	0.28	0.41	94.35	0.0

Children in Christian School

Much	Little	Not Like	Nothing	No	Blank
44	69	1	6	606	0
6.06	9.50	0.14	0.83	83.47	0.0

Christian Funeral

Much	Little	Not Like	Nothing	No	Blank
49	58	2	16	601	0
6.75	7.99	0.28	2.20	82.78	0.0

Christian Wedding

Much	Little	Not Like	Nothing	No	Blank
85	139	2	35	465	0
11.71	19.15	0.28	4.82	64.05	0.0

Church Worship

Much	Little	Not Like	Nothing	No	Blank
119	158	1	26	422	0
16.39	21.76	0.14	3.58	58.13	0.0

TABLE THREE

DISTRIBUTION OF BIBLES, PICTURES AND NATURE OF JESUS

Copy of the Bible

Whole Heartedly Agree	Agree	No Comments	Disagree	Strongly Disagree	Blank
96	377	113	123	17	0
13.22	51.93	15.56	16.94	2.34	0.0

Picture of Jesus

Whole Heartedly Agree	Agree	No Comments	Disagree	Strongly Disagree	Blank
131 18.04	302 41.60	76 9.23	190 26.17	36 4.96	0 0.0

Nature of Jesus

A God	Refor-mer	Avatar	Pro-phet	True God	Leader	Misled Man	Blank
442 60.88	38 5.23	28 3.86	70 9.64	47 6.47	59 8.13	23 3.17	19 2..6

TABLE FOUR

WHAT LEARNED FROM JESUS

Learned nothing from Jesus

Yes	No	Blank
400 55.10	325 44.77	1 0.14

Learned to pray sincerely

Much	Little	No	Blank
45 6.20	100 13.77	186 25.62	395 54.41

Learned to love others

Much	Little	No	Blank
120	176	34	396
16.53	24.24	4.68	54.55

Learned to help the needy

Much	Little	No	Blank
99	166	65	396
13.64	22.87	8.95	54.55

Learned to help the society

Much	Little	No	Blank
97	136	97	396
13.36	18.73	13.36	54.55

Learned what God wants of me

Much	Little	No	Blank
32	52	246	396
4.41	7.16	33.88	54.55

Learned to have peace and joy

Much	Little	No	Blank
50	75	205	396
6.89	10.33	28.24	54.55

Learned to receive forgiveness

Much	Little	No	Blank
56	59	215	396
7.71	8.13	29.61	54.55

Learned how to attain heaven

Much	Little	No	Blank
33	43	254	396
4.55	5.92	34.99	54.55

TABLE FIVE

BELIEFS ABOUT JESUS

Jesus a living historical person

Agree	Disagree	Don't know	Blank
573	47	103	3
78.93	6.47	14.19	0.41

He rose from the dead

Agree	Disagree	Don't know	Blank
438	107	180	1
60.33	14.74	24.79	0.14

He is alive

Agree	Disagree	Don't know	Blank
375	126	224	1
51.65	17.36	30.85	0.14

He raised the dead

Agree	Disagee	Don't know	Blank
263	132	230	1
50.00	18.18	31.68	0.14

He healed the sick

Agree	Disagree	Don't know	Blank
503	72	150	1
69.28	9.92	20.66	0.14

He drove out demons

Agree	Disagree	Don't know	Blank
432	93	200	1
59.50	12.81	27.55	0.14

Power to help His worshippers

Agree	Disagree	Don't know	Blank
513	80	132	1
70.66	11.02	18.18	0.14

TABLE SIX

PRACTICES OF PRAYER TO JESUS

Never Prayed to Jesue

Yes	No	Blank
450	276	0
61.98	38.02	0.0

Prayed, Not Helped

Yes	No	Blank
51	225	450
7.02	30.99	61.98

Prayed, Was Helped

Yes	No	Blank
219	57	450
30.17	7.85	61.98

Pray When in Need

Yes	No	Blank
139	147	440
19.15	20.25	60.61

Pray Regularly

Yes	No	Blank
41	245	440
5.65	33.75	60.61

Prayed Before

Yes	No	Blank
45	240	441
6.20	33.06	60.74

TABLE SEVEN

EXPERIENCES IN PRAYER TO JESUS

Experienced Freedom

Much	Little	No	Blank
35	40	211	440
4.82	5.51	29.06	60.61

Experienced Blessing

Much	Little	No	Blank
65	89	132	440
8.95	12.26	18.18	60.61

Experienced Healing

Much	Little	No	Blank
74	78	134	440
10.19	10.74	18.46	60.61

Experienced peace of mind

Much	Little	No	Blank
29	40	217	440
3.99	5.51	29.89	60.61

Experienced Forgiveness

Much	Little	No	Blank
104	89	93	440
14.33	12.26	12.81	60.61

Prayed for someone

Much	Little	No	Blank
72	49	165	440
9.92	6.75	22.73	60.61

TABLE EIGHT

WORSHIP OF JESUS

Worship at home privately

Yes	No	Blank
143	580	3
19.70	79.89	0.41

Worship with family members

Yes	No	Blank
20	705	1
2.75	97.11	0.14

Worship at Church

Yes	No	Blank
235	491	0
32.37	67.63	0.0

Worship along with other Gods

Yes	No	Blank
170	556	0
23.42	76.58	0.0

Worship only Jesus

Yes	No	Blnak
32	694	0
4.41	95.59	0.0

TABLE NINE

PREFERRED WAYS TO LEARN MORE ABOUT JESUS

Learn by worshipping at church

Much Interest	Little Interest	No Interest	Blank
78	98	550	0
10.74	13.50	75.76	0.0

Learn by reading the Bible

Much Interest	Little Interest	No Interest	Blank
142	107	477	0
19.56	14.74	65.70	0.0

Learn by discussion with evangelist

Much Interest	Little Interest	No Interest	Blank
173	124	429	0
23.83	17.08	59.09	0.0

Learn through an open discussion

Much Interest	Little Interest	No Interest	Blank
82	109	535	0
11.29	15.01	73.69	0.0

Learn by listening to Radio

Much Interest	Little Interest	No Interest	Blank
133	138	455	0
18.32	19.01	62.67	0.0

Learn by attending rallies

Much Interest	Little Interest	No Interest	Blank
57	65	604	0
7.85	8.95	83.20	0.0

Learn by Christian Literature

Much Interest	Little Interest	No Interest	Blank
90	142	494	0
12.40	19.56	68.04	0.0

TABLE TEN

RELATION TO NBBCs

Worship Jesus Without Being to Convert

Yes	No	Can't Say	Blank
357 49.17	235 32.37	132 18.18	2 0.28

Jesus is the Only True Way

Whole heartedly agree	Agree	No. Comments	Disagree	Strongly disagree	Blank
28 3.86	24 3.31	79 10.88	497 68.46	98 13.50	0 0.0

Christian Relatives

Yes	No	Blank
126 17.36	599 82.51	1 0.14

Non Christian Relatives Who Woıship Jesus

Yes	No	No Idea	Blank
150 20.66	551 75.90	25 3.44	0 0.0

APPENDIX III

CROSS TABLE DATA ON HINDUS, MUSLIMS AND OTHERS

TABLE ONE

CROSS TABLE ACCORDING TO AGE

Opportunities to Learn About Jesus

In a Christian School Versus Age

	15–20	21–25	26–30	31–40	41–50	51–60	61 & Above	Blank	
Much	18	17	18	24	12	12	5	0.	106
Row %	16.98	16.04	16.98	22.64	11.32	11.32	4.72	0.0	
Col %	14.06	13.28	13.64	15.69	12.90	18.75	17.86	0.0	14.60
A Little	28	17	15	16	12	5	4	0	97
Row %	28.87	17.53	15.46	16.49	12.37	5.15	4.12	0.0	
Col %	21.88	13.28	11.36	10.46	12.90	7.81	14.29	0.0	13.36

	15–20	21–25	26–30	31–40	41–50	51–60	61 & Above	Blank	
Not Like	0	0	0	0	0	0	0	0	0
Row %	0.0	0.0	0.0	0.0	0.0	0.0	0.0	0.0	
Col %	0.0	0.0	0.0	0.0	0.0	0.0	0.0	0.0	0.0
Nothing	1	2	1	2	0	0	0	0	6
Row %	16.67	33.33	16.67	33.33	0.0	0.0	0.0	0.0	
Col %	0.78	1.56	0.76	1.31	0.0	0.0	0.0	0.0	0.83
No	81	92	98	111	69	47	19	0	517
Row %	15.67	17.79	18.96	21.47	13.35	9.09	3.68	0.0	
Col %	63.28	71.88	74.24	72.55	74.19	73.44	67.86	0.0	71.21
Blank	0	0	0	0	0	0	0	0	0
Row %	0.0	0.0	0.0	0.0	0.0	0.0	0.0	0.0	
Col %	0.0	0.0	0.0	0.0	0.0	0.0	0.0	0.0	0.0
Total	128	128	132	153	93	64	28	0	726
Row%	17.63	17.63	18.18	21.07	12.81	8.82	3.86	0.0	100.00

TABLE TWO

CROSS TABLE ACCORDING TO AGE AND BELIEFS AND KNOWLEDGE ABOUT JESUS

He Rose from the Dead Versus Age

	15–20	21–25	26–30	31–40	41–50	51–60	61 & Above	Blank	
Agree	85	77	76	90	61	36	13	0	438
Row %	19.41	17.58	17.35	20.55	13.93	8.22	2.97	0.0	
Col %	66.41	60.16	57.58	58.82	65.59	56.25	46.43	0.0	60.33
Disagree	16	24	19	11	11	14	12	0	107
Row %	14.95	22.43	17.76	10.28	10.28	13.08	11.21	0.0	
Col %	12.50	18.75	14.39	7.19	11.83	21.88	42.86	0.0	14.74
Don't Know	27	27	37	51	21	14	3	0	180
Row %	15.00	15.00	20.56	28.33	11.67	7.78	1.67	0.0	
Col %	21.09	21.09	28.09	33.33	22.58	21.88	10.71	0.0	24.79
Blank	0	0	0	1	0	0	0	0	1
Row %	0.0	0.0	0.0	100.00	0.0	0.0	0.0	0.0	
Col %	0.0	0.0	0.0	0.65	0.0	0.0	0.0	0.0	0.14
Total	128	128	132	153	93	64	28	0	726
Row %	17.63	17.63	18.18	21.07	12.81	8.82	3.86	0.0	100.00

TABLE THREE

CROSS TABLES ACCORDING TO CASTE

BELIEFS ABOUT JESUS

Caste Versus He Rose from the Dead

	Agree	Disagree	Don't know	Blank	
H.C.	232	49	101	0	382
Row %	60.73	12.83	26.44	0.0	
Col. %	52.97	45.79	56.11	0.0	52.62
S.C.	55	7	15	0	77
Row %	71.43	9.09	19.48	0.0	
Col %	12.56	6.54	8.33	0.0	10.61
Others	151	51	63	1	266
Row%	56.77	19.17	23.68	0.38	
Col %	34.47	47.66	35.00	100.00	36.64

Blank	0	0	1	0	1
Row %	0.0	0.0	100.00	0.0	
Col %	0.0	0.0	0.56	0.0	0.14
Total	438	107	180	1	726
Row %	60.33	14.74	24.79	0.14	100.00

Caste Versus He is Alive

	Agree	Disagree	Don't Know	Blank	
H.C.	186	63	133	0	382
Row %	48.69	16.49	34.82	0.0	
Col %	49.60	50.00	59.38	0.0	52.62
S.C.	46	9	22	0	77
Row %	59.74	11.69	28.57	0.0	
Col %	12.27	7.14	9.82	0.0	10.61

	Agree	Disagree	Don't know	Blank	
Others	143	54	68	1	266
Row %	53.76	20.30	25.56	0.38	
Col %	38.13	42.86	30.36	100.00	36.64
Blank	0	0	1	0	1
Row %	0.0	0.0	100.00	0.0	
Col %	0.0	0.0	0.45	0.0	0.14
Total	375	126	224	1	726
Row %	51.65	17.36	30.85	0.14	100.00

TABLE FOUR

PREFERRED WAYS TO LEARN ABOUT JESUS

Caste Versus Learn by Worshipping at Church

	Much Interest	Little Interest	No Interest	Blank	
*H.C.	39	48	295	0	382
Row %	10.21	12.57	77.23	0.0	
Col %	50.00	48.98	53.64	0.0	52.62
**S.C.	1	17	48	0	77
Row %	15.58	22.08	62.34	0.0	
Col %	15.38	17.35	8.73	0.0	10.61
Others	27	33	206	0	266
Row %	10.15	12.41	77.44	0.0	
Col %	34.62	33.67	37.45	0.0	36.64

*H. C.: High Caste
**S. C. : Schedule Caste

	Much Interest	Little Interest	No Interest	Blank	
Blank	0	0	1	0	1
Row %	0.0	0.0	100.00	0.0	
Col %	0.0	0.0	0.18	0.0	0.14
Total	78	98	550	0	726
Row %	10.74	13.50	75.76	0.0	100.00

Caste Versus Learn by Reading the Bible

	Much Interest	Little Interest	No Interest	Blank	
H C	75	59	248	0	382
Row %	19.63	15.45	64.92	0.0	
Col %	52.82	55.14	51.99	0.0	52.62

S.C.	23	13	41	0	77
Row %	29.87	16.88	53.25	0.0	
Col %	16.20	12.15	8.60	0.0	10.61
Others	44	35	187	0	266
Row %	16.54	13.16	70.30	0.0	
Col %	30.99	32.71	39.20	0.0	36.64
Blank	0	0	1	0	1
Row %	0.0	0.0	100.00	0.0	
Col %	0.0	0.0	0.21	0.0	0.14
Total	142	107	477	0	726
Row %	19.56	14.74	65.70	0.0	100.00

Caste Versus Learn by Discussion with an Evangelist

	Much Interest	Little Interest	No Interest	Blank	
H.C.	79	64	239	0	382
Row %	20.68	16.75	62.57	0.0	
Col %	45.66	51.61	55.71	0.0	52.62
S.C.	26	18	33	0	77
Row %	33.77	23.38	42.86	0.0	
Col %	15.03	14.52	7 69	0 0	10.61
Others	68	41	157	0	266
Row %	25.56	15.41	59.02	0.0	
Col %	39.31	33.06	36.60	0.0	36.64
Blank	0	1	0	0	1
Row %	0.0	100.00	0.0	0.0	
Col %	0.0	0.81	0.0	0.0	0.14.
Total	173	124	429	0	726
Row %	23.83	17.08	59.09	0.0	100.00

Caste Versus Learn through an open Discussion

	Much Interest	Little Interest	No Interest	Blank	
H.C.	48	57	277	0	382
Row %	12.57	14.92	72.51	0.0	
Col %	58.54	52.29	51.78	0.0	52.62
S.C.	9	12	56	0	77
Row %	11.69	15.58	72.73	0.0	
Col %	10.98	11.01	10.47	0.0	10.61
Others	25	39	202	0	266
Row %	9.40	14.66	75.94	0.0	
Col %	30.49	35.78	37.76	0.0	36.64
Blank	0	1	0	0	1
Row %	0.0	100.00	0 0	0 0	
Col %	0 0	0.92	0.0	0.0	0.14
Total	82	109	535	0	726
Row %	11.29	15.01	73.69	0.0	100.00

Caste Versus Learn by Listening to Radio

	Much Interest	Little Interest	No Interest	Blank	
H.C.	70	79	233	0	382
Row %	18.32	20.68	60.99	0.0	
Col %	52.63	57.25	51.21	0.0	52.62
S.C.	18	17	42	0	77
Row %	23.38	22.08	54.55	0.0	
Col %	13.53	12.32	9.23	0.0	10.61
Others	45	41	180	0	266
Row %	16.92	15.41	67.67	0.0	
Col %	33.83	29.71	39.56	0.0	36.64
Blank	0	1	0	0	1
Row %	0.0	100.00	0.0	0.0	
Col %	0.0	0.72	0.0	0.0	0.14
Total	133	138	455	0	726
Row %	18.32	19.01	62.67	0.0	100.00

Caste Versus Learn by Attending Rallies

	Much Interest	Little Interest	No Interest	Blank	
H.C.	25	29	328	0	382
Row %	6.54	7.59	85.86	0.0	
Col %	43.86	44.62	54.30	0.0	52.62
S.C.	9	11	57	0	77
Row %	11.69	14.29	74.03	0.0	
Col %	15.79	16.92	9.44	0.0	10.61
Others	23	25	218	0	266
Row %	8.65	9.40	81.95	0.0	
Col %	40.35	38.46	36.09	0.0	36.64
Blank	0	0	1	0	1
Row %	0.0	0.0	100.00	0.0	
Col %	0.0	0.0	0.17	0.0	0.14
Total	57	65	604	0	726
Row %	7.85	8.95	83.20	0.0	100.00

Caste Versus Learn by Christian Literature

	Much Interest	Little Interest	No Interest	Blank	
H.C.	48	78	256	0	382
Row %	12.57	20.42	67.02	0.0	
Col %	53.33	54.93	51.82	0.0	52.62
S.C.	11	17	49	0	77
Row %	14.29	22.08	63.64	0.0	
Col %	12.22	11.97	9.92	0.0	10.61
Others	31	47	188	0	266
Row %	11.65	17.67	70.68	0.0	
Col %	34.44	33.10	38.06	0.0	36.64
Blank	0	0	1	0	1
Row%	0.0	0.0	100.00	0.0	
Col %	0.0	0.0	0.20	0.0	0.14
Total	90	142	494	0	726
Row %	12.40	19.56	68.04	0.0	100.00

TABLE FIVE

RESPONSES OF MUSLIMS

A. Learned about Jesus

	Much	A Little	Did Not Like	Nothing	No
In a Sunday School	0	1.33	0	0	98.67
In a Christian School	12.0	8.00	0	0	80.00
In a Christian Hospital	1.33	3.00	0	0	94.67
Seeing Xn Social Work	1.33	10.67	0	0	88.00
Visiting Velankanni	1.33	6.67	0	2.67	89.33
Radio Programme	20.00	22.67	0	2.67	54.67
T.V. Programmes	12.00	24.00	0	1.33	62.67
Movie Programmes	21.33	17.33	0	1.33	60.00
Reading Bible	2.67	14.67	1.33	1.33	80.00
Christian tracts	2.67	20.00	1.33	2.67	73.33
Christian Literature	5.33	12.00	1.33	1.33	80.00
Big Meetings	1.33	6.67	1.33	2.67	88.00
Street Preaching	4.00	26.67	2.67	5.33	61.33
Christian Family	26.67	10.67	0	5.33	57.33

	Much	A Little	Not Like	Nothing	No
Through marriage	0	1.33	0	0	98.67
Individual Christian	25.33	13.33	0	8.00	53.33
Discussion with Evangelist	1.33	2.67	0	1.33	94.67
Children in Xn School	4.00	8.00	0	0	88.00
Christian Funeral	9.33	5.33	0	0	85.33
Christian Wedding	14.67	12.00	0	0	73.33
Church Worship	9.33	6.67	0	4.00	80.00

B. What Accept about Jesus

	Agree	Disagree	Don't Know
Living Historical Person	69.33	17.33	13.33
Rose from Dead	37.33	33.33	29.33
Is Alive	53.33	24.00	22.67
Raised the Dead	45.33	29.33	25.33
Healed the Sick	57.33	21.33	21.33
Drove out Demons	54.67	20.00	25.33
Power to help his worshippers	54.67	25.33	20.00

C. How Worship Jesus

	Yes	No
At home privately	6.67	93·33
With family members	0	100.00
At Church	8.00	92.00
Along with other gods	5·33	94.67
Worship only Jesus	0	100.00

D. How Desire to Learn More about Jesus

	Much Interest	Little Interest	No Interest
By worshipping at Church	4.00	1·33	94.67
By reading the Bible	5·33	2.67	92.00
By discussion with evangelist	13·33	9·33	77·33
Through open discussion group	5·33	5·33	89·33
By listening to radio	5·33	5·33	89·33
By attending rallies	1.33	0	98.67
By Christian literature	6.67	2.67	90.67

TABLE SIX

CROSS – TABLES ACCORDING TO EDUCATION

OPPORTUNITIES OF LEARNING ABOUT JESUS

In a Christian School Versus Education

	None	Std. 1–8	Std. 9–11	SSLC/ PUC	Graduate	Post-Graduate	Blank	
Much	2	19	16	44	18	7	0	106
Row %	1.89	17.92	15.09	41.51	16.98	6.60	0.0	
Col %	3.51	7.57	20.51	19.30	20.00	33.33	0.0	14 60
Little	0	28	9	38	17	4	1	97
Row %	0.0	28.87	9.28	39.18	17.53	4.12	1.03	
Col %	0.0	11.16	11.54	16.67	18.89	19.05	100.00	13.36
Not Like	0	0	0	0	0	0	0	0
Row %	0.0	0.0	0.0	0.0	0.0	0.0	0.0	
Col %	0.0	0.0	0.0	0.0	0.00	0.0	0.0	0.0

	None	Std. 1-8	Std. 9-11	SSLC/ PUC	Graduate	Post-Graduate	Blank	
Nothing	0	3	1	2	0	0	0	6
Row %	0.0	50.00	16.67	33.33	0.0	0.0	0.0	
Col %	0.0	1.20	1.28	0.88	0.0	0.0	0.0	0.83
No	55	201	52	144	55	10	0	517
Row %	10.64	38.88	10.06	27.85	10.64	1.93	0.0	
Col %	96.49	80.08	66.67	63.16	61.11	47.62	0.0	71.21
Blank	0	0	0	0	0	0	0	0
Row %	0.0	0.0	0.0	0.0	0.0	0.0	0.0	
Col %	0.0	0.0	0.0	0.0	0.0	0.0	0.0	0.0
Total	57	251	78	228	90	21	1	726
Row %	7.85	34.57	10.74	31.40	12.40	2.89	0.14	100.00

Reading the Bible Versus Education

	None	Std. 1–8	Std. 9–11	SSLC/ PUC	Graduate	Post-Graduate	Blank	
Much	0	7	7	11	10	2	0	37
Row %	0.0	18.92	18.92	29.73	27.03	5.41	0.0	
Col %	0.0	2.79	8.97	4.82	11.11	9.52	0.0	5.10
A Little	4	35	19	52	22	10	0	142
Row %	2.82	24.65	13.38	36.62	15.49	7.04	0.0	
Col %	7.02	13.94	24.36	22.81	24.44	47.62	0.0	19.56
Not Like	1	1	0	0	2	0	0	4
Row %	25.00	25.00	0.0	0.0	50.00	0.0	0.0	
Col %	1.75	0.40	0.0	0.0	2.22	0.0	0.0	0.55
Nothing	0	0	1	2	1	0	0	4
Row %	0.0	0.0	25.00	50.00	25.00	0.0	0.0	
Col %	0.0	0.0	1.28	0.88	1.11	0.0	0.0	0.55

No	52	208	51	163	55	9	1	539
Row %	9.65	38.59	9.46	30.24	10.20	1.67	0.19	
Col %	91.23	82.87	65.38	71.49	61.11	42.86	100.00	74.24
Blank	0	0	0	0	0	0	0	0
Row %	0.0	0.0	0.0	0.0	0.00	0.0	0.0	
Col %	0.0	0.0	0.0	0.0	0.0	0.0	0.0	0.0
Total	57	251	78	228	90	21	1	726
Row %	7.85	34.57	10.74	31.40	12.40	2.89	0.14	100.00

Church Worship Versus Education

	None	Std. 1–8	Std. 9–11	SSLC/ PUC	Graduate	Post-Graduate	Blank	
Much	6	32	17	40	19	5	0	119
Row %	5.04	26.89	14.29	33.61	15.97	4.20	0.0	
Col %	10.53	12.75	21.79	17.54	21.11	23.81	0.0	16.39

	None	Std. 1–8	Std. 9–11	SSLC/ PUC	Graduate	Post-Graduate	Blank	
A Little	9	52	27	53	12	5	5	158
Row %	5.70	32.91	17.09	33.54	7.59	3.16	0.0	
Col %	15.79	20.72	34.62	23.25	13.33	23.81	0.0	21.76
Not Like	0	0	0	0	1	0	0	1
Row %	0.0	0.0	0.0	0.0	100.00	0.0	0.0	
Col %	0.0	0.0	0.0	0.0	1.11	0.0	0.0	0.14
Nothing	1	8	2	9	6	0	0	26
Row %	3.85	30.77	7.69	34.62	23.08	0.0	0.0	
Col %	1.75	3.19	2.56	3.95	6.67	0.0	0.0	3.58
No	41	159	32	126	52	11	1	422
Row %	9.72	37.68	7.58	29.86	12.32	2.61	0.24	
Col %	71.93	63.35	41.03	55.26	57.78	52.38	100.00	58.13

Blank	0	0	0	0	0	0	0	0
Row %	0.0	0.0	0.0	0.0	0.0	0.0	0.0	
Col %	0.0	0.0	0.0	0.0	0.0	0.0	0.0	0.0
Total	57	251	78	228	90	21	1	726
Row %	7.85	34.57	10.74	31.40	12.40	2.89	0.14	100.00

TABLE SEVEN

PREFERRED WAYS OF LEARNING ABOUT JESUS

Learn by Worshipping at Church Versus Education

	None	Std. 1–8	Std. 9–11	SSLC/ PUC	Graduate	Post-Graduate	Blank	
Much Int.	1	27	15	26	7	2	0	78
Row %	1.28	34.62	19.23	33.33	8.97	2.56	0.0	
Col %	1.75	10.76	19.23	11.40	7.78	9.52	0.0	10.74

	None	Std. 1–8	Std. 9–11	SSLC/ PUC	Graduate	Post Graduate	Blank	
Lit. Int.	11	35	12	30	8	2	0	98
Row %	11.22	35.71	12.24	30.61	8.16	2.04	0.0	
Col %	19.30	13.94	15.38	13.16	8.89	9.52	0.0	13.50
No Int.	45	189	51	172	75	17	1	550
Row %	8.18	34.36	9.27	31.27	13.64	3.09	0.18	
Col %	78.95	75.30	65.38	75.44	83.33	80.95	100.00	75.76
Blank	0	0	0	0	0	0	0	0
Row %	0.0	0.0	0.0	0.0	0.0	0.0	0.0	
Col %	0.0	0.0	0.0	0.0	0.0	0.0	0.0	0.0
Total	57	251	78	228	90	21	1	726
Row %	7.85	34.57	10.74	31.40	12.40	2.89	0.14	100.00

Learn by Reading the Bible Versus Education

	None	Std. 1–8	Std. 9–11	SSLC/ PUC	Graduate	Post-Graduate	Blank	
Much Int.	3	40	26	47	18	8	0	142
Row %	2.11	28.17	18.31	33.10	12.68	5.63	0.0	
Col %	5.26	15.94	33.33	20.61	20.00	38.10	0.0	19.56
Lit. Int.	6	37	10	41	12	1	0	107
Row %	5.61	34.58	9.35	38.32	11.21	0.93	0.0	
Col %	10.53	14.74	12.82	17.98	13.33	4.76	0.0	14.74
No Int.	48	174	42	140	60	12	1	477
Row %	10.06	36.48	8.81	29.35	12.58	2.52	0.21	
Col %	84.21	69.32	53.85	61.40	66.67	57.14	100.00	65.70
Blank	0	0	0	0	0	0	0	0
Row %	0.0	0.0	0.0	0.0	0.0	0.0	0.0	
Col %	0.0	0.0	0.0	0.0	0.0	0.0	0.0	0.0
Total	57	251	78	228	90	21	1	726
Row %	7.85	34.57	10.74	31.40	12.40	2.89	0.14	100.00

Learn by Discussion with Evangelist Versus Education

	None	Std. 1–8	Std. 9–11	SSLC/ PUC	Graduate	Post-Graduate	Blank	
Much Int	9	68	25	52	14	5	0	173
Row %	5.20	39.31	14.45	30.06	8.09	2.89	0.0	
Col %	15.79	27.09	32.05	22.81	15.56	23.81	0.0	23.83
Lit. Int.	11	42	14	43	11	3	0	124
Row %	8.87	33.87	11.29	34.68	8.87	2.42	0.0	
Col %	19.30	16.73	17.95	18.86	12.22	14.29	0.0	17.08
No Int.	37	141	39	133	65	13	1	429
Row %	8.62	32.87	9.09	31.00	15.15	3.03	0.23	
Col %	64.91	56.18	50.00	58.33	72.22	61.90	100.00	59.09
Blank	0	0	0	0	0	0	0	0
Row %	0.0	0.0	0.0	0.0	0.0	0.0	0.0	
Col %	0.0	0.0	0.0	0.0	0.0	0.0	0.0	0.0
Total	57	251	78	228	90	21	1	726
Row %	7.85	34.57	10.74	31.40	12.40	2.89	0.14	100.00

TABLE EIGHT

Income Group Versus Worship at Church

	Yes	No	Blank	
Low Income Group	76	156	0	232
Row %	32.76	67.24	0.0	
Col %	32.34	31.77	0.0	31.96
Middle Income Group	112	231	0	343
Row %	32.65	67.35	0.0	
Col %	47.66	47.05	0.0	47.25
High Income Group	47	104	0	151
Row %	31.13	68.87	0.0	
Col %	20.00	21.18	0.0	20.80
Total	235	491	0	726
Row %	32.37	67.63	0.0	100.00

APPENDIX IV

"JESUS IS THE ONLY TRUE WAY"

Table showing the response of 47 Hindus and Muslims

Whole Heartedly Agree	Agree	No Comments	Disagree	Strongly Disagree	Blank
28	13	1	5	0	0
59.57	27.66	2.13	10.64	0.0	0.0

APPENDIX V

PART I

GENERAL STATISTICS ON NON-BAPTISED BELIEVERS IN CHRIST IN MADRAS CITY

TABLE ONE: BIO DATA

Age:

15–20	21–25	26–30	31–40	41–50	51–60	61 and above	Blank
*20	11	7	5	2	7	0	0
**38.46	21.15	13.46	9.62	3.85	13.46	0.0	0.0

Sex:

Male	Female	Blank
21	31	0
40.38	59.62	0.0

Occupation

Teacher	House Wife	Business	NGO's	Executive	Professional	Others	Blank
0	18	2	0	0	1	31	0
0.0	34.62	3.85	0.0	0.0	1.92	59.62	0.0

Caste

High Caste	Scheduled Caste	Others	Blank
17	14	21	0
32.69	26.92	40.38	0.0

*Data in the first row are actual numbers of respondents

**Data in the second row give the percentage of each category

Religion

Hindu	Muslim	Ortho-dox	Prot.-Xian	R.C.	Others	Blank
51	0	0	0	0	1	0
98.08	0.0	0.0	0.0	0.0	1.92	0.0

Education

None	Std 1–8	Std 9–11	SSLC/ PUC	Gra-duate	Post Grad.	Blank
3	26	7	13	2	1	0
5.77	50.00	13.46	25.00	3.85	1.92	0.0

Income Group

Low Income Group	Middle Income Group	High Income Group
26	23	3
50.00	44.23	5.77

Native Place

Kerala	South Tamilnadu	Madras	Others	Blank
4	11	30	7	0
7.69	21.15	57.69	13.46	0.0

TABLE TWO

A. OPPORTUNITIES TO LEARN ABOUT JESUS THROUGH INSTITUTIONS:

In a Sunday School

Much	A Little	Did not Like	Nothing	No	Blank
6	1	0	0	45	0
11.54	1.92	0.0	0.0	86.53	0.0

In a Christian School

Much	A Little	Did not Like	Nothing	No	Blank
13	8	0	0	31	0
25.00	15.38	0.0	0.0	59.62	0.0

In a Christian Hospital

Much	A Little	Did not Like	Nothing	No	Blank
1	2	0	0	49	0
1.92	3.85	0.0	0.0	94.23	0.0

Seeing Christian Social Work

Much	A Little	Did not Like	Nothing	No	Blank
0	11	0	0	41	0
0.0	21.15	0.0	0.0	78.85	0.0

Visiting Velankanni

Much	A Little	Did not Like	Nothing	No	Blank
9	10	0	7	26	0
17.31	19.23	0.0	13.46	50.00	0.0

B. OPPORTUNITIES TO LEARN ABOUT JESUS THROUGH MASS MEDIA

Radio Programme

Much	A Little	Did not Like	Nothing	No	Blank
18	19	0	0	15	0
34.62	36.54	0.0	0.0	28.85	0.0

T. V. Programme

Much	A Little	Did not Like	Nothing	No	Blank
7	15	0	0	30	0
13.46	28.85	0.0	0.0	57.69	0.0

Movie Programme

Much	A Little	Did not Like	Nothing	No	Blank
17	28	0	0	7	0
32.69	53.85	0.0	0.0	13.46	0.0

Reading the Bible

Much	A Little	Did not Like	Nothing	No	Blank
9	20	0	0	23	0
17.31	38.46	0.0	0.0	44.23	0.0

Christian Tracts

Much	A Little	Did not Like	Nothing	No	Blank
10	26	0	1	15	0
19.23	50.00	0.0	1.92	28.85	0.0

Christian Literature

Much	A Little	Did not Like	Nothing	No	Blank
4	26	0	0	22	0
7.69	50.00	0.0	0.0	42.31	0.0

Big Meetings

Much	A Little	Did not Like	Nothing	No	Blank
7	·10	0	0	35	0
13.46	19.23	0.0	0.0	67.31	0.0

Street Preaching

Much	A Little	Did not Like	Nothing	No	Blank
10	26	0	1	15	0
19.23	50.00	0.0	1.92	28.85	0.0

C. OPPORTUNITIES TO LEARN ABOUT JESUS THROUGH PERSONAL CONTACTS

Christian Family

Much	A Little	Did not Like	Nothing	No	Blank
19	17	0	4	12	0
36.54	32.69	0.0	7.69	23.08	0.0

Through Marriage

Much	A Little	Did not Like	Nothing	No	Blank
1	2	0	0	49	0
1.92	3.85	0.0	0.0	94.23	0.0

Individual Christian

Much	A Little	Did not Like	Nothing	No	Blank
21	14	0	2	15	0
40.38	26.92	0.0	3.85	28.85	0.0

Discussing with Evangelist

Much	A Little	Did not Like	Nothing	No	Blank
3	8	0	0	41	0
5.77	15.38	0.0	0.0	78.85	0.0

Children in Christian School

Much	A Little	Did not Like	Nothing	No	Blank
4	3	0	0	45	0
7.69	5.77	0.0	0.0	86.54	0.0

Christian Funeral

Much	A Little	Did not Like	Nothing	No	Blank
8	10	0	3	31	0
15.38	19.23	0.0	5.77	59.62	0.0

Christian Wedding

Much	A Little	Did not Like	Nothing	No	Blank
8	13	0	3	28	0
15.38	25.00	0.0	5.77	53.85	0.0

Church Worship

Much	A Little	Did not Like	Nothing	No	Blank
19	15	0	1	17	0
36.54	28.85	0.0	1.92	32.69	0.0

TABLE THREE

ATTITUDE TOWARD BIBLE AND PICTURES:

Copy of the Bible

Whole heartedly Agree	Agree	No Comments	Disagree	Strongly Dis-agree	Blank
22	24	5	1	0	0
42.31	46.15	9.62	1.92	0.0	0.0

Picture of Jesus

Whole heartedly Agree	Agree	No Comments	Dis-agree	Strongly Disagree	Blank
22	21	4	4	1	0
42.31	40.38	7.69	7.69	1.92	0.0

TABLE FOUR

UNDERSTANDING CONCERNING JESUS

A. NATURE OF JESUS

A God	Refor-mer	Ava-tar	Pro-phet	True God	Leader	Mis-led	Blank
9	0	0	1	41	0	0	1
17.31	0.0	0.0	1.92	78.85	0.0	0.0	1.92

B. WHAT ONE HAS LEARNT FROM JESUS

Learned nothing from Jesus

Yes	No	Blank
16	36	0
30.77	69.23	0.0

Learned to pray Sincerely

Much	A Little	No	Blank
17	11	8	16
32.69	21.15	15.38	30.77

Learned to love others

Much	A Little	No	Blank
21	12	3	16
40 38	23.08	5.77	30.77

Learned to help the needy

Much	A Little	No	Blank
23	8	5	16
44.23	15.38	9.62	30.77

Learned to help the society

Much	A Little	No	Blank
18	14	4	16
34.62	26.92	7.69	30.77

Learned what God wants of me

Much	A Little	No	Blank
11	6	19	16
21.15	11.54	36.54	30.77

Learned to have peace and joy

Much	A Little	No	Blank
19	9	8	16
36.54	17.31	15.38	30.77

Learned to receive forgiveness

Much	A Little	No	Blank
18	10	8	16
34.62	19.23	15.38	30.77

Learned how to attain heaven

Much	A Littie	No	Blank
14	10	12	16
26.92	19.23	23.08	30.77

TABLE FIVE

KNOWLEDGE ABOUT JESUS

Jesus a living historical person

Agree	Disagree	Don't know	Blank
46	3	3	0
88.46	5.77	5.77	0.0

He rose from the dead

Agree	Disagree	Don't know	Blank
46	4	2	0
88.46	7.69	3.85	0.0

He is Alive

Agree	Disagree	Don't know	Blank
47	3	2	0
90.38	5.77	3.85	0.0

He Raised the Dead

Agree	Disagree	Don't know	Blank
42	3	7	0
80.77	5.77	13.46	0.0

He healed the Sick

Agree	Disagree	Don't know	Blank
49	1	2	0
94.23	1.92	3.85	0.0

He drove out demons

Agree	Disagree	Don't know	Blank
46	1	5	0
88.46	1.92	9.62	0.0

Power to help His Worshippers

Agree	Disagree	Don't know	Blank
50	0	2	0
96.15	0.0	3.85	0.0

TABLE SIX

PRACTICES OF PRAYER TO JESUS

Never prayed to Jesus

Yes	No	Blank
17	35	0
32.69	67.31	0.0

Prayed, not helped

Yes	No	Blank
3	34	15
5.77	65.38	28.85

Prayed, was helped

Yes	No	Blank
33	4	15
63.46	7.69	28.85

Pray when in need

Yes	No	Blank
35	4	13
67.31	7.69	25.00

Pray regularly

Yes	No	Blank
18	21	13
36.62	40.38	25.00

Prayed before

Yes	No	Blank
2	37	13
3.85	71.15	25.00

TABLE SEVEN

EXPERIENCES IN PRAYER TO JESUS

Experienced Freedom

Much	Little	No	Blank
14	8	17	13
26.92	15.38	32.69	25.00

Experienced Blessing

Much	Little	No	Blank
20	12	7	13
38.42	23.08	13.46	25.00

Experienced Healing

Much	Little	No	Blank
27	8	4	13
51.92	15.38	7.69	25.00

Experienced Peace of Mind

Much	Little	No	Blank
17	9	13	13
32.69	17.31	25.00	25.00

Experienced Forgiveness

Much	Little	No	Blank
26	7	6	13
50.00	13.46	11.54	25.00

Prayed for Someone

Much	Little	No	Break
23	5	11	13
44.23	9.62	21.15	25.00

TABLE EIGHT

PRACTICES OF WORSHIP TOWARD JESUS

Worship at Home Privately

Yes	No	Blank
34	18	0
65.38	34.62	0.0

Worship with Family Members

Yes	No	Blank
10	42	0
19.23	80.77	0.0

Worship at Church

Yes	No	Blank
36	16	0
69.23	30.77	0.0

Worship along with other Gods

Yes	No	Blank
10	42	0
19.23	80.77	0.0

Worship only Jesus

Yes	No	Blank
29	23	0
25.77	44.23	0.0

TABLE NINE

PREFERRED WAYS TO LEARN MORE ABOUT JESUS

Learn by Worshipping at Church

Much Int.	Little Int.	No Int.	Blank
24	8	20	0
46.15	15.38	38.46	0.0

Learn by Reading the Bible

Much Int.	Little Int.	No Int.	Blank
29	2	21	0
55.77	3.85	40.38	0.0

Learn by Discussion with Evangelist

Much Int.	Little Int.	No Int.	Blank
62	5	15	0
31.54	9.62	28.85	0.0

Learn through an Open Discussion

Much Int.	Little Int.	No Int.	Blank
16	13	23	0
30.77	25.00	44.23	0.0

Learn by Listening to Radio

Much Int.	Little Int.	No Int.	Blank
31	6	15	0
59.62	11.54	28.85	0.0

Learn by attending rallies

Much Int.	Little Int.	No Int.	Blank
24	6	22	0
46.15	11.54	42.31	0.0

Learn by Christian Literature

Much Int.	Little Int.	No Int.	Blank
21	11	21	0
40.38	21.15	38.46	0.0

TABLE TEN

OTHER ATTITUDES AND EXPERIENCES

Worship Jesus without being to convert

Yes	No	Cant Say	Blank
42	3	7	0
80.88	5.77	13.46	0.0

Jesus is the Only True Way

Whole Heartedly Agree	Agree	No Com.	Dis-Agree	Strongly Disagree	Blank
28	24	0	0	0	0
53.85	46.15	0.0	0.0	0.0	0.0

Christian Relatives

Yes	No	Blank
26	26	0
50.00	50.00	0.0

Non Christian Relatives who Worship Jesus

Yes	No	No Idea	Blank
23	28	1	0
44.23	53.85	1.92	0.0

APPENDIX V

PART II

CROSS - TABLE STATISTICS ON NON-BAPTISED BELIEVERS IN CHRIST

TABLE ONE

Non-Christian Relatives who worship Jesus Versus Age

	15–20	21–25	26–30	31–40	41–50	51–60	61 and above	Blank	
Yes	9	7	2	4	0	1	0	0	23
Row %	39.13	30.43	8.70	17.39	0.0	4.35	0.0	0.0	
Col %	45.00	63.64	28.57	80.00	0.0	14.29	0.0	0.0	44.23

No	11	3	5	1	2	6	0	0	28
Row %	39.29	10.71	17.86	3.57	7.14	21.43	0.0	0.0	
Col %	55.00	27.27	71.43	20.00	100.00	85.71	0.0	0.0	53.85
No Idea	0	1	0	0	0	0	0	0	1
Row %	0.0	100.0	0.0	0.0	0.0	0.0	0.0	0.0	
Col %	0.0	9.09	0.0	0.0	0.0	0.0	0.0	0.0	1.92
Blank	0	0	0	0	0	0	0	0	0
Row %	0.0	0.0	0.0	0.0	0.0	0.0	0.0	0.0	
Col %	0.0	0.0	0.0	0.0	0.0	0.0	0.0	0.0	0.0
Total	20	11	7	5	2	7	0	0	52
Row %	38.46	21.15	13.46	9.62	3.85	13.46	0.0	0.0	100.00

TABLE TWO

I. Caste Versus Worship at home privately

	Yes	No	Blank	
High Caste	9	8	0	17
Row %	52.94	47.06	0.0	
Col %	26.47	44.44	0.0	32.69
Scheduled Caste	13	1	0	14
Row %	92.86	7.14	0.0	
Col %	38.24	5.56	0.0	26.92
Others	12	9	0	21
Row %	57.14	42.86	0.0	
Col %	35.29	50.00	0.0	40.38
Blank	0	0	0	0
Row %	0.0	0.0	0.0	0.0
Col %	0.0	0.0	0.0	0.0
Total	34.	18	0	52
Row %	65.38	34.62	0.0	100.00

II. Caste Versus worshipping with Family Members

	Yes	No	Blank	
High Caste	4	13	0	17
Row %	23.53	76.47	0.0	
Col %	40.00	30.95	0.0	32.69
Scheduled Caste	3	11	0	14
Row %	21.43	78.57	0.0	
Col %	30.00	26.19	0.0	26.92
Others	3	18	0	21
Row %	14.29	85.71	0.0	
Col %	30.00	42.86	0.0	40.38
Blank	0	0	0	0
Row %	0.0	0.0	0.0	
Col %	0.0	0.0	0.0	0.0
Total	10	42	0	52
Row %	19.23	80.77	0.0	100.00

Caste and worshipping at church

	Yes	No	Blank	
High Caste	12	5	0	17
Row %	70.59	29.41	0.0	
Col %	33.33	31.25	0.0	32.69
Scheduled Caste	11	3	0	14
Row %	78.57	21.43	0.0	
Col %	30.56	18.75	0.0	26.92
Others	13	8	0	21
Row %	61.90	38.10	0.0	
Col %	36.11	50.00	0.0	40.88
Blank	0	0	0	0
Row %	0 0	0.0	0.0	
Col %	0.0	0.0	0.0	0.0
Total	36	16	0	52
Row %	69.23	30.77	0.0	100.00

Caste and worshipping Jesus along with other Gods

	Yes	No	Blank	
High Caste	2	15	0	17
Row %	11.76	88.24	0.0	
Col %	20.00	35.71	0.0	32.69
Scheduled Caste	3	11	0	14
Row %	21.43	78.57	0.0	
Col %	30.00	26.19	0.0	26.92
Others	5	16	0	21
Row %	23.81	76.19	0.0	
Col %	50.00	38.10	0.0	40.38
Blank	0	0	0	0
Row %	0.0	0.0	0.0	
Col %	0.0	0.0	0.0	0.0
Total	10	42	0	52
Row %	19.23	80.77	0.0	100.00

Caste versus worship only Jesus

	Yes	No	Blank	
High Caste	7	10	0	17
Row %	41.18	58.82	0.0	
Col %	24.14	43.48	0.0	32.69
Scheduled Caste	11	3	0	14
Row %	78.57	21.43	0.0	
Col %	37.93	13.04	0.0	26.92
Others	11	10	0	21
Row %	52.38	47.62	0.0	
Col %	37.93	43.48	0.0	40.38
Blank	0	0	0	0
Row %	0.0	0.0	0.0	
Col %	0.0	0.0	0.0	0.0
Total	29	23	0	52
Row %	55.77	44.23	0.0	100.00

TABLE THREE

Caste versus worship Jesus without being converted

	Yes	No	Can't Say	Blank	
H.C.	13	1	3	0	17
Row %	76.47	5.88	17.65	0.0	
Col %	30.95	33.33	42.86	0.0	32.65
S.C.	12	0	2	0	14
Row %	85.71	0.0	14.25	0.0	
Col %	28.57	0.0	28.57	0.0	26.92
Others	17	2	2	0	21
Row %	80.95	9.52	9.52	0.0	
Col %	40.48	66.67	28.57	0.0	40.38
Total	42	3	7	0	52
Row %	80.77	5.77	13.46	0.0	100.00

TABLE FOUR

Church worship versus education

	None	Std. 1–8	Std. 9–11	SSLC/ PUC	Graduates	Post-Graduates	Blank	
Much	0	8	2	7	1	1	0	19
Row %	0.0	42.11	10.53	36.84	5.26	5.26	0.0	
Col %	0.0	30.77	28.57	53.85	50.00	100.00	0.0	36.54
A Little	1	8	3	3	0	0	0	15
Row %	6.67	53.33	20.00	20.00	0.0	0.0	0.0	
Col %	33.33	30.77	42.86	23.08	0.0	0.0	0.0	28.85
Did not Like	0	0	0	0	0	0	0	0
Row %	0.0	0.0	0.0	0.0	0.0	0.0	0.0	00
Col %	0.0	0.0	0.0	0.0	0.0	0.0	0.0	0.0

	None	Std. 1–8	Std. 9–11	SSLC/ PUC	Graduates	Post Graduates	Blank	
Nothing	0	1	0	0	0	0	0	1
Row %	0.0	100.00	0.0	0.0	0.0	0.0	0.0	
Col %	0.0	3.85	0.0	0.0	0.0	0.0	0.0	1.92
No	2	9	2	3	1	0	0	17
Row %	11.76	52.94	11.76	17.65	5.88	0.0	0.0	
Col %	66.67	34.62	28.57	23.08	50.00	0.0	0.0	82.69
Blank	0.	0	0	0	0	0	0	0
Row %	0.0	0.0	0.0	0.0	0.0	0.0	0.0	00
Col %	0.0	0.0	0.0	0.0	0.0	0.0	0.0	0.0
Total	3	26	7	13	2	1	0	52
Row %	5.77	50.00	13.46	25.00	3.85	1.92	0.0	100.00

TABLE FIVE

Income group versus preference to learn about Jesus by reading Christian Literature

	Much Interested	A Little Interested	No Interest	Blank	
Low Income Group	18	3	5	0	26
Row %	69.23	11.54	19.23	0.0	
Col %	58.06	50.00	33.33	0.0	50.00
Middle Income Group	12	3	8	0	23
Row %	52.17	13.04	34.78	0.0	
Col %	38.71	50.00	53.33	0.0	44.23
High Income Group	1	0	2	0	3
Row %	33.33	0.0	66.67	0.0	
Col %	3.23	0.0	13.33	0.0	5.77
Total	31	6	15	0	52
Row %	59.62	11.54	28.85	0.0	100.00

Income group versus preference to learn about Jesus by listening to radio

	Much Interested	A Little Interested	No Interest	Blank	
Low Income Group	13	5	8	0	26
Row %	50.00	19.23	30.77	0.0	
Col %	61.90	45.45	40.00	0.0	50.00
Middle Income Group	8	5	10	0	23
Row %	34.78	21.74	43.48	0.0	
Col %	38.10	45.45	50.CO	0.0	44.2
High Income Group	0	1	2	0	3
Row %	0.0	33.33	66.67	0.0	
Col %	0.0	9.09	10.00	0.0	5.77
Total	21	11	20	0	52
Row %	40.38	21.15	38.46	0.0	100.00